Social Welfare Policy

Second Edition

Social Welfare Policy

ANALYSIS AND FORMULATION

Charles S. Prigmore
University of Alabama

Charles R. Atherton
University of Alabama

D. C. Heath and Company
Lexington, Massachusetts
Toronto

FOR SHIRLEY AND ZOE

Acquisition Editor: James Miller
Production Editor: Rosemary Rodensky
Designer: Mark T. Fowler
Illustrator: Carmela Ciampa

PHOTO CREDITS
page 7   J. Beandt/Stock, Boston
page 27   Ginger Chih
page 45   Ellis Herwig/Stock, Boston
page 63   Bohdan Hrynewych/Stock, Boston
page 89   Bobbi Carrey/The Picture Cube
page 117   Paul S. Conklin
page 145   Marion Bernstein
page 167   Marion Bernstein
page 191   Paul S. Conklin
page 205   Marion Bernstein
page 219   Owen Franken/Stock, Boston
page 241   Sam Sweezy

Published simultaneously in Canada.

Printed in the United States of America.

International Standard Book Number: 0-669-06745-8

Library of Congress Catalog Card Number: 85-60969

Preface

In this, the second edition of *Social Welfare Policy*, our central task remains the presentation of a rational set of criteria to guide social welfare policy analysis and formulation. It remains our belief that social workers can and should be more involved in the policy process. Therefore, we have tried to provide an approach that will assist both instructor and student (as well as the general social work reader) in building a base for the analysis and formulation of alternatives to present social welfare policies.

This book is intended for use in professional foundation courses in social welfare policy analysis. The undergraduate and the first year graduate student are usually newcomers to formal policy analysis, but we assume that both have some knowledge of the major social welfare programs currently in force in the United States. In some of the chapters, we have deliberately taken some extreme and controversial positions. Sometimes we may sound quite radical while at other times we are fairly conservative. This is done deliberately in order to provoke a dialogue. It is not important that the reader agree with our stand in any chapter. We want to offer the student and the instructor a place to start in their interactions. It is our belief that we will have succeeded if the reader is stimulated into thinking through his or her own position. We have found this to be a sound educational approach.

The first three chapters lay the groundwork. In these chapters, we explain our viewpoint toward the importance of social welfare policy, discuss the relationship of social and professional values to policy analysis and formulation, and present our approach to policy analysis. The next five chapters look at specific policy areas: income maintenance, poverty, health and mental health care, housing and neighborhood living space, and the general problems of service delivery. We analyze what we perceive to be the current policies that guide programs in these areas and suggest alternative policies for discussion. The last three chapters introduce the student to social action, social planning, and administration. These chapters are intended to act as a bridge from social welfare policy analysis and formulation to the implementation of policy. Each chapter can only serve as a brief introduction, since these are complex subjects. We assume that students in schools of social work will take courses in these subjects later in their professional preparation. Other readers may find these chapters useful as a general road map that may suggest directions for independent study.

We are indebted to Professors Jerry Griffin and Richard Crow for their contributions to this volume. Professor Griffin wrote Chapter 10 and Chapter 11 is the work of Professor Crow.

We would also like to thank Professor Philip B. Coulter, Director of the Institute for Social Science Research of the University of Alabama. Mr. Coulter and the Institute provided much needed technical support for the preparation of the manuscript.

C. S. P.

C. R. A.

Contents

6

Major Policy Problems in Health and Mental Health Systems   117

7

Policies for Problems in Living Space   145

8

Social Welfare Policy and Social Service Delivery   167

Introduction

◼

Social welfare policy is an exciting and complex subject. Unfortunately, some students and some educators are less interested in policy than they ought to be. For them, treatment is more immediate in its challenges because results can be seen more quickly. Policy seems ethereal and remote. Some of our own students have argued that there is little that they can do to affect policy decisions unless they reach positions of influence. They have argued that most policy decisions are reached in the state capitol or in Washington, rather than on the "firing line." We argue that policy is influenced at all levels.

First of all, while final policy decisions are made by legislators, administrators, or judges, they are not made in a wholly arbitrary way. Decision makers are political animals. Because the decision maker usually wants to go on making decisions, he or she must be sensitive to influence. While social workers are not the most powerfully influential group in the world, they can affect some policy some of the time, either on their own or in concert with other interest groups. In the past, social workers have, in fact, participated in successful policy changes with respect to children's programs, the handicapped, and the mentally ill. While social workers do not win every battle, they have made important contributions to social welfare policy decisions.

Second, not all policy is made in the capitols. Most agencies make allowance for participation from line personnel in the decision-making process. In the agencies that we know best, staff serve on task forces and committees that have something to say about what the agency does. While other decision makers may set ground rules governing the structure and services of a given agency, much of the actual operative patterns and service delivery principles will be worked out within the agency. Therefore, line social workers often have opportunities to influence how the agency will actually operate.

Third, the line social worker is, in a sense, in the most important of policy positions. He or she is the one who has direct contact with the clientele. Whether or not clients get services and the kind of services they actually get are both determined by the social worker's understanding of agency policy. In effect, what the social worker does reflects the actual policy of the agency. Social workers, then, can and do affect social welfare policy. They can do more.

Certainly more help is needed by policymakers, for the policy arena is a confusing place. Fifteen years ago the late Richard Titmuss pointed out that "concepts and models of social policy are as diverse as contemporary concepts of poverty." Little has happened to alter the truth of this remark. There is still a vast amount of confusion about what "good" social welfare policy ought to look like. There remain a number of conflicting value positions. Consensus is most unlikely.

Many important needs continue to go unmet, and the country's efforts continue to be misshapen and fragmented. Clearly, time is being lost in the constant war that must be fought against the effects of poverty, injustice and the meaninglessness that characterizes so much of so many people's lives.

Why has policy development been so fragmentary and confused? Ronald Dear has leveled three criticisms at the process of policy development in the United States.[1] First, the United States has often waited too long to recognize problems or has made no response at all. The United States was the last Western industrial nation to develop a social security program. We still have no coherent population policy. Second, when policies have been formed and implemented, they are often in conflict with each other. Third, welfare policy makers tend to oversimplify complex problems and look for simplistic solutions.

Beyond these problems, there are others. Proposals are often selected without regard to political and economic feasibility. When former Senator George McGovern embraced the proposal of a guaranteed family income of $6,500 for a family of four during the 1972 campaign, he encountered a great deal of opposition. Although this seems like a trifling amount today, it was well above the poverty line in 1972 dollars and the cost would have been prohibitive in the federal budgets of the time. McGovern hastily withdrew his proposal, but not before it had been milked dry for the benefit of his opponents.

Those who propose policy do not always relate their proposals to research findings. While it is true that research in the social sciences is seldom conclusive, it makes no sense to disregard it on those occasions when there is consistency. A good example is the research on the rehabilitation of prisoners. Some who should be knowledgeable continue to argue for the expansion of traditional treatment services despite repeated findings that such services have had limited success in preventing recidivism. Clearly, something should be done about the American penal system. It is equally clear that more of the same is not the answer.

Too often decision makers have not thought enough about the criteria by which alternatives can be measured. There is a tendency toward embracing some version of cost-benefit analysis as the sole criterion of a policy's worth. This leaves out any consideration of other values.

Finally, some changes are selected for their cosmetic effect, and do not reflect any actual improvement.

Despite the difficulties that greet those who enter the policy arena, we think that it is important for social workers to devote more of their professional energies to the policy process. We have no quick and easy solutions. The central question that we address is: How does one analyze and formulate social welfare policy? The answer that this book provides focuses on what we think has to be done when considering policy issues.

REFERENCES

1. Ronald Dear, "The Current Crisis in Social Welfare," in *Social Work in Transition* (Seattle, Wash.: School of Social Work, University of Washington, 1974), pp. 24–26.

Part I

The Basis for Social Welfare Policy and an Approach to Policy Analysis and Formulation

The first three chapters lay the groundwork that we believe is necessary to an understanding of our approach to policy analysis and the formulation of alternatives. In the first chapter we present our view of the importance of social welfare in human affairs and the historical and philosophical approach upon which our approach rests. The second chapter discusses the crucial question of values and choices in social welfare policy. It is our contention that the kind of social welfare policy that a society has depends ultimately on convictions and beliefs that are part of the cultural context.

Chapter 3 presents our outline for policy analysis. We believe that we have included in this schema the essential factors that must be considered if the social worker is to successfully analyze current policies and suggest useful alternatives.

1

The Context of Social Welfare

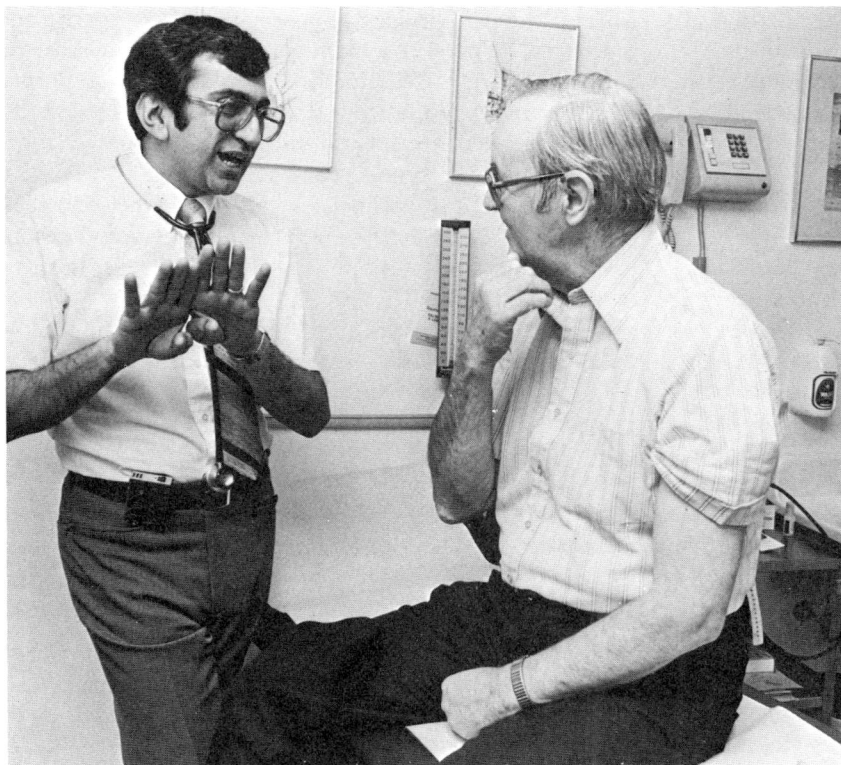

Social welfare policy is always related to the social, political, economic and cultural context in which it exists. To provide a background for what we have to say about analyzing and formulating social welfare policy, we will describe our understanding of that context in this chapter. We think that it will help if the reader has some idea of our presuppositions. The chapter will also reveal some of our biases!

Social Welfare and Mutual Aid

To begin, let us look briefly at the status of social welfare in the modern world. While many people are very critical of social welfare, there is still the expectation that society should provide for the delivery of a secure level of basic life supports (food, housing, health care, education, and various kinds of counseling and protective services) to people as benefits of citizenry. Alfred Kahn has made this observation. "Social services appear everywhere in the modern world. They continue to exist and even expand as productivity increases and as average standards of living are raised. Indeed, they are seen as part of the improved standards."[1] Some societies provide a wider range of programs and services than do others. There is great variation in the mix between government sponsored and voluntarily sponsored delivery systems. While some societies' services are viewed more enthusiastically than others, virtually all societies accept the principle that society ought to provide resources against problematic social situations, downturns in the economic cycle, health crises and unfavorable living conditions.

The idea of providing social services and programs is not new. It has its roots in a very old idea in human affairs—that cooperation rather than competition is necessary for group survival in the face of an uncertain and often hostile world.

The anthropologists tell us that the basic historical unit of society is the tribe or clan. It seems fairly certain that the earliest people on earth lived a nomadic existence, surviving by food gathering and hunting. While much popular literature depicts these early cave dwellers and nomads as constantly at war with each other, there is little evidence to support that view. Rather, the historical evidence supports the idea that survival was possible through cooperation. The historian, Stewart Easton, supplies an important summary:

> It used to be thought that man in a state of nature was forced to compete with all other human beings for his very subsistence, or, in the famous words of Thomas Hobbes, that his life was "solitary, poor, nasty, brutish, and short." We have no record of such a way of life, either in early times, or among present-day "primitive"

men. And it no longer seems as probable to us as it did in the nineteenth century, under the influence of the biological ideas of Darwin, that human survival was a matter of success in the constant struggle for existence, if this struggle is conceived of as a struggle between human beings. It now seems much more probable that survival has always been due to successful cooperation between human beings to resist the always dangerous forces of nature.[2]

Mutual aid, then, is a key characteristic of human society. It has been so since the early history of people on this earth.

The Function of Social Conflict

Some years ago, Lewis Coser explored the adaptive function of social conflict as a basic human process.[3] At first glance, the ideas of Coser and other conflict theorists seem to suggest that human social organization is formed and even held together through the clash of cultures and personalities. In the seminal work of Robert E. Park and Ernest W. Burgess, the groundwork was laid for the notion that there are four basic processes in the interaction of social groups: competition, conflict, accommodation, and assimilation. These processes are thought to form a rough continuum of the development of human social organization. Briefly, the notion is that humans begin by competing for scarce resources. This competition is carried on without necessarily involving social contact as in the simple example of two tribes who inhabit the same general territory, hunting the same animals, but avoiding each other. At the point when the tribes identify each other and engage in any struggle for scarce resources, they move into a situation of conflict. It is possible for one tribe to survive by killing off the other. If this happens, it is obvious that survival has only come about at the expense of the nonsurvival of another group. While there are a few examples of this process in history, this is not usually the case. What usually happens (and this must be true, or we would all be Huns or Mongols) is that the people involved eventually realize that conflict is expensive, wearisome, and, in the long run, counterproductive. At this point, they seek to accommodate each other and begin to work out adjustments that will permit the survival of both groups. Ultimately, this accommodation leads to assimilation:

> Accommodation has been described as a process of adjustment, that is, an organization of social relations and attitudes to prevent or to reduce conflict, to control competition, and to maintain a basis of security in the social order for persons and groups of divergent interests and types to carry on together their varied life activities. *Accommodation in the sense of the composition* (resolution) *of conflict is invariably the goal of the political process.*
>   Assimilaton is a process of interpenetration and fusion in which persons and groups acquire the memories, sentiments, and attitudes of other persons or groups, and, by sharing their experiences and history, are incorporated with them in a common cultural life. *Insofar as assimilation denotes this sharing of tradition, this*

*intimate participation in common experiences, assimilation is central in the histor-
ical and cultural processes.*[4] (emphasis added)

Conflict, then, is a stage in the process of development of human society, but not the end process. Coser says:

> In loosely structured groups and open societies, conflict, which aims at a resolution of tension between antagonists, is likely to have stabilizing and integrative functions for the relationship. By permitting immediate and direct expression of rival claims, such social systems are able to readjust their structures by eliminating the sources of dissatisfaction. The multiple conflicts which they experience may serve to eliminate the causes for dissociation and to reestablish unity.[5]

It is important to notice that the various conflict theorists do not describe conflict as a permanent condition. It is rather a part of a larger process that is a stage on the way to a more stable relationship.

We can see the working out of these social processes in two contemporary examples. There is a long history of conflict in the relationship of many of those who live in the state of Israel and the Arab world. This conflict is literally centuries old. In 1977 we saw what looks like the beginning of accommodation as a result of the peace process that came out of negotiations in which Premier Begin of Israel, President Sadat of Egypt, and President Jimmy Carter played major roles. It is far too soon to claim that the conflict phase is winding down. Recent events in Lebanon show that many Arab leaders are still mistrustful and angry, and many Israelis are watchful and uncertain. However, from a sociological point of view, the meetings that began in 1977 contain the elements of the accommodative process. One is encouraged to take the hopeful view of the future, although it is clear that accommodation and assimilation are certainly far down the road.

Parenthetically, we need to point out that assimilation does not necessarily mean the merging of all cultural, political, or religious differences. Assimilation involves a sharing of tradition and a participation in common experiences according to Park and Burgess. This can occur as a social process without forcing people to give up important ethnic and religious identifications and traditions.

Another example of conflict resolution in the making can be found in the changing relationship of blacks and whites in the United States. The history of racial conflict is a long and bloody one. In 1968, The National Advisory Commission on Civil Disorders published a report which went so far as to say that the country was moving toward two nations, one black and one white. While we do not claim that race relations in the United States are ideal, there are signs that some progress toward accommodation has been made, however slow and grudging. Like the Arab-Israeli example, however, genuine assimilation is still far off.

People cannot survive and grow healthily in a constant state of conflict. They must either find ways of avoiding contact or move to some kind of accommodation. It is one of our biases that social welfare concerns must be based on values that support mutuality and accommodation. Human survival becomes hollow if it can be achieved only at the expense of others.

To most of us, "survival" may not seem to be a relevant concept to use in this context. Most citizens in the industrialized nations generally live well above survival levels. However, the ecological movement has raised our consciousness of the delicate balance of human life and the fragility of our security. We think that welfare planning must de-emphasize the "we-they" kind of relationship that has characterized much of our past. Catastrophic illness, economic turmoil, natural disaster, emotional problems, and loss of meaning are not just things that "they" face. We must learn to live together on this planet, because threats to any of us are threats to us all. We are becoming more aware of the interrelatedness of life. Dust from atomic explosions in one country falls across its borders. We have learned to trade with the Eastern bloc and popular American soft drinks are now available in the People's Republic of China. We may have at last come to the realization that we are interrelated and the failure to reach some kind of understanding can result in the mutual destruction that all would prefer to avoid. It is clear to us that despite their ideological differences, the people of the earth are "all in one boat" and it will not do for any one of us to punch a hole in the bottom of it.

Is There a Need for Social Welfare?

This is a perennial question. Curiously enough, social welfare programs are unpopular with both the political left as well as the right. On the right, the argument is that people ought to take care of themselves. The traditional exhortation to the poor is "Lift yourselves by your own bootstraps." Since hardly anybody today knows what a bootstrap is, the phrase has become a very hollow cliché. Back in the old days, when most people wore boots instead of shoes, there were straps at the back or sides of the boot that enabled the wearer to pull them on. The idea of "pulling yourself up by your own bootstraps" was to advance yourself through your own efforts. The "self-made man" was one who needed no help from anyone but who depended upon his own "rugged individualism" in order to succeed. This image is still dear to the heart of the arch-conservative. It is naive in that it ignores the inability of many—the old, the very young, those who are victims of various forms of discrimination—to succeed without some type of support services. In the "old days" we didn't have all these services and programs. In the "old days" a lot of people suffered extreme privation, too.

Those on the extreme left oppose social welfare, too. Their argument is that the social system is unjust and that welfare is just another form of control of the poor and the oppressed. Instead of a punitive and limiting welfare system, the left argues that we need a total reform of the system in order for a new and more just social order to be formed. We find this approach to be equally naive. If the left were to find themselves in power tomorrow morning, we doubt if all the social evils would pass away and all the wrongs would be righted. Besides, it is highly unlikely that there will be popular revolutions of the sort that the left espouses. The revolutions that have taken place have not brought about the kinds of reforms that the revolutionaries expected. Rather, what has happened is that the power has shifted from group A to group B without the subsequent ennobling of the common person that was supposed to result. The chief beneficiaries of the revolution have been those most closely allied with it.

It should be clear to the reader that the authors are moderates who believe that social welfare programs and services provide important answers to many of the personal and social perils that threaten human life. We recognize that social welfare programs and services improve the lot of many people who would otherwise be denied access to goods and services that make life meaningful. We choose not to exhort the poor to "tough it out" as best they can and we think that the left looks for "pie in the sky" that is simply not there.

It is our belief that modern human beings need socially provided support systems—just as our ancestors needed mutual support—or life would indeed be the "solitary, poor, nasty, brutish, and short" proposition that Thomas Hobbes described. The Judeo-Christian religious tradition and its secular cousin, humanitarianism, have given social welfare, as we know it, a distinctive coloration and shape, but the need for mutual aid and the facts of human interdependence are not limited to Western civilization. Non-Western peoples have a number of similar religious and philosophical systems that emphasize the mutuality of human needs. It is our conviction that no human society anywhere can survive for very long without some provision for mutual support systems. The rationales and the values may differ throughout the world but the common awareness is there. In industrial—and industrializing—societies, it is expressed through increasingly larger and more complex public and privately financed social welfare systems. Mutual aid in the modern world is more complicated than helping to rebuild a neighbor's barn when it burns or sharing a pot of chicken soup with a sick friend, but the essence of mutual concern for others is still very much a part of authentic humanity. Before we explore the complexity, we need to define some terms.

What Is Social Welfare?

We recognize that social welfare has been defined in many ways and that no one definition is entirely satisfactory to everyone. We have chosen to use Friedlander and Apte's statement:

> Social welfare is a system of laws, programs, benefits and services which strengthen or assure provisions for meeting social needs recognized as basic for the welfare of the population and for the functioning of the social order.[6]

We like this definition because it leaves room for the inclusion of both public and voluntary programs and services. It recognizes that certain needs are basic for the welfare of people. We also like this definition because it is consistent with our belief that social welfare is an essential part of organized social life. We interpret the definition to mean that a society that does not recognize and plan for some way of meeting basic needs is not really a functional society.

We recognize that there are elements of social control or, to use Talcott Parsons' phrase, "boundary maintenance" in most definitions of social welfare. These elements are most readily apparent in child welfare services and mental health treatment programs. We have chosen to interpret most welfare services as social utilities—social provisions to meet common human needs, rather than as social control mechanisms.

What Is Social Welfare Policy?

We are going to use a very simple definition: Social welfare policy is a generic term for the guidelines used for decision making on social welfare programs and issues. This is a derivation of Kahn's statement:

> A policy is a "standing plan," a "guide to future decision making," or a "continuing line of decisions . . ." It is the implicit or explicit core of principle that underlies specific programs, legislation, priorities.[7]

Kahn emphasizes the idea that social welfare policy has to do with the principles on which specific social welfare programs and service delivery systems are based over time. Effective and appropriate social welfare policy is not just an impulsive response to a problem, but a reasonably well thought out long-range plan. There is a subtle warning in Kahn's definition. He notes that policies may be implicit rather than explicit. A good part of accurate policy analysis depends upon one's ability to recognize implicit factors and make them explicit.

In this book we will limit our discussion to "social welfare policy" in order to focus on our major concerns. Other writers use the term "social policy" to mean the same thing. We think that "social policy" is a broad term that encompasses a wide range of policies that have to do with things not limited to social welfare. Other policies, including economic policy, population policy and agricultural policy are also social policies and we do not want to venture very far into those fields.

We also need to point out that we have tried to avoid confusing social welfare policy by identifying it with any particular viewpoint. Richard Titmuss, for example, seems to have used the term "social policy" as synonymous with economic redistribution. That is, if a nation has a social policy then, by definition, it has a policy that redistributes income and/or wealth from those who have more to those who have less. We think that this is a misuse of the term in that social policy is a generic term. A nation might have a social policy that requires economic redistribution—but, on the other hand, another nation might have a very conservative social policy that was anti-redistribution. The mixing of policy-as-a-thing and policy-as-a-specific-meaning is confusing, so we avoid it.

Just as we have avoided relating our use of "social welfare policy" with any political view, we also do not identify one set of values that is permanently related to social welfare. That is, we cannot say that only one set of beliefs about the human condition is consistent with support for social welfare programs. It is clear that in the contemporary United States there is support for social welfare from both liberal and conservative people. There are differences about how much should be committed to social welfare and who should receive benefits, but neither side can claim moral superiority over the other as long as there are genuine elements of concern for the human condition on both sides. In short, we want to try to avoid being captured by any one ideology and to be free to cast a critical eye at both liberals and conservatives.

It is important to repeat that social welfare policy (or any other type of social policy for that matter) is formed in a context. To forget that there are connections between social welfare concerns and the rest of the social system is disastrous. Quite often it seems as if those who are interested in social welfare set priorities for action as if there were no other interests to be considered. This naiveté is surely related to the failure of many humane proposals.

Accordingly, as we discuss the context in which to think about social welfare policy, we will be interested in a number of elements that bear on the decision-making process.

Social Welfare and Humanitarianism

But is it all this complicated? Isn't it enough to recognize that social welfare is based on humanitarian concerns and let it go at that? Is not social welfare policy merely a matter of making decisions about programs and services on the basis of what is right and humane? Let us examine the case for humanitarian philosophy (putting on one side the problem that we may not all agree on what is right and humane) as the only important variable.

It can be argued that the appearance of social services everywhere is indicative of a growing sense of the love of humanity. Certainly, social welfare and social work have deep roots in religion and humanitarianism. The welfare agencies and programs that we have today have been described as the institutionalization of the philanthropic impulse and love of mankind:

> Social work as an identifiable profession had its point of origin in the final decade of the nineteenth century. The feeling of charity toward one's fellow man and actions based on that feeling, however, had their origins in antiquity. The philanthropic impulse, the love of mankind that is manifested in beneficent deeds, has, it appears, always been a part of human nature—an essential ingredient of the mixture of emotions and beliefs that makes man human . . . The performance of charitable acts has been carried out under the aegis of voluntary and governmental organizations throughout history; the need for giving help and the acceptance of responsibility to do so has been a constant in human society.[8]

In many cases welfare programs and services have come about because of people's compassion. Much about social welfare reflects genuine unselfishness.

Using the charitable impulse as the *sole* basis for social welfare, however, leads in the direction of trusting to human nature to do charitable acts. But social welfare must be more pragmatic than that. Consider those words of Orville Brim in his presidential address to the American Orthopsychiatric Association:

> How much more than the price of a lunch will it cost society over the long term in lost productivity, and in the need for institutionalization, of children damaged by nutritional deficiencies? This is a cold-blooded way to make the case for the care of children in our society, but I say again that the competition for goods and services in the American economy is economic and political, and *we can no longer rely solely on good will and individual acts of charity and kindness to provide for children in this country.*[9] (emphasis added)

We share Brim's cynicism. Over the years it has not been enough to appeal to legislatures, public administrators, contributors, and taxpayers to provide social welfare programs out of humane motives. It is often necessary to resort to lawsuits, political pressure, and citizen action to compel society to live up to "the feeling of charity" that is supposedly embodied in its institutions. Therefore, we think the case for social welfare must rest on more than the philanthropic impulse, although that may be an important value. We would suggest that justice is an equally important value.

The Shift from Informal to Formal Welfare System

In the pages ahead we will argue that social welfare institutions as we now know them have deeper historical roots than we ordinarily think about. A crucial question was raised some years ago by Wilensky and Lebeaux. The problem that they were addressing was whether social welfare was a matter of giving aid to people in emergency situations or providing services as a normal, ordinary function of society. They put it this way:

> Two conceptions of social welfare seem to be dominant in the United States today; the *residual* and the *institutional*. The first holds that social welfare institutions should come into play only when the normal structures of supply, the family and the market, break down. The second, in contrast, sees the welfare services as normal, "first line" functions of modern industrial society.[10]

We think that Wilensky and Lebeaux have missed an important point. They looked at the formation of *formal* social welfare organizations as the beginnings of social welfare. Since most agencies as we know them had their start in industrial times, it may seem logical to assume that social welfare had its beginnings at that time. It is true that orphanages, poorhouses, and hospitals are products of industrial societies. But an institution in the sociological sense of the term (and this is the way Wilensky and Lebeaux were using the word) is more than a formal organization. As defined by the late sociologist Arnold Rose, an institution is a "number of culturally defined and evaluated behavior patterns, closely related to each other logically and culturally, which are transmitted continuously to individuals who come into an expected social role for what the institution is relevant."[11]

If an institution is a set of behavior patterns, then welfare as an institution existed long before the orphanages, poorhouses, and hospitals. Welfare functions had been institutionalized in the family, clan or tribe. What happens is that they gradually shift into organizations outside the family as the nature of society changes during industrialization. If the institutional view (as Wilensky and Lebeaux define it) is that social welfare should be thought of as a pattern of behaviors which continues over time, then social welfare as an institution has been around for a long time. What is different is that during the Industrial Revolution the *structure* in which welfare programs and services were provided was changed, but the *function* had been institutionalized all along.

An example may help clear up this point. Consider the situation of the mentally ill. Nonindustrial societies all have an institutionalized (or culturally patterned) way of dealing with those whose behavior is bizarre in its appearance to the mass of people. Some of these societies have a very harsh policy (which, like it or not, is still an institutionalized way of dealing with the problem), but there are other societies that venerate the mentally ill and create special roles for them. If the society industrializes, these special roles tend to disappear. The mentally ill are left without social support. They may wander about to live as best they can. At some point, these people become an annoying problem. Usually, someone suggests confinement or banishment. These "services" may be very crude and cruel—but they are clearly "residual" in that they are socially sponsored responses to a perceived problem. They would be the thing that society elected to do when the traditional role failed. Over time, because the problem of the mentally ill does not go away, more effective and efficient solutions might be proposed. Our hypothetical society might devise a more sophisticated solution because the society is humane. It might devise a new solution because people believe that the mentally ill are a resource that is too valuable to be allowed to go to waste or because the society believes it has a moral obligation to its citizens. Whatever the motive behind the policy, the new provision for the mentally ill becomes institutionalized and becomes a "first line function" to which people turn because of its sophistication.

It was Wilensky and Lebeaux's belief that, as industrialization continued, the institutional view would prevail over the residual. Our analysis leads us to concur. We think that the institutional approach is historically the one that prevailed prior to industrialization. That is, most societies had a patterned way of dealing with the problems of the poor, the mentally ill, the old and other identifiable special groups. The traditional pattern breaks down during the process of industrialization. Once a society industrializes, the welfare functions again become institutionalized in a new form. In the United States, now that industrialization has advanced to the point it has, we think that welfare has returned to its institutional status—even though there are changes due to specialization, bureaucratization, and the urban character of modern society. To put it as simply as we can, it can be said that humans in a "state of nature" recognize their interdependence and generally work together—at least within their own ethnic groups. However, people lose sight of this interdependence during the early dislocations that come with social change and industrialization. The strain toward interdependence is regained when industrialization has taken hold. Therefore, after a brief hiatus (as history goes) of two hundred or so years, we humans in the Western world seem to be regaining an understanding of the need to reach out to each other and to find ways to be mutually supportive in what has turned out to be a very fragile world. We do not naively believe that all conflict has ceased or will cease in the near future. We do think, however, that if the world is to operate to the optimum benefit of human beings our interdependence must be recognized or our civilization will decay.

A Brief History of Mutual Aid

We will trace the idea of mutual aid in Western society in order to point out that a concern for human welfare was a part (in some degree) of the historical and cultural situation and cannot be understood apart from that situation.

When early humans discovered the use of tools, this knowledge enabled them to have alternatives to hunting and food gathering. Eventually early society began to take on a more formal and geographically permanent structure:

> At the next stage of development, called the Neolithic Revolution, man ceased to be totally dependent upon nature and began in some degree to control it. He learned to breed and to tend animals, so that they were always available to him for food when he needed them, and he taught them to work for him and supplement his own labor. He learned to plant crops and harvest them, laying down seeds in some spot cleared for the purpose and in which such plants did not grow by nature. He learned to build himself a home where none had been provided by nature, and he even discovered how to grow special crops such as flax from which he could make himself clothing.[12]

Generally, the core institution in this early agricultural society was the extended family. Planned cultivation, which replaced food gathering, allowed the family to provide its members with more goods and services as well as relatively consistent social statuses and roles. Human beings could stay in one place long enough to begin to develop a more complex culture than was possible before. One was protected from the hazards of the old life (as well as could be, given the state of technology) by the resources of the family. Villages and tribes composed of several families could now acquire a more or less permanent home and a distinctive social shape. Unemployment was not a societal or personal problem except for those who had no family or who had left their families. Those without a family usually turned to begging or stealing. A member of an extended family had certain welfare-like provisions. When a person was ill, the family provided care. Children whose parents died would be cared for by another relative as a matter of course. There was no need for a formally organized welfare system for most members of this kind of a society. The informal system worked for most of the people for most of the time. Of course, it must be remembered that the general level of living was not very high. The distinction between the "haves" and the "have nots" was not great except for a very privileged few.

A clear example of this built-in mutual aid provision can be seen in Scottish Highland society. The clans of Scotland are important today only as sentimental symbols, but historically the Highlanders were held together by bonds of kinship and territoriality. Tribal organizations in other cultures were based on farming or fishing, but the Scots' society was primarily organized around warfare, primarily against the English. The clans also functioned as mutual aid societies. In theory at least, no clan member starved so long as the chief had resources in land or food. Work, either in the form of maintenance of the land or in warfare, was available. Some of this "work" involved piracy and theft from the English, but this was considered legitimate under the mores of the culture. There were risks of injury and disease, but one was protected against them as far as resources allowed. The clans protected their members because it was necessary for the clans' purposes. The chief, of course, was an autocrat, hence his or her protection was paternalistic.[13] But each member of the clan was important, a member of an "honorable community" as they called it, and could claim clan support as a right of kinship.

As a footnote to the above discussion, it should be pointed out that the Scottish and the English have reached a fairly stable state of accommodation while preserving important cultural differences. This accommodation came only after several hundred bloody years and is still marred by rumblings from Scottish groups who say that they want separate Scottish nationhood.

While other tribal organizations differ from that of the Highland clan, they share the principle of mutual aid. In Europe, support from one's society or clan as a matter of mutual aid was supplemented by the actions of organized religion up through the end of the Roman Empire. It is important to repeat that receiving assistance from one's extended family was a right firmly enmeshed in the web of custom. It was a first line function of the tribe, clan, or community and not just a residual service that depended on some vague philanthropic impulse. This firmly institutionalized system of mutual aid worked well enough through the Middle Ages until the beginnings of industrialization. It continues to work to some extent today in rural communities and among closely knit ethnic and religious groups.

Welfare and the Medieval World

With the decline of Rome as a world power, a great source of unity and universality disappeared from the Western world. Without the Roman empire, life was much more uncertain. Roads, the major means of travel and communication, were no longer safe because of roving bands of outlaws. People tended to travel less and trade was curtailed. Civilization and learning did not come to a standstill, however, and it is entirely wrong to describe the medieval period as the "Dark Ages." This term refers to a darkening of the lamp of learning and culture, and despite its popularity it is misleading. People did, however, become more localized in their dealings with their environment, and as a result new economic and political systems evolved that were appropriate for the day.

"Feudalism" is properly used to describe the political system of the medieval period. Theoretically, in feudalism the king controlled all the land. He dispensed it to the aristocracy and the gentry in return for loyalty. In actuality, no very neat distribution of the land was possible. No medieval king was ever really in a position to parcel out the land to his followers since it was not easy to set aside the decisions of previous kings. The king could only award land that he controlled. The kings had to depend on their own personal land and retainers for power and wealth, and none could enforce their will much beyond the immediate area that they could control militarily. Effectively, each small landholding was a relatively independent unit.

The economic system that supported feudalism is usually referred to as "manorialism." Each aristocrat held a piece of land in trust. These parcels of land ranged from a few acres to great estates of thousands of acres. The poor knight on a few acres was barely able to pay for a horse and armor. A rich duke might have a fairly large retinue of relatives on horses and a group of foot soldiers. Peasants or serfs worked the land. The serf was not a slave in that he did not belong personally to the master, but he and his family were bound to the land. The typical manor also had a mill, a blacksmith's shop, and a church. The manor was, for all practical purposes, a self-supporting economic unit.

Medieval men and women had certain rights under this system. The serf could not leave the land, but he could not be made to leave it either. He had a right to a certain amount of land for his own use. If he died, his widow and children had certain rights to support. These rights were among the few feudal laws that were observed relatively faithfully throughout Europe. Although there were some bad masters, most were reasonably honorable about their obligations to take care of those who were servants or serfs.

Descriptions of the medieval peasant's life indicate that the peasant lived under miserable conditions. It was common, for example, for the pigs to live in the hovel with the serf's family. Actually, the masters were not much better off. Most people's image of the medieval noble are romanticized, as in the novels of Sir Walter Scott, and do not show how little social distance there was between master and serf. Manor houses were great drafty things without proper windows, heated by enormous fireplaces which were very inefficient. Privileges were unequal, of course, but the noble and the serf drank from the same well, and the fever killed them both with great equality.

Town life was somewhat different from that of the manor. There, freemen, merchants, and craftsmen worked out their own unique social system. Most relevant to our discussion were the welfare-like arrangements made by the gilds for their members. The gilds (or guilds) were associations of independent craftsmen. As entrepreneurs, the gild members regulated the market by setting wages and prices. They also regulated entry into the crafts. Each gild had a kind of social insurance scheme that provided for members unable to work and for the families of deceased members. These benefits were limited to members and did not benefit the city populace as a whole. They represent an attempt to provide a basic kind of economic and social protection against economic insecurity on the basis of mutual aid.

The Role of Religion and Philanthropy

What has been described so far represents only a rough attempt to provide a resource system. Early humans aided and protected those within their identifiable social groups because they had to do so in order to survive in a hostile environment. In the medieval period, the rights of the serfs were limited and were protected only up to a point. This protection was a minimal provision of resources and there was little in the way of anything that could be recognized as a social service. The gilds provided for their members at points of stress, but they had nothing to do with the urban poor or the small tradesmen.

Large numbers of people were not part of a network in which they could benefit from a system of mutual aid. The treatment of the emotionally ill, the care of children who had no close family, and the survival of large numbers of people who had no secure place in the system were uncertain. It was the existence of these large numbers of "outsiders" that prompted the social consciousness of organized religion to respond with programs and services.

Others have traced the history of the contribution of organized religion and philanthropic societies. For our purposes it is important to see how these contributions relate to the development of the concept of social welfare as a social utility. It was religion that gave social welfare its moral and ethical flavor in the Western world.

The Jews have a long tradition of concern for the poor and homeless among them. The Christian church developed a similar concern, although hampered at times by a certain moralistic puritanism:

> Among the peoples of antiquity, the Jews made the care of dependent children a special duty under the law. Their practice of placing orphans in selected family homes was carried over into the early Christian Church where the necessity to care for many children made dependent by the persecutions of emperors led the Church to begin boarding children with "worthy widows," paying for a child's care by collections taken in the various congregations.[14]

For centuries, this concern was somewhat parochial. The church basically took care of its own. It only became concerned about the "heathen" at the point of conversion. The development of human services for those outside one's own religious group did not come about until the Industrial Revolution forcibly brought to public attention the enormity of the problems faced by many human beings. As problematic situations became visible, both Judaism and Christianity broadened their concerns and provided (and still provide) many needed services to the community in general, particularly in the area of families and children. Religion and its secular cousin, humanitarianism, responded to the needs directly but also played an important role in motivating governments to provide social welfare programs and services. Religious bodies were forced to recognize the social implications of their theology by the tremendous needs that occurred as the character of social life changed. The obligation of mutual aid for all who share the human condition was always there as a theological imperative. It was not acted upon beyond one's own group until the societal needs became compelling.

The Modern World

As we said in the last section, it is not accurate to think of the medieval era as the "Dark Ages." Learning, trade and manufacture advanced during this period. The thing that was lacking was better communication between social units. This difficulty was overcome when the Italian merchant princes swept the pirates from the Mediterranean and reopened trade routes with the East that had been closed for years. The reopening of international trade unleashed, ultimately, several forces that transformed the Western world. One area in which there was a great deal of change was social welfare.

As trade and manufacturing increased, a merchant class gained ascendency over the traditional nobility. The bankers, merchants, traders, and manufacturers challenged the traditions of the aristocratic society, and eventually this challenge brought about a revolution in life that eclipsed the changes of the neolithic revolution. Increased trading opportunities brought about an increase in demand. This increase in demand influenced the invention of labor-saving machinery. Machines meant factories and the gradual shift of population from rural areas to urban centers.

The rising middle class's attack on the landed aristocracy involved more than the transformation of the economy from an agricultural to a manufacturing base. Business does better in a politically stable climate. The middle class initially supported strong kings, and the kings therefore tended to favor the middle class. The cooperation between kings and merchants involved no magic. They were simply two parties who needed each other. Business people were willing—up to a point—to pay taxes to the central authority. Kings expanded their power, pacifying the countryside as their influence increased. This created the stable climate that allowed trade to thrive. Trade routes became relatively safe and secure except during wartime. The monarchies became far more stable than they had been in the medieval era. While individual kings might be deposed or assassinated on occasion, the institution of a strong central government came about because it was good for business.

An important factor involved in the rise of the middle class was the development of liberalism as a political philosophy. It must be emphasized, however, that eighteenth- and nineteenth-century liberalism is not the same thing as contemporary liberalism.

Liberalism has always been hard to pin down in any version. This is not the place to try to offer a comprehensive definition. However, there are certain common elements in Classical Liberalism (nineteenth-century liberalism) that are important for this discussion. Basically, Classical Liberals believed in the rights of the individual, the sacredness of private property, representative government, a free press and laissez-faire in the market place.[15] This viewpoint today is generally called "conservative" but a hundred and fifty years ago, it was revolutionary. One always has to understand a social movement in the historical context in which it occurs. Classical Liberalism *was* liberal compared to the prevailing social thought of the time.

The Classical Liberal's belief in "individual rights" is not the same thing as today's belief in fairness and social justice. To the Classical Liberal, "freedom" did not mean freedom for all. It meant freedom for the middle class as opposed to the privileged status of the aristocracy. The middle class wanted representation in constitutional assemblies as opposed to the concentration of power in a landed aristocracy. The notions of the free market and the desire to have enforceable laws of contract have to be seen as a desire to be free in business affairs so that profit could be maximized.

In short, the middle class merchants and industrialists were no more democratic than were the aristocrats. They gradually substituted parliaments for kings when they had used the monarchy as far as they could. For the traditional supports built into the medieval world, the middle class substituted the vagaries of the free market and the factory system. With the rise of Classical Liberalism the sense of community diminished, as did the built-in welfare provisions. As we shall see later, welfare became a function of the state as opposed to being a function of the custom of the community.

The Factory System

The industrial world was a wholly different place when compared with its predecessor. The basis of European life in the Middle Ages had been agriculture, and the relative abundance of low-cost labor (except during war or famine) may have retarded the development of machinery. The manufacturing that was done usually took place in the home or in small industries. However, as demands for goods increased due to trading opportunities, there was a demand for procedures that would increase production. The new machines were more efficient than hand labor and more profitable because of the high volume of goods that could be produced.

There has been much disagreement about the effects of industrialism. Wilensky and Lebeaux have reviewed the arguments.[16] They concluded that industrialism and its concurrent forces, urbanism and bureaucratization, are not as intrinsically evil as some writers at the turn of the century believed. In an analysis originally published in 1925, M. Dorothy George, after a careful review of historical records, made the same point for industrial London in the late eighteenth century:

> London had become healthier; the dangers and uncertainties of life had been lessened, partly by a change of manners, greater cleanliness, less drinking, partly by a

better police and by the reform of some gross abuses in poor law administration. Crimes of violence were fewer and different in kind, and there have been a great reduction in the number of prisoners for debt. The traditional violence and brutality of the London populace was gradually diminishing. At the end of the Century it is no longer a subject of comment by foreign visitors.[17]

While most contemporary writers no longer consider industrialism and urbanism as automatic evils, no one denies that they have had an effect on human behavior and social organization. Rosalind Mitchison notes that:

the movement of the population and the big scale of the towns broke the bonds that hold a man into society, his local community, the widespread kinship, the religious congregation, even the band of regulars at an alehouse, and it was only slowly that these would be reformed.[18]

It is apparently true, then, that when industry moves from the cottage to the factory, from generalization to specialization, from country to city, something happens to make human life different for at least a transitional period.

The effect is not limited to history. Modern emerging nations are going through some of the dislocations of industrialization. For example, traditional tribal relationships in parts of Nigeria have broken down to the extent that it has been necessary to organize a child welfare service to contend with the problems of homeless urban children. It is possible that the dislocations are temporary and limited in their effect. However, one could expect that services will continue in forms appropriate to industrial societies if these nations continue to develop modern institutions.

The United States and Mutual Aid

The case can be made that the United States is moving toward the practical realization of the provision of welfare programs and services on the basis of mutual aid. Many programs and services now exist to offer assistance to a wide variety of problems and conditions. Even with the austerity of the current administration in Washington, public and private health, education and welfare programs and services spend over 500 billion dollars—an amount that is slightly over 25 percent of the Gross National Product of the United States.[19] Most of this sum goes to services that benefit nearly everybody in some way including income maintenance for older people, the Public Health Service, and most of the schools and colleges in the country. Public aid, which is what most people think of when the word welfare is mentioned, is only a very little part of this huge amount.

Despite this outlay of funds, many social problems remain. So, while there is movement, there are signs that we have not yet arrived at the realization that social welfare programs and services are not simply matters of charity, but a matter of necessity because of human interdependence. In modern societies, we cannot do without welfare services any more than we could do without fire or police services. The quality of life would decline for everybody. Welfare reform continues to be a popular topic, but hardly anyone suggests that all forms of social welfare be discontinued. The crucial question, then, is not whether or not there should be some kind of welfare system. The question that is really before us is, what should the social welfare enterprise do and how should it be done? We think that it helps to answer this question if one has the ability to analyze and formulate constructive social welfare policy. We have to make the most effective choices that we can. The choices that we make are obviously dependent upon the knowledge and values that we use as the basis for decision making. We will look more closely at the role of values in social welfare policy in the next chapter.

REFERENCES

1. Alfred J. Kahn, *Social Policy and Social Services* (New York: Holt, Rinehart and Winston, 1964), p. 14.
2. Stewart C. Easton, *The Heritage of the Past* (New York: Holt, Rinehart and Winston, 1964), p. 4.
3. Lewis A. Coser, *The Functions of Social Conflict* (Glencoe, Ill.: The Free Press of Glencoe, 1956).
4. Robert E. Park and Ernest W. Burgess, *Introduction to the Science of Sociology*, 2nd ed. (Chicago: The University of Chicago Press, 1924), pp. 735–736.
5. Coser, *op. cit.*, p. 154.
6. Walter A. Friedlander and Robert Z. Apte, *Introduction to Social Welfare* (Englewood Cliffs, N.J.: Prentice-Hall, 1974), p. 4.
7. Kahn, *op. cit.*, p. 69.
8. Russell E. Smith and Dorothy Zeitz, *American Social Welfare Institutions* (New York: John Wiley, 1974), p. 3.
9. Orville G. Brim, Jr., "Macro-Structural Influences on Child Development and the Need for Childhood Social Indicators," *American Journal of Orthopsychiatry*, Vol. 45, No. 4 (July 1975), pp. 518–519.
10. Harold L Wilensky and Charles N. Lebeaux, *Industrial Society and Social Welfare* (New York: The Free Press, 1965), p. 138.
11. Arnold Rose, *Sociology* (New York: Alfred A. Knopf, 1965), p. 727.
12. Easton, *op. cit.*, p. 3.
13. Chiefs were often women, since it was the general rule for leadership to descend to the oldest child, not just to the oldest male. A woman who was chief performed the same duties as a man even to active participation in warfare, including command in the field. See, Sir Thomas Innes of Learney, Lord Lyon King of Arms, *The Tartans of the Clans and Families of Scotland*, 6th ed. (Edinburgh: W. & A. K. Johnson and G. W. Bacon, Ltd., 1958).
14. Lela B. Costin, *Child Welfare: Policies and Practice* (New York: McGraw-Hill, 1972), p. 323.
15. For one of the most durable and provocative treatments of the rise and change of liberalism, see Harry K. Girvetz, *The Evolution of Liberalism* (New York: Collier Books, 1963).
16. Wilensky and Lebeaux, *op. cit.*, Chs. 3, 4, and 5, pp. 49–133.
17. M. Dorothy George, *London Life in the Eighteenth Century* (New York: Harper & Row, A Harper Torchbook, 1964), p. 3.

18. Rosalind Mitchison, *A History of Scotland* (London: Methuen and Company, 1970), p. 381.
19. U.S. Bureau of the Census, *Statistical Abstract of the United States: 1981*, 102 ed. (Washington, D.C. 1981), p. 319.

QUESTIONS FOR DISCUSSION

1. Critically examine the viewpoint taken toward social welfare in this chapter. What would you add or subtract from the concept that is used?
2. Take the position that social welfare services and programs are optional and should rightly depend only on the level of goodwill in society. What kind of services do you see growing out of this position and what kind of policies do you think that they would follow?
3. This chapter argues that formal social welfare programs and services are products of forces that exist only in modern industrialized societies. Why do the authors think this is so? Why could not, for example, the ancient Babylonian empire have the same kind of social welfare programs and services that we have today?
4. What would be the difference in social welfare policy if a given program was defined as "residual" as opposed to "institutional"?
5. Discuss the limits of coverage of social welfare services. That is, try to decide what kinds of problems should be included as objects of society's concern. What risks should be left strictly to the individual?
6. The authors take the position that social welfare is a necessary institution in modern industrial societies. Criticize this argument. Isn't voluntary humanism enough to assure that needs will be met?
7. Is there greater social distance between the classes in America than was true twenty years ago? What implications does your answer have for social welfare planning and policy?
8. What difficulties do you see in considering social welfare policy as an equal partner to social work treatment? Has there been any movement in this direction?

SUGGESTED PROJECTS

1. Describe in a short paper a present-day example of mutual aid in action. How do the mutual aid provisions operate to enable the members of the group or neighborhood to get on with satisfactory living?
2. As an exercise, study some previous period of European or American history. Select a problem area, for example, mental health, the status of women, or medical care. Given the constraints that exist at the time you have selected, try your hand at devising a social welfare policy that you think may have worked better than the one that apparently was followed.

Share your proposal with the class and discuss the adequacy of your proposed policy.

FOR FURTHER READING

Edward P. Cheyney. *The Dawn of a New Era*. New York: Harper & Row, A Harper Torchbook, 1962. First volume of the "Rise of Modern Europe" series that is still one of the best historical series ever produced. Cheyney's book is an excellent general survey of the transition from the medieval world to the modern era.

Nathan E. Cohen. *Social Work in the American Tradition*. New York: The Dryden Press, 1958. Traces social work and social welfare in the framework of humanitarianism and American democracy. Cohen relates the development of social work and social welfare to important social, economic, and political developments in U. S. history. Unfortunately, the book ends with the Eisenhower administration and has never been revised, but it is still worth reading.

Harry K. Girvetz. *The Evolution of Liberalism*. New York: Collier Books, 1963. A provocative view of the development of liberalism as political and social thought.

Harold L. Wilensky and Charles N. Lebeaux. *Industrial Society and Social Welfare*. New York: The Free Press, 1965. An extremely influential book outlining the relation of the development of social welfare programs and services to industrialism. The paperback edition cited here contains Wilensky's views on the prospects for the welfare state from the vantage point of the middle 1960s. Some aspects of the book are dated, of course, but it is still worth reading for its analytical merit.

2

Values and Choices in Contemporary Social Welfare Policy

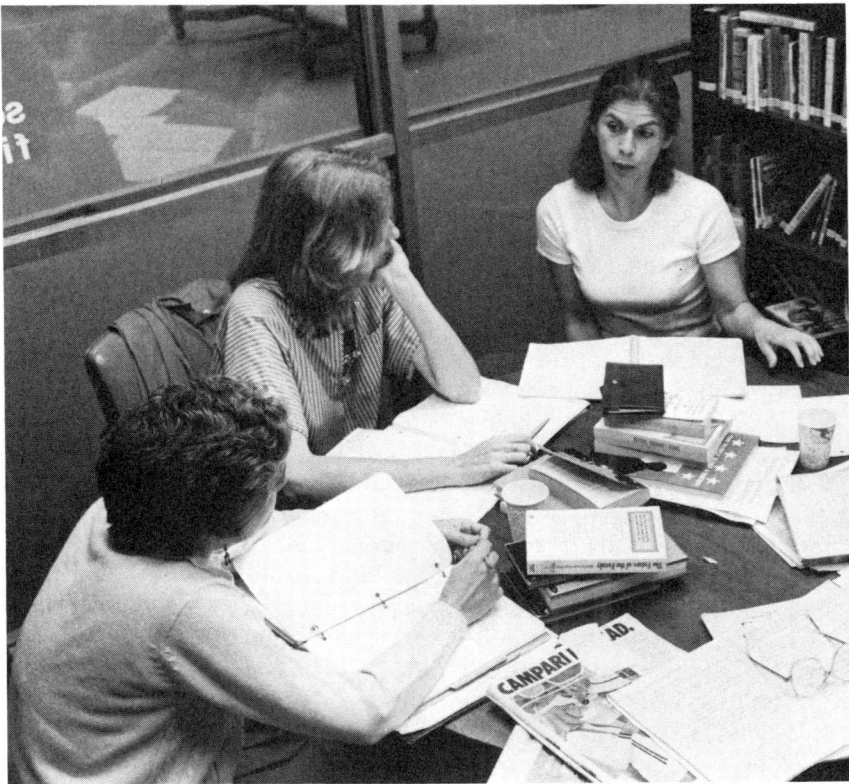

IN THIS CHAPTER WE WILL DISCUSS some beliefs that affect social welfare policy decisions in the United States. Decision making of any kind is ultimately a matter of choosing among various alternatives. The choice hinges upon values. A value, as defined by Milton Rokeach, is "an enduring belief that a specific mode of conduct or end-state of existence is personally or socially preferable to an opposite or converse mode of conduct or end-state of existence."[1] These "enduring beliefs" about the preferability of certain means over ends are the bases for deciding whether a given alternative is "good" or "bad."

David Gil, who writes from an egalitarian perspective, makes the point that choices in social welfare policy are heavily influenced by the dominant beliefs, values, ideologies, customs and traditions "shaped and guarded by cultural and political elites recruited, mainly, from among the more powerful and privileged strata."[2] If Gil is correct in his analysis, then one could expect that public policy in the United States tends to reflect a heavy conservative (in the sense of traditional) influence. Although the social welfare planner may want to operate from a liberal position (and not all do), he or she must be aware of the durability and influence of some major traditional values. Further, the social welfare planner needs to recognize that a number of these values clearly are in conflict. Some are easier to share than others. Some act as constraints on policy formulation and implementation.

The Relationship of Values and Knowledge

Many social workers who have shared their opinions with us believe that we have overemphasized the role of values and suggest that knowledge is an equally important input to policy choices. Pincus and Minahan discuss the relationship of values and knowledge to social work practice. By implication, the same distinction applies to social welfare policy. They define values as "beliefs, preferences, or assumptions about what is desirable or good for man."[3] Knowledge consists of "observations about the world and man which have been verified or are capable of verification."[4]

The problem is that the policy formulation process is not as rational as one might like. Knowledge is itself a value, after all, based on a set of beliefs about what constitutes truth. Readers with a background in philosophy will recognize that Pincus and Minahan's distinction between values and knowledge only holds so long as one is an empiricist, and that empiricism is only one way of looking at reality.

There are others who take a less idealistic view of rationality in decision making:

Those who look to evaluation to take the politics out of decision making are bound to be disappointed. Within every organization, decisions are reached through negotiation and accommodation, through politics . . . Evaluative facts have an impact on collective decisions only to the extent that program effectiveness—inevitably and justifiably—competes for influence on decisions with considerations of acceptability, feasibility and ideology.[5]

In short, one cannot take the politics out of social welfare planning and political decisions are based upon what people believe in and are willing to support emotionally.

At the heart of the problem is the question of whose values (or whose knowledge) are to be used in making decisions. A number of interested publics are involved in social welfare policy decisions. Politicians, business people, farmers, members of the professions, and the public all have a stake in social welfare policy. Nearly everyone seems to have a set of beliefs about what should be done and how it should be done. All believe that they are guided by the facts. Few suspect that they are really often operating solely in the realm of values. The decision-making process is further complicated because some of the people interested in the decisions have more influence than others.

Social workers—who we believe have not been a major factor in social welfare policy decisions—can play a larger role in the decision-making process if they are aware of the role of values in the process.

Central Values in the United States

Although the United States may not have achieved a complete pluralism in all areas of social and political life, there is certainly pluralism in the realm of social and personal values. Over the past hundred years or so, the country has moved from what seemed a fairly unified and perhaps simplistic set of values into an incredible array of diverse viewpoints. The United States has always included groups who marched to a different rhythm—the Puritans, the Anabaptists, the Shakers and more recently the "flower children," the "Jesus freaks," and Greenpeace. Each of these (and other) social, ethnic and cultural movements has added something to the richness of life in the United States. While these movements—and especially recent ones including those of blacks, youth and the feminists—have had a significant impact on American values, much of the core of the traditional value system remains intact and continues to receive widespread support.

Thus, a number of traditional value orientations are commonly shared in the United States. These values are not accepted by everyone, and some are clearly in conflict with others. We do not claim that social welfare policy must be governed by all of these values—but we do argue that they must be recognized and taken into account. A number of major social values were identified over twenty years ago by Robin Williams.[6] We have summarized Williams' discussion below, but we have added some of our own comments and what we see as the implications for social welfare policy.

Achievement and Success

Most Americans view the accumulation of money and the achievement of high social status as symbols of success and personal worth. Part of the discontent with public welfare stems from the notion that it is something for the nonachiever and the unsuccessful. People still generally equate public welfare with incorrect interpretations of the word "charity." We do not wish to digress into a long discussion here, but charity (from the Latin *caritas*) originally meant esteem or high regard for one's fellow human beings.[7] Charity has come to mean something that "we" do for "them." We no longer see the recipients of charity as fellow beings, but as inferiors. Obviously, if social welfare services are to be seen as a "first line" service, social welfare policy needs to focus on the mutuality of the human condition and avoid the "us vs. them" trap. One of the reasons that the Old Age, Survivors, Disability and Health Insurance provisions of the Social Security Act have been successful is that these programs take into account the American beliefs about achievement and success. One appears to "earn" benefits, and the beneficiary can identify his or her eligibility as something that is deserved because of participation in the work force. Economically secure retirement allows one, so the belief goes, to live on the fruits of a successful life.

Activity and Work

There is general agreement that the United States is a busy place. Visitors from other countries sometimes have difficulty adjusting to the continual noise and bustle of American cities. Williams suggests that this American characteristic came about because our population was largely recruited from the more aggressive and active members of the working classes of Europe. This accent on work was intensified with the struggle for survival on the frontier. In welfare planning, the high value that Americans put on work has usually surfaced in making work requirements a condition for eligibility for public welfare. Some social workers have argued that requiring work is punitive and should not be a feature of American welfare policy, but it is unlikely that Americans would accept a program that does not acknowledge the importance of work. It is important to note that the poor, when they are asked, almost always state a preference for work over "going on welfare." In Chapter 5 we will give some more attention to this theme.

Value Orientation

Americans tend to see the world from a moral perspective. Although there is great individual and group diversity in moral values in the United States, virtually all Americans believe that their view of events is morally responsible.

Few publicly espouse an amoral or totally hedonistic way of life. This strong sense of morality has led to a number of value conflicts, some with considerable violence.

Despite the diversity in personal values, there is a kind of "public morality" that more or less pervades the culture. True, there is a good deal of ritualism, hypocrisy, and cynicism in public morals, but there are some broad areas of agreement. Currently, for example, there seems to be a general agreement that honesty in public office is an important moral value. We are not surprised, because of our cynicism, that there are dishonest officials. Most Americans expect a certain amount of corruption in public office, and we will apparently tolerate a moderate amount of it. However, we do have limits of toleration. If the violation is flagrant enough, the official will be called into account. If the behavior goes beyond a certain point, the official will eventually be removed from office. Usually, the limits of toleration are reached when the official's behavior is seen to interfere seriously with his or her performance in the public interest.

Unfortunately, one of the more widely shared beliefs in this country is a warmed-over seventeenth-century puritanism that is often directed at the poor, the unemployed, and other groups who often are included in the clientele of the social worker. This moralistic attitude has a powerful effect on social welfare policy, as we shall see later.

It is impossible to analyze and formulate social welfare policy without paying attention to the moral values of this culture. However, it is important to emphasize that the social welfare planner should focus on positive values that involve responsibility for others rather than on the narrow puritanism that seeks reasons for moral disapproval of others.

Humanitarian Mores

Although Americans generally take a "hard-nosed" attitude toward the chronically poor and unsuccessful, they are often generous toward the victims of natural disasters and temporary distress. There is a certain value conflict between the willingness to contribute to private philanthropy through the United Way or a service club and the punitive approach to handling of public assistance. To most Americans, humanitarianism means private support for those who are in trouble "through no fault of their own." Public assistance is not seen as a worthy humanitarian program but as a governmental dole for those who are in trouble *through* faults of their own. Humanitarianism in the popular mind does not seem to extend to mass governmental programs. Because of the orientation of the average taxpayer in this country, an effective welfare policy cannot be sold on the basis of humanitarian concern. Perhaps if public assistance were not seen as a dole and the short-term nature of most assistance were emphasized, it would be possible to gain public support for more constructive policies.

Efficiency and Practicality

The stress on technology, expedience, novelty and getting things done has led to the glorification of engineering in the United States. The trouble is that technical efficiency tends to become valued for its own sake, rather than for what it serves to accomplish. Williams observes that such a concentration on practicality tends to de-emphasize intellectual, contemplative, ascetic, or mystical concerns. In order to have appeal to Americans, social welfare policy probably ought to address practical concerns and should emphasize efficiency, particularly in administration. In doing so, we need not neglect the humanity of those who will benefit. Social workers may have made a serious tactical error in not responding to the taxpayer's legitimate concern for an efficient use of funds. We should be in the forefront of those who want a streamlined administration with a maximum emphasis on the actual delivery of service.

Progress

The faith that things will surely get better over time, and that we can fashion the best of all possible worlds if we but have the will, is a central belief to many Americans. While this belief is threatened on occasion, it remains a sturdy element in the American creed. It is this value that leads to faddishness in social welfare programs as in other things. Part of the hostility that is shown toward social welfare may be related to the public's inability to see progress. While we do not advocate pandering to those who would argue for progress at any cost, we do think that social welfare personnel have not been sensitive to the public's desire to see things get better. It often appears that as more money is plowed into a program things get worse. While this is not true in all cases, it is often the appearance of things and it may be believed. Therefore, social workers should support programs that achieve demonstrable results, not those that are simply "trendy."

Material Comfort

The wealth and resources of the United States have led its citizens to achieve a high standard of living. Americans seem highly motivated by the desire to constantly improve their material position. A few decades ago, automobiles, televisions sets, and dishwashers were luxuries. Now, they have virtually become necessities for most of the population. Increased leisure time has accelerated the drive for material comfort.

For Americans, the achievement of a gadget-filled existence seems to have become a moral goal. It might be said that it is now more important that people live ostentatiously than that they live well. Few people would be willing to actually sacrifice in order to build a new library, support a symphony, or finance a new free medical clinic. It is part of the general moral climate to reduce the scope of benefits for those who are unemployed or marginally employed even though the country as a whole possesses enormous wealth. In this kind of an atmosphere, it is difficult to convince state legislatures that benefits for health, education and social welfare should be maintained on an adequate level.

Equality

The United States Constitution was written by people who deliberately rejected the traditional social stratification of Europe. Consequently, Americans have a formal commitment to equality before the law. Over time, the concept of equality before the law has been extended to mean an equality of formal rights and obligations and equality of opportunity for social and economic rewards.[8] Williams emphasizes the notion that inequalities resulting from achievement have not been seen as violations of the American concept of political equality. For many years, rewards not resulting from achievement, including those related to sex or race, were considered the natural order of things. Now, because of the activity of blacks, feminists, and other groups, rewards not related to achievement have become largely unacceptable. It is interesting to note that with a very few exceptions, activists have not wanted to disturb the basic opportunity and achievement structure. Their efforts have largely been concentrated on opening it, but not eliminating it. Equality before the law and equality of opportunity are palatable to most Americans, but social policies that encourage economic equality have not gained much of a foothold in the United States (or anywhere else including the Soviet Union for that matter). There have been periodic flare-ups of socialistic sentiment in the country (in the 1920s and to a lesser extent in the 1960s) but these movement have been more rhetorical than successful. There are a few people prominent in social welfare policy circles that claim to have egalitarian economic ideas, but it is unlikely that this point of view will be popular in the United States. We have seen the electorate swing toward the right in recent years, particularly in presidential politics, with the elections of Mr. Nixon and Mr. Reagan. Even Mr. Carter was clearly more conservative than previous Democrats. In the face of this tendency to periodically shift to conservative leaders, social workers who espouse radical economic policies run the considerable risk of becoming an embattled minority with little public support and little impact on public policy.

Freedom

The American concept of freedom finds its expression in "a tendency to think of rights rather than duties, suspicion of established (especially personal) authority, a distrust of central government, a deep aversion to acceptance of obviously coercive restraint through visible social organization."[9] American citizens characteristically demand rights to privacy, engage in various forms of civil disobedience, and flout unpopular laws. Whereas Americans appear to accept diffuse controls over their behavior (as in the case of impersonal markets) they object to any really strict personal control through law and regulation. Personal autonomy is of high value and a certain amount of variant behavior is tolerated unless it is perceived as publicly threatening.

All Americans, from the John Birch Society to the Socialist Workers' Alliance, prize freedom though their views may differ on what it is. It is this strong tradition of personal freedom that has complicated the development of coherent social welfare programs and services in the United States. Each new proposal is seen by someone as an inhibition of personal freedom. This, we believe, is an unfortunate misunderstanding of the motives of most social welfare planners. Most personnel in social welfare believe that they are *enhancing* freedom by increasing the life chances of the clientele. The social welfare enterprise probably needs to clarify its goals and be more conscious of the public's need to know what they are. The aims of social welfare policy should not deprive Americans of personal freedom, but should provide supports that open up choices for people. The idea is to increase the opportunities to secure jobs, housing, and services that enable people to maximize their life chances.

External Conformity

There is a strong tendency for Americans to conform, at least in external ways, to their contemporaries. This tendency toward conformity is not necessarily an evil (although there are critics who say that it is), but there is a problem here because the clientele of social welfare programs are usually seen as "different" rather than as fellow humans. Social welfare policy makers should, we think, stress that clients have many of the same needs and problems that might be faced by other human beings if circumstances were altered. Emphasizing personal differences tends to widen the distance between client groups and the rest of society.

Science and Secular Rationality

Under this heading, Williams discusses the concern with "order, control and calculability" characteristic of an engineering society. This interest in order and predictability is closely related to the values of progress, equality and practicality. Science is believed to be rational and disciplined. It has become part of a "secular religion" aimed toward control of a disordered world. The scientist is seen as one preoccupied with efficiency, technology, pragmatism, and expediency. To the extent that rationality is important, it is clearly in the interest of social welfare policy makers to support a more efficient system. It should not be expected, however, that social welfare be dehumanized and secularized in the interests of order and control.

Nationalism-Patriotism

This value does not impinge on social welfare policy to any great extent. Under this heading, Williams discusses two types of nationalistic values in the United States. In the one, the nation becomes the end, and criticism of any feature of American life may be considered treasonous. In the other, the nation is regarded highly because of its identification with the ends of democracy and freedom which supports dissent. These two points of view inevitably clash. Those who see the nation as an end perceive the need for increasing control over individual behavior. Those who see the nation as a means to an end tend to protest any compromise with the values of freedom, individualism and democracy.

About the only time that there is any connection between this value and social welfare policy is when a policy is believed to be similar to a European practice. It is generally disastrous to try to sell a policy to Americans on the basis of how well it works in Europe. This is most curious in a country that is quick to buy German automobiles, import French wines and perfumes, and store spare cash in Swiss and Norwegian banks! It appears to us that people will use the "it works in Europe" argument when it supports what they want to do and reject it when it does not. So far, there are few contemporary European welfare practices that appeal to our current decision makers.

Democracy

Williams lists major themes in the democratic creed as including "equality of certain formal rights and formal equality of opportunity, a faith in the rule of impersonal law, optimistic rationalism, and ethical individualism."[10] Many of these themes relate to other American value orientations, but they are uniquely tied together as part of the democratic value system. Underlying all these themes is the "agreement upon procedure in the distribution of power and in the settling of conflicts," and agreement on the chief aim of government as the maximizer of individual self-direction as a means of ensuring worth, dignity, and the creative capacity for individual human beings.[11]

Interestingly enough, although nearly every American thinks of the United States as a democracy, it is not. It is, as our friends on the right have pointed out, a republic. The people do not rule directly, but voice their opinions through the kind of representatives whom they elect. While a few states do make use of the referendum and vote directly on some issues, for the most part the political decisions of the people are indirectly rendered. This is an important distinction, particularly when it comes to social welfare policy. As a general rule, those senators and members of congress that tend to support social welfare are from states and districts where a pro-welfare stance will give them votes. While it may be tempting to stress democratic values in social welfare, it is important to realize that ultimately social welfare policy is a major power issue.

Individual Personality

Americans are taught from birth that the individual personality is of high intrinsic worth. The individual is viewed as a responsible, independent, decision-making unit. Although at times this value orientation may clash with other values, such as the achievement-success orientation, it remains a deeply imbedded value in our culture. The length to which our society goes to protect the individual can be seen, according to Williams, in our firm legal stance that an individual is not free to take his or her own life, since an individual personality would thereby be destroyed. Clearly, this value conflicts with the value of external conformity. This tends to force those who would support social welfare concerns to balance a belief in individual differences with the idea that beneficiaries of social services and programs are not so different that they become "them" rather than part of "us."

Racism and Related Group Superiority Themes

The values of equality, humanitarianism, democracy and the worth of the individual are in a recurring conflict with pervasive patterns of racism, sexism and other group superiority themes. No American social welfare policy should be based on notions of group superiority. Policymakers, however, must be aware of these themes in American society. They must be prepared to counter opponents whose objection to a given social welfare policy is merely a thinly disguised bigotry.

Another View

Williams' list of dominant American values is, as we have said, over twenty years old. Has the passage of time made a difference? Surely, one would think, some of the values noted above have changed radically or at least have been significantly modified. W. Andrew Achenbaum, whose interest is in federal programs for the aging, has re-examined this problem in the light of his concern for the values that influence program decisions relating to the aging American. He concludes that American values are still largely based on a "continuing commitment to Judeo-Christian ideals and Enlightenment principles, to a democratic form of government and to a capitalistic economic system (which) has enabled a civic culture to flower, which has been remarkable for its resilience and longevity."[12] Achenbaum, like Williams, recognizes the inconsistencies and ambiguities in the American system. These inconsistencies are related, in his view, to a number of value dilemmas that have affected the programs for the aged in this country. Although Achenbaum does not do it this way, the issues that he identifies can be restated as questions that have a wider application.[13]

1. Should all Americans be expected to be self-reliant under all circumstances or do we have to take into account the fact that some people are going to be dependent on others for survival for all or part of the time?
2. Should people work for everything they get or are there things to which they are entitled by virtue of being human beings?
3. Is work always a virtue and leisure always a vice?
4. Should individual rights be stressed or should family rights be paramount?
5. Should social programs be supported by private or public means?
6. Should social programs provide benefits on the basis of equity and fairness or should they focus on providing adequate benefits regardless of whether or not a person has earned benefits?
7. Should programs follow tradition or should they try for novel and inventive solutions?

As can be seen, the kinds of value dilemmas that Achenbaum identifies in the 1980s do not differ fundamentally from those listed by Williams in the 1960s. We conclude that while there are some broad areas of general agreement among Americans (that is, the majority of Americans accept some form or another of Judeo-Christian ethics, a belief in technological and scientific progress, a general orientation to "democratic" principles and individualism, and an ideal of free market capitalism) there are also areas of inconsistency and many unresolved issues when one gets down to specifics. That is, everybody believes in progress, but there is great disagreement about just what that is. It should come as no shock, therefore, to find that the American welfare system is confusing and controversial. At least we can take comfort in the realization that there is unanimity among social workers. Or can we?

Social Work Values

If one takes the position that social work is a major profession in the welfare enterprise, then social workers' values figure to be important factors in social welfare policy choices. We have noted elsewhere that this has not always been the case for a variety of reasons. We can now add another reason: There is no single consistent value position with which all social workers agree. Charles Levy, who has probably studied this problem more than anyone else, has observed that social work values are not simply a mirror of the values of society, but that there are only some values that are shared at least in part.[14]

Levy suggests that what is shared includes the ideas that human beings are changeable, self-actualizing, and equal in opportunity and that they deserve equal treatment, support, opportunities for participation in their own government, and nonjudgmental acceptance. This listing roughly parallels Williams' values of humanitarianism, equality, freedom, democracy and the worth of the individual.

Martin Rein takes a more complex and certainly a less sanguine view.[15] He argues that there are a number of creeds and belief systems among social workers. He identifies four major ways in which social workers look at their primary job.

1. *The traditional casework view.*

   The aim of the traditional caseworker is to enable people to meet the standards of society by learning to conform to traditional behavioral norms.

2. *Radical casework.*

   The radical social worker rejects traditional standards as normative and challenges hurtful norms through appeals to alternative standards and by challenging institutions to be more humane.

3. *Community sociotherapy.*

   Those who follow this belief system encourage self-help among community groups on the principle that as people become involved in activity they displace their hostility and learn to become conformists.

4. *Radical social policy.*

   This is a reformist creed which focuses on the notion that changing political, economic, and social institutions is a precondition for individual change.

Other value positions can be added. There are social workers who see their activity and the purpose of social welfare as extensions of the ministry of a religious body. Some social workers see their mission in terms of protecting society against the deviant. Others see social welfare as a highly personalized activity that expresses their own creativity. These additional views only confirm Rein's point: there is no general agreement among social workers about values.

Pincus and Minahan point out that the social worker is often caught in value dilemmas and complex, ambiguous moral situations. They identify a number of such situations. Examples include the issue of self-determination versus manipulation of the client and the problem of encouraging clients to plan for constructive change where the client perceives the world in fatalisic terms and believes that nothing can change.[16] Their best counsel is to maintain a balance between flexibility and integrity and to develop self-awareness, technical expertise, and a tolerance for ambiguity.[17] We add that we think that social workers need to be clear at least about their own value systems and need to be able to recognize that others' value systems are meaningful and should not be demeaned.

We have no resolution to the problem of the diversity of values in social welfare and among social workers. In the next chapter, the reader will find that professional values are elements in one of the criteria for evaluating social welfare policy. In the absence of a clear and universally accepted set of social work values, we suggest that the only practical approach is to keep abreast of the positions taken by the National Association of Social Workers. These positions represent a good-faith attempt to reach consensus within the profession, and they are periodically reviewed for their relevancy. This is not an entirely satisfactory solution, we admit, but it will have to do unless social workers come to a general agreement about professional values. Such an agreement is unlikely in any realistic short term because of the diversity of persons who enter the field. This problem is not exclusive to social work. A diversity of personal and even professional values exists in the ranks of other occupational groups.

Values and Problems Addressed by Social Welfare Policy

The nature of social welfare policy has something to do with the way in which problems are defined. The sociologists Robert K. Merton and Robert Nisbet have defined social problems as "the substantial, unwanted discrepancies between what is in a society and what a functionally significant collectivity within that society seriously . . . desires to be in it."[18] In other words, a social problem is publicly defined when people who have enough influence to be listened to, realize that there is a discrepancy between their perception of what society values and the actual life conditions in the society. As can readily be seen, American social problems are closely related to American social values. For instance, since a high value is placed on work, achievement, and money, it follows that when the unemployment rate is considered high and poverty becomes visible, the poor will be seen to be problematical. Whether or not poverty will be seen as a social problem or merely as a personal problem for those who are poor will depend on whether or not those who perceive poverty as a problem are in a position that will ensure that their views will be heard and whether or not they are concerned enough about the condition to act publicly. If a significant segment of the public does not see the discrepancy as a problem, it will remain in the public mind as only a personal problem for those who are afflicted and little or no public action is likely.

This point may need further explication. To many social workers, social problems are considered something more than matters of opinion. They are definite conditions whose seriousness is obvious. How can there be any doubt that poverty is a problem? Social workers must remember that their view of certain conditions as problematic stems from their espousal of whatever values they may hold. Those who are not social workers may not share the same values, or they may have a conflict among values that the social workers involved do not have.

Like it or not, a social problem is whatever people with enough "clout" say it is. Sometimes many people are in agreement. Almost everybody would join in saying that crime is a social problem—except for those for whom crime is a business. Sometimes something can be defined as a social problem by relatively few people if they are powerful and well organized. In the 1920s, an extremely well-organized group defined alcohol consumption as a major social problem, even though it soon became apparent that this was a minority definition that was not popular in the long run.

To complicate things, it is also true that the size and importance of the group that defines problems changes over time. In the middle 1960s, a very large number of people who had influence saw poverty as a major problem in our society. Poverty is no longer central as a major social problem. It has been replaced by unemployment, high interest rates and the federal budget deficit. In the public view, these problems are more pervasive and threatening.

Generally, social welfare policy is devised in response to a problem that has been identified by society or some significant segment of society as appropriate to social welfare. As a rule, the problem has reached a fairly serious stage before it gets significant attention. There have been suggestions that social work, as a major service delivery profession, ought to think in terms of prevention. While we agree that this would be an ideal approach, it is not really viable. We cannot readily anticipate many of the social problems that will be defined and funded in the future. Since the social welfare enterprise is not entrepreneurial or well endowed, it has to wait on social definitions of problems and funding. So far, society as a whole has not seen fit to finance preventive social welfare planning on any wide scale.

Social Problems, Social Welfare Policy and Social Work

As we have said, the kinds of things that a society considers problematical depend very much on the values of that society. The nonindustrial nation might define its problems as hunger, lack of pure water and disease. Because these problems are such a clear threat to survival, they would seem to claim the center of attention. Such a society might place the highest social value on identifying an effective means of producing food, finding a clean source of fresh water and building a comprehensive health enterprise. However, this may not be what happens. Those of us who have grown up in Western-oriented industrial nations would probably think in these terms. It is important to recognize that the values that are important in the Western world may have nothing to do with either problem formulation or problem solution in non-Western society. Instead, another set of values might govern the whole problem-definition-solution process. In a given society, the major decision makers might conclude that the people are hungry because it is fate. Therefore, the central problem of the society might well be the need to spend more time in contemplating the nature of fate or the propitiation of the forces of nature. In such a framework, hunger may be viewed as a secondary problem.

Defining any behavior, condition, or circumstance as a social problem is ultimately a value judgment. For another example, before 1914 the United States perceived drug abuse and addiction as a medical matter. In an era of widespread concern about "moral decay," the nation redefined that condition during the period from 1910 to 1930 as a social problem rather than as the problem of a number of individuals. The "drug problem" has by now become a law enforcement problem that grows more serious and more tragic every day. Unfortunately, the law enforcement approach appears to have led to a number of new social problems, including widespread crime in urban areas and a great deal of cultural conflict.

If we are correct in our understanding of the nature of social problems, then the charge to social work and other helping professions must be enlarged to include skills beyond those of the clinic. Appropriately prepared social workers can help groups and communities to redefine problems into more manageable components. They can aid in the formulation of more appropriate policies and help to educate the public in effective problem definition and policy formulation. The social worker of the future, then, needs to be prepared to take on a number of roles: educator, value changer, social institutional change agent, broker of services, advocate on behalf of those who need services and therapist.

Most of the present approaches to policy analysis and formulation start from the premise that since many social agencies already exist, policies are most likely to be formulated and implemented by them. We take the position that social workers should focus on a broad range of possible policy alternatives, some of which may lead entirely outside the context of existing agencies. Some alternatives may involve organizations and institutions other than those ordinarily seen as part of the social welfare enterprise. In order to participate in policy formulation and implementation in the present era, social workers must learn to use influence, build coalitions and engage in problem redefinition. Social workers will have to be freed from their present professional and organizational biases in order to work in this broader social context.

In our next chapter, we offer a system of policy analysis that we think will help expand the social worker's competence in the policy arena. It is a pragmatic system and is not limited in its usefulness to any one ideological position.

REFERENCES

1. Milton Rokeach, *The Nature of Human Values* (New York: The Free Press, 1973), p. 5.
2. David G. Gil, *Unraveling Social Policy*, Revised edition (Cambridge, Mass.: Schenckman Publishing Co., 1976), p. 28.
3. Allen Pincus and Anne Minahan, *Social Work Practice: Model and Method* (Itasca, Ill.: F. E. Peacock, 1973), p. 52.

4. *Ibid.*

5. Carol Weiss, *Evaluation Research*, (Englewood Cliffs, N.J.: Prentice-Hall, 1972), p. 4.

6. Robin Williams, *American Society: A Sociological Interpretation*, 2nd edition (New York: Alfred A. Knopf, 1957).

7. Melancthon W. Jacobus, Elbert C. Lane, and Andrew C. Zenos, eds., *A New Standard Bible Dictionary*, 3rd rev. ed. (New York: Funk & Wagnalls company, 1936), pp. 126–127.

8. Williams, *op. cit.*, pp. 440–442.

9. *Ibid.*, p. 446.

10. *Ibid.*, p. 461.

11. *Ibid.*, pp. 461–462.

12. W. Andrew Achenbaum, *Shades of Grey,* (Boston: Little, Brown and Company, 1983), p. 19.

13. *Ibid.*, pp. 20–23.

14. Charles S. Levy, "The Value Base of Social Work," *Journal of Education for Social Work*, Vol. 9, No. 1 (Winter 1973).

15. Martin Rein, "Social Work in Search of a Radical Profession," *Social Work*, Vol. 15, No. 2 (April 1970).

16. Pincus and Minahan, *op. cit.*, pp. 42–52.

17. *Ibid.*, p. 52.

18. Robert K. Merton and Robert Nisbet, *Contemporary Social Problems,* 2nd ed. (New York: Harcourt, Brace and World, 1966), p. 799.

QUESTIONS FOR DISCUSSION

1. Why are there so few examples of decision making, whether in school, job, or family life, that do not involve value judgments?

2. Select a social problem not specifically discussed in the chapter and explore the value judgments involved in its definition and management.

3. Why can an advanced or post-industrial society address itself to social problems that are different from those in developing societies?

4. List examples (other than drug abuse) in which a policy designed to cope with a social problem has either led to a new problem or the aggravation of an existing problem.

5. Try your hand at redefining a social problem so that it might be more manageable. Consider prostitution or gambling since they are highly value-laden, legal in some places and illegal in others.

6. Discuss the differences between societal values and social work values. Are there more similarities than differences?

SUGGESTED PROJECTS

1. Talk with a social worker about professional values that are most relevant to social work practice.

2. Discuss societal values with a sociologist or an anthropologist. Does he or she agree with Williams' list?

3. Ask a state legislator or a member of Congress about the societal values that he or she considers most important in contemporary policy making.

FOR FURTHER READING _____

Nathan E. Cohen. *Social Work and Social Problems.* New York: National Association of Social Workers, 1964. Although seriously dated, this is an early effort to develop a model for the analysis of social problems that is heavily oriented toward recognition of the role of societal and social work values in problem definition and resolution.

Charles S. Levy. *Social Work Ethics.* New York: Human Services Press, 1976. A thoughtful book by the most influential scholar of ethics in social work.

Roy Lubove. *The Professional Altruist.* Cambridge, Mass.: Harvard University Press, 1965. A book that is surely well on its way to becoming a classic in its field. Discussion of value considerations and choices occurring throughout the development of social work practice.

Milton Rokeach. *The Nature of Human Values.* New York: The Free Press, 1973. Written by the leading American sociologist in the field of societal values.

3

The Systematic Process of Policy Analysis and Formulation

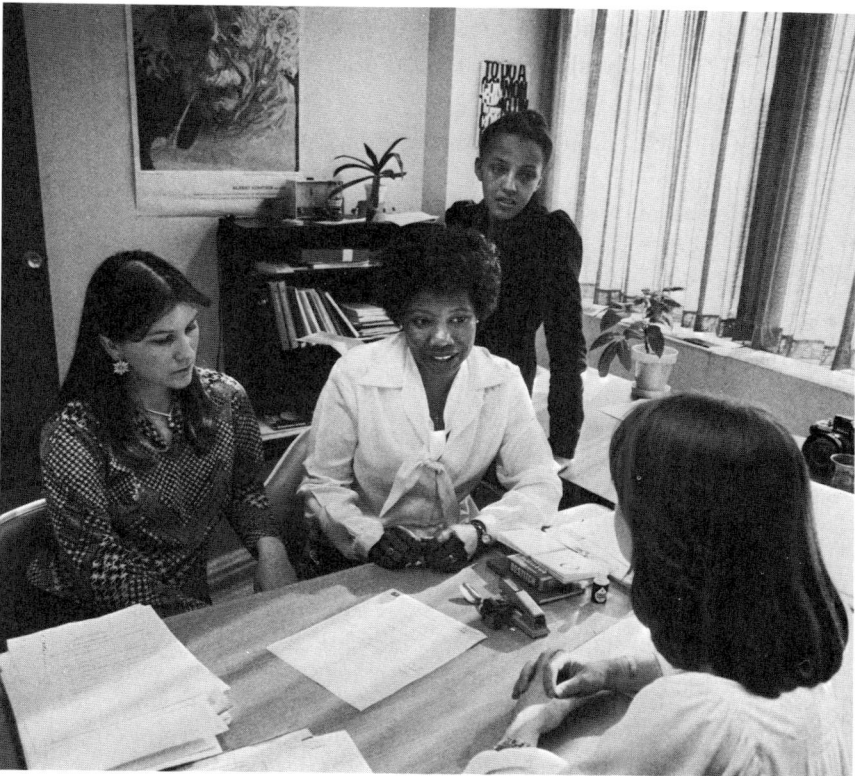

IN THIS CHAPTER WE PRESENT A relatively systematic way of analyzing social welfare policy. As we said in the last chapter, social welfare policy is closely related to the values of the culture. There are other important factors that must be taken into account. The factors that we will discuss fall into four categories:

- **Considerations Related to Values**

   Is the policy under consideration compatible with contemporary "style"?

   Is the policy compatible with important and enduring cultural values, particularly equity, fairness and justice?

   Is the policy compatible with social work's professional value and ethical system?

- **Dimensions of Influence**

   Is the policy acceptable to those in formal decision-making positions?

   Does the policy satisfy relevant interest groups?

- **Knowledge Considerations**

   Is the policy based on knowledge that has been tested to some degree?

   Is the policy workable? That is, can the programs that flow from the policy be carried out in the real world?

   Does the policy create few problems for both the public and the intended beneficiaries?

- **Elements Related to Costs and Benefits**

   Is the policy reasonably effective?

   Is the policy efficient?

We will discuss these questions in some detail later. It should be evident that in addition to their usefulness in analyzing a current policy, they also serve as a basis for evaluating alternatives that may be proposed.

We think that the ideal social policy would produce a "yes" to each question. In the real world, however, few (if any) policies would satisfy all criteria. Some of these factors are obviously more important than others, but we have been unable to develop a satisfactory weighting system that would make the task of policy analysis easy. Our experience suggests that one who is doing policy analysis has to live with some uncertainty. Taking these factors into account should result in a better policy decision than if one did not. The closer a given policy satisfies these criteria, the more effective it will be in achieving its goals. Perhaps the chief use of a scheme of this kind is not the comparison of a given policy with an absolute standard but the comparison of one policy with an alternative. If one policy more nearly meets these criteria than another, we think it is more likely to work for human benefit.

Necessity for Criteria for Evaluation

It is helpful to look at the way policies have been selected in the past. The determination of which policy to use has not always been approached systematically. Braybrooke and Lindblom discuss two frequently used but primitive approaches to policy analysis and formulation.[1] In one, the "naive criteria" method, it is assumed that all one needs to worry about are a few general values, such as "security" or "full employment." In this approach, if a policy to gain "full employment" is developed, then it must be all right, since full employment is a desirable value. It is apparently not necessary to worry about the inflationary effect of full employment or whether or not everyone is prepared and able to work. Another example of the naive criteria approach is the notion that the solution to the problem of fathers not supporting their children is to "lock the bastards up." This policy panders to a very naive criterion for problem solution. It does not take into account a whole series of very complex issues. More importantly, most simple solutions have been tried and do not work. In this case, a father (if he can be found) does not earn any money in jail.

The second primitive approach is the "naive priorities" method. This consists of merely ranking the priorities of one's own interest group and using them as a guide to policy determination. It is as if one operated in a situation where no other group had conflicting priorities. Like it or not, we do have to make policy in a world in which other priorities exist—and we must take them into account.

In social welfare, these unsystematic approaches have kept us from improving policymaking through more creative efforts. Yehezkel Dror has written on this topic; he describes the current situation:

> Misery, poverty, war, the gap between the haves and the have-nots (individuals and countries alike), the utilization of limited space for increasing humanity, environmental issues, human and community relations, distribution of health services, individual and public safety, recreation, transportation, telecommunication, and so on and so forth—these are among the areas and issues for policymaking, all and each one of which are filled with difficult problems that, at present, we are quite incapable of handling.[2]

What are the requirements of a more sophisticated process of policy analysis and formulation? First, it should be rational. The evidence for decision making should rest on tested knowledge rather than uninformed opinion. Second, the method should be clear and explicit. Any person using the same method should reach the same conclusion.[3] Third, the objective should be to reach the solution of maximum benefit for the least social cost. The ecologist Ian McHarg calls this "the solution of maximum social utility."[4] What is needed is to produce a new policy which avoids as many social costs as possible while creating or enhancing as many social values as possible. Fourth, one must be able to understand the ecological consequences circumscribing the process of policy analysis and formulation. What is the range of effects on surrounding social structures and people? What is the impact on the total environment? The essential precondition of planning, according to McHarg, is the formulation of choices related to goals, as well as the criteria for assessing them and the means for their realization.[5] Fifth, good public policy should coincide with individual self-interest, insofar as this is possible. If one is to establish the largest base of support as well as to ensure the greatest opportunity for individual benefit, this is a clear requirement. Sixth, if planning requires the posing of alternatives with the costs and benefits of each, it is necessary to be able to demonstrate the consequences of allowing the present policy to continue.[6] The future of each alternative, including the presently used one, needs to be forecast as accurately as possible. Seventh, successful policy must be consistent with relevant social and personal values. Eighth, social welfare personel must be concerned with creating an environment in which people can function in self-fulfilling ways rather than endlessly coping with social problems.[7] This last requirement suggests, for example, that efforts should be made to create a climate in which people can develop in healthy ways rather than spending much of their time in treatment for pathology.

The requirements above are based on the work of an ecologist. We have much to learn from the discipline of ecology. It is a guiding principle in ecology that "every time a decision is made, countless other decisions are simultaneously precluded."[8] The traditional courses in social welfare policy and services in schools of social work have been criticized for failing to observe this principle: "Our most fruitful guide for selecting materials from the past comes from ecology. Our need, I think, is to implant the idea of the complex interrelatedness of variables over time, space, and systems, to alert students to social change processes and the unique role of values in human decision making."[9]

Other Frameworks for Policy Analysis

Most writers on social welfare policy have traditionally taken an ideological position on a social problem, often poverty, or have directed their attention toward some goal, such as income maintenance or health provision, and then devoted the discussion to interpreting or defending their position. More recently, a growing number of writers have addressed the analysis of social welfare policy as a process without necessarily infusing it with a specific ideological stance.

The approach of breaking social welfare policy into a number of key areas of concern may be of more help in an analytical understanding of social policy as a phenomenon than in knowing how to formulate a policy. Neil Gilbert and

Harry Specht look at social policy analysis in this way. Their framework follows. We have added our interpretation in the parentheses.

> The four major dimensions of choice in this framework may be expressed in the form of the following questions:
> 1. What are the bases of social allocations? (That is, who should benefit and why?)
> 2. What are the types of social provisions to be allocated? (What should they get?)
> 3. What are the strategies for the delivery of these provisions? (How will they get it?)
> 4. What are the methods of financing these provisions? (Who will pay for it and how?)[10]

A framework of this sort helps to analyze existing policy and to visualize its components. It may be less helpful in evaluating alternatives to existing policy because it does not look at factors outside the social welfare enterprise.

Perhaps the consideration of alternatives is just as important. David Gil argues that "the development and study of alternative social policies is perhaps the most important aspect of policy analysis." [11] He suggests that to analyze policy alternatives, one must consider: (1) the way in which resources are developed and the priorities that are given to various goods and services; (2) the way societies allocate positions, functions and tasks to its members; and (3) the way privileges are distributed.[12]

Gilbert and Specht's work and Gil's book are important contributions to social work's maturity in the policy area. We differ from them primarily in the position that we assign to the roles of values and politics in the policy process. We support Alfred Kahn's contention that "large social policy changes are made in value terms and political perspective, not through the weighing of effectiveness." [13] Others agree. Perlman and Gurin comment that "decisions are based ultimately on commitments to certain values or value systems." [14] They recognize that practitioners juggle three main considerations in reaching decisions (values, patterns of influence or power, and rationality), but the first consideration—values—seems to be the most important.

Needs, Goals, and Policies

We are ready now to present our approach to policy analysis and formulation. This chapter will sketch out the general outline. Later chapters will show the application both to existing policies and to problems that need coherent policy.

We believe that one should plan social welfare policy only after a careful needs assessment in which as many relevant persons as possible are invited to participate. It seems to us that social welfare programs are often planned simply because the money is there or because a relatively small number of vocal people support the idea. These approaches can lead to the imposition of unwanted or unneeded programs which the beneficiaries use grudgingly, if at all.

A good needs assessment leads to the setting of goals. Goals are broad statements of desired outcomes. If the people involved in the needs assessment are broadly representative of the community, then the goals should reflect some degree of community consensus about needs. The goals can be long-term or short-term, but are more likely to be successful when they are reachable and immediate. It is workable to suggest that any policy formulator have long-term goals that act as a general guide to the future, but to set within the long-term goals a series of short-term goals which are compatible. Having set the immediate goals, the next step is to consider the alternatives that are available in reaching them. It is important to point out that the social worker should not confine his or her planning to existing organizational frameworks. One should be alive to the possibility of opportunities for the development of entirely new approaches. Good policy formulation should not be constrained by existing institutions or organizations and their present modes of operation. There are enough constraints to consider already, as we shall point out.

A Framework for Policy Analysis and Formulation

The reader should note that each of the questions that we pose can be asked of a current policy as one attempts to analyze its effectiveness. The same questions should also be asked of any proposed alternative. The questions follow the same order as the list at the beginning of the chapter.

1. *Is the policy under consideration compatible with contemporary "style"?*

   Political scientists have noted that communities and nations have "climates" or "styles" in public matters (and private matters too) and that people expect things to be done accordingly. The brief presidency of John F. Kennedy was characterized by a youthful, innovative enthusiasm that was sometimes praised for its dynamism and sometimes criticized for its frivolous "Camelot" mystique. The Johnson administration was perceived as bold and daring in the conception of new programs, yet it was derided for expectation of "quick fixes" for serious, long-standing problems. During the Nixon years, there was a positive accent on localism in planning and program development, but a negative overtone of mistrust and suspicion. The Ford presidency was recognized as decent and honest, but cautious and tentative. The Carter years reflected the president's fundamental humanness, but the constructive atmosphere was flawed by a lack of political sophistication and by indecisiveness. The Reagan administration, in the field of social welfare, has stressed voluntarism and private initiative, rather than governmental responsibility.

   While these characterizations of recent national administrations are admittedly facile oversimplifications, they do exemplify the kind of thing that we think must be done in some depth around a given policy proposal. Any policy innovation that is too drastic a departure from the prevailing style probably will not be given much attention and will have little chance of acceptance.

At the local level, communities vary from arch-conservative to progressive, and styles vary from a preference for the quiet and cautious approach to a stormy and aggressive one.

An assessment of the climate or style of a situation may not be as important as other features, but it is important and a necessary aspect of a thorough analysis. It is hard to suggest a totally dependable way of ascertaining political climates since there is a certain subjectivity involved. One can only be sensitive to the statements and behaviors of community, state, and national decision makers.

2. *Is the policy compatible with important and enduring cultural values, particularly equity, fairness and justice?*

There are strong reasons why a policy should move the society toward a condition of equity, fairness and justice. These concepts have a great deal of historical potency. They are positively regarded by all Americans. If a policy moves toward equity, it provides for a fairer distribution of opportunities before the law. As we noted in Chapter 2, most Americans want to identify with a moral position. Equity, fairness and justice are important moral values that people want to see reflected in public life even if private life does not always contain them. Policies that aim at fairness and impartiality are more generally acceptable than policies that create obvious privilege. As a general rule, one can tell if a policy is just and equitable if it fails to attract legal challenges, particularly challenges based on the principles of "due process" or "equal protection." Policy makers would do well to anticipate the likelihood of violation of these principles as a gauge of the legitimacy of any proposal. While we believe that equity, justice and fairness are paramount, the policy analyst needs to be aware of other important values. The list in Chapter 2 may be useful as a rough checklist. Because values do change, this list will need to be revised over time, although values do not change as rapidly as styles.

3. *Is the policy compatible with social work's professional value and ethical system?*

We noted in Chapter 2 that there is not a consensus among social workers on all value questions. The entire issue of compatibility between societal values and professional values is particularly acute in social work.[15] The social worker often finds it difficult to choose between professional values and broader social values, since they are often at variance.[16] Very often, the policy alternatives considered by most social workers will be more compatible with a fairly liberal ideology than with the more conservative values of most Americans. Even without the ideological component, there are often differences between professionals and the public over purely instrumental values having to do with the way social workers do their jobs. Charles Frankel, the philosopher, considers it important that social workers retain the tension between professional values and societal values in order to avoid purely political solutions to problems.[17] We think that it would be equally desirable, on the other hand, to avoid clinging to ideological positions when clearly a political solution is needed. In short, we think that both professional values and societal values need to be given consideration.

Examples of the discontinuity between social work values and societal values are not hard to find. A frequent clash arises over the societal value of parental responsibility and rights, on the one hand, and the professional's view that children have rights that supersede parental rights. This particular tension has led some social workers to distrust courts that tend to lean more toward parental rights.[18]

Since it is clear that social workers operate from a number of different value positions, it is not a simple matter to suggest a way of identifying a clear standard of social work values. Our best suggestion here is to look at the position taken by the National Association of Social Workers (NASW) in their frequent position papers. Although all social workers are not in agreement with NASW, the professional association represents the best attempt to bring people to some agreement on highly charged issues.

4. *Is the policy acceptable to those in formal decision-making positions?*

By this we mean, is the policy acceptable to the working politicians that serve in legislatures and administrative structures at various levels of government? Many social workers and persons in leadership roles in social welfare have tended to be fearful, suspicious, and uncomfortable with politicians and the political process. This response, of course, was justified by the political scandals of the seventies that culminated in the events that have come to be known collectively as the Watergate affair. This distrust of the political process was not always typical. Many of the early social workers, Jane Addams for example, turned freely and often to political action. In the past several years, it has become clear that political power can be used to achieve social welfare ends, that political interests are not necessarily opposed to professional interests, and that politicians and social workers can work effectively together.[19]

Social workers' willingness to move toward the political arena has been reinforced by their increasing recognition that the political process can be responsive to people when they work together to achieve mutually beneficial ends. It seems clear that social workers need to understand political institutions and processes, if the policies that they endorse are to get any kind of favorable consideration. Consequently, social workers need to know a great deal about the timing of policy efforts, the legislative process, techniques of forming coalitions with other groups (even though the price might be some change in timing or in content of policy), and the techniques of influencing public opinion.[20]

In terms of social policy analysis and formulation (as opposed to implementation) it is obvious that no policy alternative, however humane in its motivation, is apt to receive serious public consideration unless it is politically feasible. One needs to take the current political patterns into consideration because the attitudes and ideology of political figures and groups are crucial factors.

The question of political feasibility involves an assessment of what is possible today and what might need to be deferred until next year or ten years from now. We will need to become comfortable with conflict strategies, techniques for conflict resolution, skills in working with interest groups, and methods of dealing with politicians and their staffs.

Fair and equitable social welfare policy may involve the inclusion into the decision-making process of those who are currently disadvantaged and powerless. So we would ask not only: Will the decision makers accept this policy and work for its adoption? We would also ask: Does it open up the possibilities for some degree of participation to more of the citizens of a pluralistic society? All persons in the society need to have access to decision-making processes in order for American society to operate as well as it can. It is in the long-term interest of all groups in the society to see that the poor, the disadvantaged, and the currently powerless gain such access. It is not in society's best interest to create large collections of discontented people who are outside the mechanisms of shared decision making.

Assessing political feasibility must be done by appealing to strategically placed persons who are knowledgeable about current political trends. It is not necessary that these advisors be sympathetic. They do need to be accurate. It may even be good if they are opponents. Friends tend to oversympathize and in this instance, we need hard advice.

Examples of the importance of political feasibility abound in social welfare policy. President Roosevelt succeeded in getting the Social Security Act of 1935 through the United States Congress. It was revolutionary in its acceptance of federal responsibility for social insurance and partial responsibility for public assistance. The nation, desperate with up to a quarter of its citizens unemployed, could accept a reversal of the centuries-old policy of strict local responsibility for the care of the aged and the poor. President Nixon, on the other hand, could not get his welfare reform through Congress in the seventies because there was no similar feeling of imminent catastrophe and because the nation believed that the Family Assistance Plan would be contrary to the work ethic and damaging to personal incentive.

One aspect of the acceptability of a policy is its legality. This may seem to be so obvious that discussion of it would seem unnecessary. At various times, some policies followed by state welfare departments have been found illegal. Costin notes the danger of unwarranted and illegal invasions of privacy that may occur when agencies providing protective services become overzealous in investigating child neglect or abuse.[21] She also points out the violations of legal rights that have occurred in juvenile courts, ultimately necessitating redress by the Supreme Court of the United States.[22] Social welfare policymakers should consider the legality of both present and alternative policies. There are a number of attorneys (some of whom are also social workers) who can assist in this aspect of policy analysis and formulation. Social workers do not need to find themselves in the position of advocating a policy that is patently illegal, so they should use the services of a knowledgeable attorney when there is any question about the legality of a policy or program.

5. *Does the policy satisfy relevant interest groups?*

This consideration is somewhat closely linked with political feasibility, but our earlier discussion was mainly in terms of formal institutions. We think that it is best to examine other interest groups under a separate heading. You may recall that a major assumption in this book is that a good test of policy is the amount of agreement about whether or not it is responsive to certain values. It stands to reason that if a policy offers some benefit to an interest group, it will tend to look with favor on that policy. Of course, any interest group will want the policy that has the most to offer in advantages, services, or goods. Most interest groups, however, are smart enough to realize that no groups get everything they want, and they know the value of bargaining.

It can be argued that the delay in providing some form of control over rising health costs is due to the lack of attention to this criterion. No change in the health care pricing system is apt to be effective unless it is acceptable to the medical profession, business, insurance companies, labor and other powerful groups. Medicare and Medicaid were finally passed when changes were made that removed many of the objections of opposing interests and after compromises were made that offered advantages to the various groups involved. It is naive to think that an opponent (in social welfare policy or anything else) will surrender something to you just because you ask. There has to be a compelling reason—and the best one in politics is that everybody wins something. This involves compromise. Compromise is not a dirty word, but is rather the hallmark of civilized political processes. We will say more about the techniques involved in Chapter 10.

Obviously, the only way that one can analyze a policy along this dimension is to ask major interest groups for their judgments. Formulation and promotion of alternative policies will be enhanced if social workers build coalitions with interest groups who share common concerns. Social workers run a considerable risk if they follow the "naive priorities" approach to social welfare policy. They would do better to acknowledge the priorities of other interest groups and to try to build cooperative efforts whenever possible.

6. *Is the policy based on knowledge that has been tested to some degree?*

The formulation of social welfare policy has not historically been closely related to scientific research for a number of reasons. Verifiable data in the social sciences are harder to acquire than in the natural sciences. Social scientists cannot do many kinds of experimental research for humane reasons. Many value premises are hidden or unexplained. Social research involves attitudes and institutions that are complex and fluid and it is usually impossible to hold them still long enough to get a good look at them. Sometimes the experimenter's own influence on research situations may cause outcomes to shift in one direction or another.

Even more significantly, the discoveries and inventions of social scientists are not readily accepted by the groups and individuals who make decisions at the local, state and national levels. These groups and individuals have their own ideas and interests, and do not have as much regard for the findings of social scientists as they have for those of the natural and physical scientists. Furthermore, social scientists have not come together on their ideas in a solid front, nor have they won over support from lay society. When we try to translate new ideas and knowledge into social reform, we face the extremely difficult problem of promoting change in people's institutionally anchored attitudes, and a planned and organized effort is required. It will take time and work to convince the decision makers and the public that efficient and effective social welfare policies are good for everybody.[23]

As we have seen in an earlier chapter, social welfare policies have been very closely tied to economic, political, and social developments. While the institutions that render services change their operations in response to changing conditions, it appears that old policies are often dragged along without the revisions that would seem to be dictated by contemporary needs and present day research findings.

In short, there are very little hard data underlying most social welfare policy and it would be hard to get the data used constructively if they were available. There are few good examples of social science data that are used in public decision making. One exception is that Myrdal's research on American race relations is considered to have been influential on the Supreme Court's ruling in *Brown vs. Topeka Board of Education* in 1954.

It is possible, within limitations, to measure whether or not a social welfare policy is sound. The measuring instruments are not perfect, but there are evaluative research procedures that are available to test social welfare programs and social treatment techniques. Clearly, imperfect as they are, they should be used to inform judgments about whether or not things will work and how well.

Even though there may be no scientific research on a given issue, there are instances where policy decisions must be made. In these cases, one can at least ask that policy be the result of a process of rational thinking and that it be a rational solution in the light of the goal.

7. *Is the policy workable? That is, can the programs that flow from the policy be carried out in the real world?*

Essentially, what we are talking about here is simple common sense, knowing that we are referring to a most uncommon virtue. This is a rather global question, and we acknowledge that there is a certain vagueness about it. In a sense, we are talking about workability when we ask about the political feasibility, cost and rationality of a proposed policy. However, there is a dimension beyond these more specific criteria. We simply want to know, given that other criteria are satisfied, whether or not a given idea can actually be put into practice with the technology available. An example may help.

Suppose that Congress decided to provide major medical insurance for every American regardless of their ability to pay. Suppose further that the American Medical Association, the AFL-CIO, the Republican Party, the Democratic Party, the National Organization for Women, the NAACP, the U.S. Chamber of Commerce, the Urban League, the National Conference of Mayors, the John Birch Society, the Americans for Democratic Action, all the major religious bodies, the American Association of Retired Persons and the National Association of Manufacturers all enthusiastically supported the plan. Now, since this is just an example, suppose that the public was willing to pay the amount necessary to finance the plan.

Even with all this agreement and support, there remains the problem of whether or not the policy can be carried out. Does the technology exist to handle all the claims with sufficient speed? Or will vendors have to wait for years to get reimbursement? The point is that it is conceivable that a policy can be politically, economically and socially acceptable and yet so difficult to field that it cannot be acted upon. Our point is that supporters of a given policy are obliged to worry about the common-sense workability of any alternative that they may propose. While some form of major medical insurance probably is workable, there are undoubtedly other ideas that are not and for which we must wait for the necessary technology.

8. *Does the policy create few problems for both the public and the beneficiaries?*

It should be clear that a solution that creates more problems than it solves is really not a very good solution. Insofar as it is possible, one doing policy analysis and formulation should try to take into account the possibility of the cure being worse than the disease. Prohibition serves as a good example, although in all fairness, it is unlikely that decision makers could have anticipated all the negative consequences that occurred. In 1920, an amendment to the United States Constitution was passed which made the sale and manufacture of alcoholic beverages illegal. The idea behind the amendment was to eliminate the social and personal consequences of drinking. Did this policy achieve its goal? Clearly, the answer is no. An enormous illegal industry arose to service the demand for beverage alcohol. Drinking illegal alcohol in unlicensed "speakeasies" became fashionable. In effect, a social policy that was designed to make one thing more manageable turned out to have unintended consequences. It did not stop people from drinking and also created the climate for a crime problem that may very well be said to have made the general conditions of society a whole lot worse.

It seems reasonable to ask that each policy alternative be examined in the light of all available knowledge in order to reduce the likelihood of creating serious new problems or of exacerbating existing problems.

Deciding on a way to answer this question is risky at best. There is no foolproof way to do it, since it is a judgment based on wisdom and experience. The effort to estimate the negative impact of a policy still needs to be made and the possibilities weighed as to their risk.

9. *Is the policy reasonably effective?*

This criterion at first glance may seem to be encompassed by the notion of workability, but it is different as we see it. The criterion of workability has to do with whether or not a policy could be carried out from a practical standpoint. Effectiveness speaks directly to whether or not the policy will actually do anybody any measurable good. In plain language, we would like to know if an approach works to achieve a desired outcome. If a proposal is designed to deal with the problem of poverty, then there ought to be some outcome or set of outcomes that shows that either the poor are less poor or that there are fewer poor people. If a program is designed to cope with the problem of child abuse, then there should be less child abuse as a consequence of the program. In short, something beneficial ought to happen and it ought to be measurable in some way. If a policy cannot be shown to have a positive effect, then it is suspect. This may sound simplistic at first reading. However, it is clear that both the clientele and the public hope for concrete results and we think that results are a perfectly reasonable expectation. It is not good enough to say that social workers and others who are connected to the social welfare enterprise are well intentioned. There ought to be some evidence of effectiveness. There are a number of research techniques that can be used to measure effectiveness of a program or of a treatment technique. As we mentioned earlier, these techniques are not perfect, but they are good enough to answer a number of questions having to do with effectiveness. In this day and age, it would be a "cop-out" to argue that the state-of-the-art was too primitive to be able to evaluate effectiveness.

10. *Is the policy efficient?*

There are two aspects to this criterion. First, can the society afford to pay for the programs based on the policy? Second, does society get the most for its money? These questions, as is the case with all the others, should be asked of current programs as well as any programs based on any new policy. A policy must lead to economically feasible programs. A good program should deliver the maximum benefit for the least amount of money to do the job right. Please notice that we are not saying that social welfare programs should be carried out in a cheap, slipshod way. What we are saying is that a policy that is perceived as "too expensive" will not have a chance of enactment. Further, a policy that results in programs that cost too much for what they deliver will also be looked upon with disfavor. In our view, a good social welfare policy will be one that can be shown to be efficient and cost-effective. A program that has enormous costs and provides benefits to only a few people will usually be rejected by decision makers, interest groups and the public.

Techniques are available to measure efficiency. Social workers sometimes bristle at the thought of subjecting what they do to cost/benefit analysis. Naive and sentimental planners may believe that a policy that results in helping a few alcoholics in a demonstration project is worth trying as a general rule even though the evidence is slim. We think that the time has come for us to do better than this. Therapists must master their fears about being evaluated. Planners must be willing to subject their programs to examination. If people who are part of the social welfare enterprise cannot find ways to show that what they do benefits a fair number of people and generally improves the quality of life in the society, they will not receive the support necessary and the enterprise will suffer. This may not be pleasant to think about, but it appears to be a fact of life and it must be taken into account when analyzing current social welfare policies and considering alternatives.

The framework that we have presented is certainly not the last word. There is some refinement over the scheme as it was presented in the earlier edition of this book. As we suspected would be true, our experience caused us to do considerable meddling with the criteria that we had previously devised. Although we are not nearly satisfied yet, we believe that these considerations have utility. In the next chapters we will apply this framework to several important areas of social welfare policy. We will look at present policies and, on the basis of the criteria presented in this chapter, suggest some alternatives for your consideration. Because this is a textbook and not actually a position document, we will warn you that we have deliberately included some proposals that we think fit the criteria fairly well and some that do not. The reader should stay on his or her toes because there are a few "curve balls" in the mix. Life is that way, too.

REFERENCES

1. David Braybrooke and Charles E. Lindblom, *A Strategy of Decision* (New York: The Free Press of Glencoe, 1963), pp. 6–8.
2. Yehezkel Dror, *Design for Policy Sciences* (New York: Elsevier, 1971), p. 141.
3. These requirements adapted from Ian L. McHarg, *Design with Nature* (Garden City, N. Y.: The Natural History Press, 1969), p. 105.
4. *Ibid.*, p. 34.
5. *Ibid.*, p. 52.
6. *Ibid.*, p. 80.

7. *Ibid.,* p. 188, 197.
8. Winifred Bell, "Obstacles to Shifting from the Descriptive to the Analytical Approach in Teaching Social Services," *Journal of Education for Social Work,* Vol. 5, No. 1 (Spring 1969), p. 7.
9. *Ibid.,* p. 8.
10. Neil Gilbert and Harry Specht, *Dimensions of Social Welfare Policy* (Englewood Cliffs, N. J.: Prentice-Hall, 1974), p. 29.
11. David Gil, *Unravelling Social Policy,* Second edition (Cambridge, Mass.: Schenkman, 1976), pp. 15–16.
12. *Ibid.*
13. Alfred J. Kahn, *Social Policy and Social Services,* (New York: Random House, 1973), p. 56.
14. Robert Perlman and Arnold Gurin, *Community Organization and Social Planning* (New York: John Wiley, 1972), p. 153.
15. See Charles Frankel, "Social Values and Professional Values," *Journal of Education for Social Work,* Vol. 5, No. 1 (Spring 1969), p. 35.
16. See Nathan E. Cohen, ed., *Social Work and Social Problems* (New York: National Association of Social Workers, 1964), pp. ix–xiv and 369–372 for an analytical scheme in which there is a built-in recognition of the disparities between professional values and social values.
17. Frankel, *op. cit.,* p. 35.
18. Elizabeth G. Meier, "Child Neglect," in Cohen, *op. cit.,* pp. 156–160.
19. See, for example, Franklin M. Zweig, "The Social Worker as Legislative Ombudsman," *Social Work,* Vol. 14, No. 1 (January 1969), pp. 30–31.
20. Charles S. Prigmore, "Use of the Coalition in Legislative Action," *Social Work,* Vol. 19, No. 1 (January 1974), pp. 96–102.
21. Lela B. Costin, *Child Welfare: Policies and Practice,* Second edition (New York: McGraw-Hill, 1979), pp. 215–216.
22. *Ibid.,* pp. 52–58.
23. Gunnar Myrdal, "The Social Sciences and Their Impact on Society," in Herman D. Stein, ed., *Social Theory and Social Intervention* (Cleveland, Ohio: The Press of Case Western Reserve University, 1963), p. 159.

QUESTIONS FOR DISCUSSION

1. Give one or two examples of the "naive criteria" and "naive priority" methods of policy formulation. What limitations for the development of useful and viable policies do you see in these examples?

2. What do you think McHarg means by the "solution of maximum social utility"? Can you think of a policy that meets this criterion?

3. Can you think of any public policies that clearly coincide with the self-interest of most individuals in the society? Can you think of examples of clashes between public policy and individual self-interest?

4. Is assessment and comparison of the cost of social welfare programs a criterion that can be reconciled with social work goals?

5. How would you characterize the contemporary "style" in social welfare policy in your state or community?

6. Describe a social problem that is caused or aggravated by a policy that is designed to ameliorate a problem.

7. Give an example of a social work goal that appears to conflict with the general values of the community.

8. Can you think of a social welfare policy that appears to be based on sound scientific knowledge?

SUGGESTED PROJECTS

1. Choose a policy that deals with a social problem of contemporary interest. Examine it using the criteria proposed in this chapter. Does the policy meet the criteria? Can you suggest alternatives that would appear to be better?

2. Interview a mayor, state or federal legislator, political reporter or a political scientist. Ask him or her to list the important factors that he or she believes are present in policy decisions. Is the list different from the one in the chapter?

FOR FURTHER READING

Winifred Bell. "Obstacles to Shifting from the Descriptive to the Analytical Approach in Teaching Social Services," *Journal of Education in Social Work,* Vol. 5, No. 1, (Spring 1969). Still a useful discussion of the need to systematically incorporate social welfare policy and services into the social work curriculum.

David Braybrooke and Charles E. Lindblom. *A Strategy of Decision.* New York: The Free Press of Glencoe, 1963. In a book that is considered a classic of its kind, the authors discuss traditional methods of decision making which they find inadequate. They offer a strategy that they call "disjointed incrementalism" which is simply the process of making policy choices through a series of small steps in the direction of a long-term goal.

Alfred J. Kahn. *Social Policy and Social Services,* Second edition. New York: Random House, 1979. An important analysis of the relationship of social welfare policy to social services by one of the most respected social welfare analysts of our time.

Richard M. Titmuss. *Social Policy.* New York: Pantheon, 1974. A posthumous collection of Titmuss' most provocative ideas. Titmuss was one of the leading theoreticians of the welfare state in Britain. Whether you agree with him or not, he is essential reading for those who want to be informed on the major traditional issues in social welfare policy.

Part II

Challenges to
Policy Analysis
and Formulation:
Five Examples

In the next chapters we look at specific areas of interest to social welfare policy: income maintenance, poverty, health care, housing and service delivery. We discuss current policies that guide programs in the area. We use our policy analysis scheme to show why some policies have not worked and why others have. We also examine some alternatives to present policies. These exercises are not intended to indoctrinate the reader, but are intended to provide take-off points for the reader's own attempts at analysis and formulation.

4

Income Maintenance
in a Money Economy

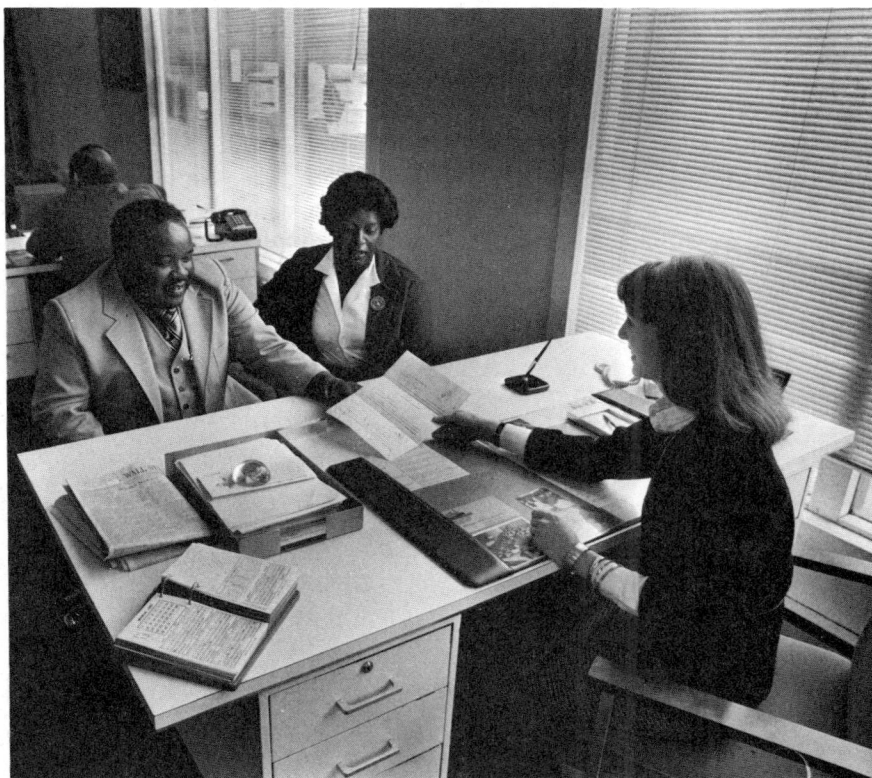

THE LOSS OF EARNINGS THAT RESULTS from retirement, chronic illness, disability, unemployment, industrial accident, or death of a spouse is usually a severe problem for people whose income is solely from wages. These contingencies not only may be catastrophic for the individual, but their impact is potentially great upon the whole society. Consequently, most nations have developed social welfare programs that maintain the income of workers when these emergencies arise. The rationale for these programs is simply that there are certain risks that accompany life in a modern industrial society. It is in the best interest of both the society and the individual to transfer resources from the part of the population that is currently earning to the part of the population that is not earning because one of these contingencies has occurred.

Some writers include all governmentally sponsored programs that pay cash or provide service benefits under the heading of income maintenance. We make a distinction between programs designed to maintain income from those primarily intended for the control of poverty. Under income maintenance we will address policies and programs for those who ordinarily have earnings, but have had an interruption in their working careers. In Chapter 5 we will address the problem of poverty and the policies and programs designed to benefit those who either have no income from work or who are underemployed. We recognize that the problems of income maintenance and poverty are often interrelated, but we believe that separate treatment is justified since the policies that address the continuance of income are offered on quite a different basis from those aimed at the problem of poverty.

Definition of Social Insurance

The programs designed to maintain income by replacing earnings are generally known as the "social insurances." Social insurance differs considerably from the kinds of insurance that people know most about (life, annuities, private pensions) in several important ways. First, participation in social insurance is compulsory. Regular insurance is voluntary and may be purchased from a number of companies. Second, social insurance programs are, by and large, on a pay-as-you-go basis and there is no cash value built up in the individual's account over time. Private retirement insurance (an annuity, for instance) involves the investment of the purchaser's premiums in stocks, bonds, property, or other income producing ventures. The customer's claim on the company is identifiable in the company's accounting system and the insured is clearly paying for his or her own future benefits. Third, because social insurances are governmental programs, legislatures can change the rules if they are willing to take the political risk. In privately purchased insurance, the policy is a contract that is binding on both the company and the consumer. Finally, social insurances tend to redistribute income from those who have it to those who no longer have it. Private insurance does not.[1]

The redistribution of income occurs as either a cash or an "in-kind" (goods and services) transfer. For example, older workers who retire at comparatively low salaries gain the benefits of the taxes paid into the Social Security system by present workers. Because Congress has continually raised the benefits out of proportion to a given worker's taxes, income is redistributed from those who have an income to those whose income is reduced. As we will see later, this approach is not without problems.

The result of governmentally sponsored income maintenance programs is that the worker (and the worker's family or survivors) will be able to meet their bills, at least for a time, and the family's creditors will be satisfied. Further, from an economic standpoint, income maintenance programs insure that there will be some cash flowing in the economy from workers who have suffered one of the contingencies that social insurance is designed to alleviate. Although not all Americans fully support the aims of social insurance, it is clear that a majority are still satisfied with the programs, at least up to a point.

It should be clear that "social insurance" is similar to ordinary insurance only in very general terms. In both, the risks of certain contingencies are spread over a large population, but beyond this the similarity is somewhat forced. Why use the term "social insurance" if what we are talking about is really an income transfer program? Because the originators wanted the transfer programs to be acceptable to the American public and they believed that acceptance would be easier if the insurance analogy were used. The idea was to sell the public on the idea that social insurance was a combination casualty insurance and annuity. While this device may have made social insurance easier to accept in the beginning, it has also obscured the real purpose and caused a certain amount of confusion. In the long run, the strategy may be working against the social insurances.

In this chapter we will discuss the major policies that govern income maintenance programs in the United States. We will examine them using the scheme that we developed in Chapter 3 and we will use this analysis as the basis for suggesting some different policy formulations. We want to remind the reader that our formulations are not necessarily recommendations of any kind. Some of our proposals may look attractive (and some may not), but they are primarily for the purpose of illustrating the policy analysis and formulation process and are designed to open rather than close the discussion.

Income maintenance programs have developed in a piecemeal fashion in the United States. We can best understand the present income maintenance policies by briefly reviewing the major programs. This review is not a detailed description of the programs or their history. For these the reader should consult other sources. Our purpose is to focus on what we think are important policy issues.

Workers' Compensation is a program by which states require employers to compensate workers who are injured in industrial accidents or who contract occupational diseases. There are two kinds of benefits: (1) cash benefits to partially replace lost earnings and (2) payment of medical and rehabilitative care. All jurisdictions place limits on the amount of cash paid and the length of time for which benefits will be paid. There are also restrictions on the medical and rehabilitation benefits in all jurisdictions. Private employers usually meet the state's requirements by purchasing insurance from companies that specialize in workers' compensation insurance. In many states, the law requires the employer to carry insurance. In others, insurance is not specifically required by law, but since employers must be able to meet employee claims, some form of risk pooling is effectively required. In some states, the state itself acts as insurer and collects the money and pays the benefits.

There is also a workers' compensation plan for federal employees, the Federal Employees' Compensation Act, first passed in 1908 and revised in 1949. Unlike the acts in the states, the federal act is financed directly by congressional appropriation. Most European countries had workers' compensation laws before the United States. The earliest was provided in Germany under Bismarck in 1883. Bismarck, an arch-conservative, did not promote workers' compensation because of his humanitarian concern, but to "cool down" the growing socialist opposition. According to Hood and Hardy, the first state law in the United States was passed in Maryland in 1902.[2] This law paid death benefits for a limited number of workers and was declared unconstitutional in 1904. Although the states were reluctant to do it, they eventually all discarded the common law principles that had governed such situations and accepted the principle of workers' compensation. There are now laws in all fifty states and the District of Columbia.

Originally, any compensation that a worker got for an accident on the job came as a result of being able to prove that the employer was negligent according to common law standards. Under common law, the employer had the duty to provide "the safety precautions that a reasonably prudent man would take if he himself were in the employees' situation."[3] This included providing a safe place to work, proper tools and equipment to do the job, adequate warning of the dangers of the job, a set of safety rules and a suitable number of co-workers who knew what they were doing.[4] If an employee sued, the employer could take refuge in a set of common law defenses.[5] First, the employer could defend himself by showing that the injury was the result of something done by a fellow worker. The employer was not liable if this were the case. Second, the employer was not liable if the employee did not use proper discretion in the course of his or her employment. If it could be shown that the employee had contributed in any way to the accident, through wrong use of a tool for example, then the employer could argue that the accident was hardly his responsibility. Third, the argument could be made that certain jobs were risky and that the employee had to accept a certain amount of risk when he agreed to accept the job.

Gradually, because of an increasing number of industrial accidents that left workers injured and financially insecure, it was decided to shift the burden for compensation from the worker to the employer without determining fault. This decision was made during the reform era shortly after the turn of the century and reflects a general reaction against "big business" that was prevalent at the time. In effect, this policy change meant that the employer was given sole responsibility for the consequences of industrial accidents (and later, occupational disease) even if the worker were clearly at fault. Under the present system, there is usually no exhaustive search for negligence. The assumption is that industrial accidents or occupational illness is a social risk to be handled as a social cost of the industrial process. Chelius points out that since the current system focuses almost entirely on income maintenance, there is little incentive for workers to be concerned about safety or accident prevention.[6] While this may be true in a strictly economic context, it is unlikely that very many workers actually adopt a totally cavalier attitude toward accidents.

The "no fault" nature of Workers' Compensation has not meant the end of lawsuits, however. As one might expect, the problems come at the borders. Generally, the state laws require that an injury or occupational disease arise "out of and in the course of employment." In most cases, this legal requirement causes no problems, but in a fair number of cases, the connection between the accident or the disease and the workplace is not clear and the matter may end up in the courts. Over the years, a good deal of case law has helped define the boundaries. Generally speaking, an accident that occurs during working hours when one is engaged in the legitimate business of the employer, either on the employer's property or elsewhere, will be compensated. If the accident occurs on the way to or from work, or when the accident is not a consequence of work, it probably will not be compensated. The same is generally true of occupational disease, but the definition of occupational disease appears to be difficult in some cases. Heart disease, for example, seems to have historically been difficult to define as a work-related illness.

There is another large area in which litigation occurs. Who benefits in the case of the death of the worker? Ordinarily, the worker's spouse and children will—provided that they have been living in a dependent relationship with the deceased. If there were some complication about the legal relationship between the spouses, the right to claim survivorship benefits might have to be tested in court. For example, if John deserts Mary and then Mary dies in an industrial accident, can John collect survivor benefits? If Mary is still legally responsible for part of John's support, he may be able to collect, but it may take legal action to find out.

There are advantages to the present system (or systems since there is a system for each state, the District of Columbia and for federal employees). First of all, the current procedures work for most people most of the time. The courts are not absolutely jammed with Workers' Compensation suits. Second, employers, attorneys, and courts usually understand the system and can work with it with a minimum of bother except in unusual cases. There is surprisingly little complaint from injured workers, although it is often dramatic when a complaint occurs and a suit is given widespread publicity. Third, coverage is now nearly universal. Recent figures suggest that over ninety percent of American workers are covered by Workers' Compensation, the Federal Employer's Liability Act, or, in the case of coal miners, the "black lung" benefits program.[7] Finally, it appears that the laws generally tend to favor the worker, who has several levels of appeal if he or she is not satisfied.

On the other hand, there are still a few problems. Workers' Compensation programs are state programs. While employers must pay for the benefits, the levels are set by the state. As one would expect, there is considerable difference in benefits from state to state. In most states, there are limits both as to the amount of compensation that one can receive and to the length of time one is eligible for benefits. Second, the benefits do not entirely replace earnings and the benefit levels have not kept up with the cost of living. Further, they do not usually cover the full cost of rehabilitation or re-education.[8]

In 1970, Congress passed the Occupational Safety and Health Act (OSHA). The primary purpose of the Act was to provide a set of standards for safety in the workplace. It appears that the Act has had uncertain results and horror stories abound about the unreasonableness of the way in which safety rules were applied by the investigative staff. One of the writers knows a small businessman who alleges that he was advised by an OSHA inspector to install on a machine a guard which would have rendered the machine inoperative. When the businessman pointed this out, the inspector agreed, but said that the guard would have to be installed anyway! In any case, the literature does not provide uniformly positive evidence that gains under the Act have outweighed losses.

One provision of the Act set up the National Commission on State Workmen's Compensation Laws. In 1972, the National Commission presented its report. The report contained eighty-four recommendations of which nineteen were said to be essential. Generally, the National Commission recommended that the states should expand the coverage to include virtually all employed persons regardless of their occupation or the size of the businesses for which they worked. Present laws exempt very small businesses, agricultural workers (in most states), domestic workers (in most states) and certain special classes of workers (professional athletes for example). Further, the National Commission recommended extending coverage to a wider range of occupational diseases, replacement of 100 percent of lost income, payment for the total cost of health and rehabilitative care and the elimination of time limits for benefits of all kinds.

The states have not followed all the National Commission's recommendations, although they have used them as guidelines for reform. One of the National Commission's recommendations was that if the states did not voluntarily comply in two years then a federal law ought to be passed that would ensure compliance.

Accordingly, the National Workers' Compensation Act of 1975 was introduced by Senators Williams and Javits. The bill was co-sponsored by Senators Hathaway, Humphrey, Kennedy, Mondale and Pell. Essentially, this Act proposed a set of federal standards for state Workers' Compensation laws. This bill did not pass in the session in which it was introduced, but it continues to find sponsors and to be reintroduced periodically. Like the National Commission report upon which it is based, the bill would include more workers than do the present state requirements, increase the benefits in the direction of full earnings replacement and require full coverage for health and rehabilitation services. Further, the bill would generally require benefit payments over a longer period of time than is now the practice in most of the state plans. Chelius has reviewed some of the problems that he sees in this bill and the reader is referred to his treatment which can be found in the "Suggestions for Further Reading" at the end of this chapter. One problem that Chelius notes, for example, is that the language of the federal bill is such that a great deal of litigation is likely to occur if the bill is passed because of language changes from the traditional legal way of defining coverage.[9]

The National Commission did not recommend nationalization of the Workers' Compensation program. The proposed National Workers' Compensation Act also stops short of nationalization, but confines itself to setting minimum standards for state programs. Since these proposals would seem to be humane in their effects, why have they not received wider acceptance? Let us try to answer this question by using the policy analysis scheme developed in Chapter 3.

Analysis of Proposed Workers' Compensation Policy Changes

1. *Is the policy under consideration compatible with contemporary "style"?*

   No. Clearly, the Reagan administration leans in the direction of supporting solutions on a local basis. Even though the proposed reforms preserve state interests in form, an act that sets national standards turns effective decision making over to the federal government for the most part. Increasing centralization is not in keeping with the style of the national administration nor is it likely to appeal to a wider audience. The United States is in a fairly conservative mood and there is little national interest in increasing the federal government's role in affairs that the states appear to be handling satisfactorily.

2. *Is the policy compatible with important and enduring cultural values, particularly equity, fairness and justice?*

   The answer here is a qualified yes. The qualification is because the present system is not seen as patently unjust and there is no dramatic reason to substitute a policy that is not particularly superior with respect to values.

3. *Is the policy compatible with social work's professional value and ethical system?*

Yes, but social workers have not recently seen the Workers' Compensation system as in need of serious reform. Traditionally, the social workers of earlier generations supported the notion that employers should be responsible for industrial accidents and disease, but contemporary social workers have not found serious reasons to quarrel with what is currently being done. Since the current system is compatible with professional values, there is no particular impetus to replace it.

4. *Is the policy acceptable to those in formal decision-making positions?*

Obviously, no. The proposed act has not passed in Congress and as we pointed out above, there is little likelihood that there will be much support from the President. There is also a noticeable lack of public agitation from governors or state legislatures.

5. *Does the policy satisfy relevant interest groups?*

Again, no. It would be expected that organized labor might have taken a strong public stand in favor of broader coverage, higher benefits and a longer period of rehabilitation, but labor has not really taken up the cudgels for reform. On the other hand, this reform will not likely have the support of either industrial or insurance interests. There is simply not enough dissatisfaction with the present system on the part of relevant interest groups.

6. *Is the policy based on knowledge that has been tested?*

Not particularly, although it can be argued that there are other programs that are operated by the states using federal standards that could serve as models.

7. *Is the policy workable?*

Probably, and for the same reason given above.

8. *Does the policy create few problems for both the public and the intended beneficiaries?*

It is impossible to answer this question definitely. If Chelius's criticisms are well founded, there would be several problems. We have already mentioned the possibility of an increased amount of litigation.[10] Another example from Chelius's study may be of interest. He says that it might be possible that since the law covers virtually all employers, even persons who hired a babysitter might have to purchase workers' compensation insurance.[11] Of course, any actual law that is passed would probably be cleaned of some of the more obvious ambiguities and objectionable features, so that Chelius's objections would be moot. Certainly a law that created a number of annoyances would not be popular and would either be changed or repealed. We have to answer this question with a no on the basis of the present law.

9. *Is the policy effective?*

Probably the proposed law would be effective, assuming that its major provisions were left intact. If the goal were total income replacement and an injured worker's income were replaced and his or her medical and rehabilitation bills were paid, then the Act would be effective. This question can be answered with a yes.

10. *Will programs derived from the policy be efficient?*

This is another difficult question. The proposed federal standards would replace 100 percent of income lost to industrial accidents or occupational disease. The current state programs replace something around two-thirds of a worker's income. The Act would, therefore, increase the benefits by a minimum of one-third for any given year. In fact, the cost could go much higher since the Act would also pay the benefits for longer periods of time. Further, there would undoubtedly be higher administrative costs since there would have to be occasional compliance surveys to make sure that a state was in fact meeting federal standards, more reports, and more staff needs. The increased costs would have to be reflected in higher product costs and ultimately the consumer would be affected. Further, it is unlikely that a federally supervised system would be notable for its efficiency if other federal programs are indicative. It is simply difficult for a program with nation-wide scope to work as if it were a hometown operation. Our best guess here is that the proposed Act does not hold out any particular hope for results that are more cost-effective than the present system. When one adds in the potential cost of the lawsuits that would result if Chelius is right, efficiency would appear to be extremely low.

In summary, we suggest that the National Workers' Compensation Act has not become national policy because it does not fit with contemporary style, has no particular value advantage at this time, is not politically acceptable, has insufficient support from important interest groups, may cause problems that outweigh its benefits, and is very expensive to boot. Although we have not been asked, we would suggest that the present sponsors of the bill should address some of these problems and either change the proposal so that it has advantages over the present system or else abandon it. A cynical view is that it may not matter whether the act passes or not since it has the effect of establishing the liberal credentials of its sponsors and the credit may be useable in some other arena. Unless the national mood changes to something like that which existed during the years of the Great Depression, we would not expect this Act to be high on the national agenda. However, we have certainly been wrong before! From our point of view, we think that the contemplated policy change provides good practice in policy analysis. We will offer a slightly different example in the next section of the chapter.

Unemployment Insurance (UI) is a federal-state program designed to maintain the income of a worker during short periods of unemployment. A number of European countries including Great Britain, Germany and Italy had already made some form of social provision for the unemployed earlier in the twentieth century. In 1932, Wisconsin passed the first law of this type in the United States.

The current Unemployment Insurance program is authorized by the Social Security Act of 1935. It is a good example of the combination "carrot and stick" approach in federal policy. So that there would be coverage in all states, a provision of the Social Security Act imposed a tax on payrolls for the purpose of providing compensation for workers who were laid off. This was the stick. The carrot was the provision that if a state enacted its own program, the federal government would refund 90 percent of the tax. Very quickly, all of the states (and later the District of Columbia and Puerto Rico) enacted unemployment insurance laws. As a general rule, each state taxes each employer a percentage of the wages of each employee up to a maximum limit. As of this writing, four states (Alaska, Alabama, New Jersey and Pennsylvania) also levy a tax on the employee. In most of the literature on UI, these taxes are invariably referred to as "contributions," but this is part of the euphemistic concealment of taxation by calling it "social insurance."

The Social Security Act imposes the tax on wages in industry and business. Excluded from the federal tax are farm workers, domestics, the self-employed, state and local government employees and those who work for charitable and religious organizations. A number of states, however, tax the employers of wage earners in these occupational fields and provide benefits for their employees even though they are not required to do so by federal guidelines.

All states define Unemployment Insurance as a matter of right. While there are differences in coverage across state lines, there are general similarities resulting from the standards imposed in the Social Security Act. To be eligible for benefits, a worker must be ready and able to work, unemployed, registered for work at the state employment service, and must have been employed in a job covered by the UI law of the state for some period of time. In addition to a requirement that a beneficiary must have been employed for a definite period of time in order to qualify for benefits, some states require that the unemployed person must have earned a certain amount of money over the previous work period. The intent of these kinds of provisions is to include persons who ordinarily have fairly steady employment and exclude those whose work is irregular and casual.

One cannot receive unemployment benefits if he or she quits a job without a legally acceptable reason, is fired for misconduct on the job, fails to register with the state employment service, refuses a job equal to or better than the one previously held, or goes on strike. Critics have argued that an unemployed worker should be required to take any job offered, but the law does not require a worker to switch occupations nor to take a lesser job than that for which he or she is qualified. Supporters of the present policy believe that if this provision were changed, it would have a depressing effect on wages and would, therefore, not be good policy.

Benefits are not equal to previously earned income. Although each jurisdiction sets minimum and maximum cash benefits, an unemployed worker generally gets about half as much in benefits as he or she previously earned. The way it works out, the low-paid worker who is unemployed for a relatively short time actually gets only slightly less cash than when working. This is because he or she does not pay income tax on the benefits from UI and may be eligible for food stamps (see Chapter 5) while unemployed. The benefits of UI approach adequacy only if income is low and unemployment only lasts a short while. The longer unemployment persists and the higher one's income, the more difficulty one has in making ends meet during periods of unemployment.

The program is not designed to deal with chronic unemployment. In most states, the maximum time that one can ordinarily receive UI is twenty-six weeks, although many states have an emergency provision that will allow an extension of thirteen more weeks. During the recession in the early 1970s, the federal government provided additional funds which allowed for longer extensions if the state's unemployment figure exceeded a rate specified in the federal guidelines. Under these special circumstances, benefits have been paid for as long as sixty-five weeks—but this kind of coverage has only been seen during nationwide recessions. Under normal unemployment circumstances, the unemployed individual will (in most states) get benefits for twenty-six weeks—half a year.

Some believe that the system is generous enough to increase unemployment and that unemployed persons may delay seeking work. This opinion rests on the premise that there is really no shortage of jobs:

> The large pool of long-term unemployed workers has been replaced by a much smaller relative number whose durations of unemployment are also much shorter. *Almost every unemployed person can now find a job in a very short time.*[12] (emphasis added)

We think that urban black youth, whose unemployment rate has run as high as 40 percent for a number of years, may find this statement incredible.

By and large, the Unemployment Insurance system has worked to maintain income during a given individual's periods of unemployment, but the system is obviously strained during recessions when unemployment is general.

Recent policy shifts in the UI program in Alabama provide a useful example for analysis.[13] Prior to the recession of the early 1980s, the Unemployment Insurance program in Alabama (officially, the Unemployment Compensation Trust Fund) was not a source of controversy. However, Alabama was one of the states hardest hit in the country during the recession. The unemployment rate was in the 10 to 15 percent range for a fairly long time. The Unemployment Compensation Trust Fund was drained and was reported to be in debt to the federal government for 82 million dollars. As is often true, the decision makers were motivated to analyze the current policies and devise alternatives when the situation became critical.

Under the pre-1983 program, employers paid a tax of 1/2 to 4 percent on the first $7,000 of each employed wage earner's pay. The actual rate paid by an employer was based on the firm's prior record of layoffs. An employer who had not laid a worker off for three years paid a tax of 1/2 percent. An employer with a high number of claims paid the maximum 4 percent rate. A new business started off with a tax rate of 2.7 percent which was adjusted up or down as the pattern of layoffs varied. Since 1975, Alabama workers have been taxed 1/2 of a percent of their wages up to $7,000. In effect, this meant that a wage earner paid a maximum of $35 a year into the Unemployment Compensation Trust Fund while the employer paid the bulk of the tax.

The benefits were among the lowest in the nation. The minimum benefit was $15 a week and the maximum was $90. It was, however, relatively easy to qualify for benefits. In addition to the usual qualifications (able and ready to work, registered for work, etc.) the laid-off worker only had to have earned $522 during the first four quarters of the five last calendar quarters prior to filing for benefits. During one of these quarters, the wage earner had to make at least $348. The base benefit period was twenty-six weeks, but there was a current state extension of an additional thirteen weeks. For those whose benefits were exhausted, it was possible to qualify for a federally provided extension of an additional sixteen weeks.

Here, then, were several elements that added up to a crisis situation. The trust fund was overspent. Further, it was agreed by all concerned, the benefits were too low. Finally, the qualifications for benefits were so low that virtually anybody who had any kind of work record in business or industry could receive at least minimum benefits. The trouble with this latter factor was that the program was not intended to cover people who were essentially part-time or casual laborers. It was intended to provide income maintenance for people who were fully involved in the work force. Even though the benefits were low for these people, the trust fund was being drained by a large number of very marginally employed people who were receiving benefits. In order to protect the intended beneficiaries, reform was needed.

The state legislature passed a revised program in early 1983. First of all, the maximum tax rate on employers was increased to 5 percent of the first $8,000 of each wage earner's salary. This rate rose to 5.4 percent as of the first of January of 1985. Because the fund is "in the red," a temporary surcharge of 25 percent was added to each employer's tax. This surcharge was scheduled to end when the fund built back up to around 300 million dollars. While the tax rate on the employee was left at 1/2 of one percent, the base against which it was levied was increased to $8,000. This immediately increased the maximum tax on the wage earner to $40 per year. After the first of January of 1984, the employee's tax doubled to 1 percent of the first $8,000 or a maximum of $80 annually. Once the fund is built up to the 300 million dollar level, the tax on the wage earner is scheduled to end.

This increase in the tax rate and the base against which the rate is levied should, unless there is a prolonged future recession, cure the problem of a shortage of money in the trust fund for the foreseeable future. The problem of low benefits has been addressed by raising the minimum benefit to $22 per week and the maximum to $120. The amount is still low by national standards, but it compares more favorably with benefits paid in the Southeast.

A major feature of the new law is that very marginally employed people will not benefit from Unemployment Insurance. Under the new law, a worker must have earned $792 in the previous year and there is a formula to determine how much of this must have been earned in any one quarter.

There are several elements of interest to the policy analyst in this situation. First of all, a minor precedent was set by raising the tax rate on employers. Previous remedies had been limited to a rise in the salary base against which the tax was levied. A second feature of interest is the provision for the direct tax burden to be lifted from the worker when the fund is back to its normal reserves. Of course, there is more appearance to this provision than substance. From an accounting point of view, any fringe benefit is charged to labor costs. A third point to be considered is the elimination of the very marginal employee from any benefit.

The new law was passed with a minimum of public struggle. We will offer an explanation using our policy analysis model to show why this law passed while the more sweeping reforms proposed for Workers' Compensation did not.

1. *Is the policy compatable with contemporary "style"?*

   Yes. The problem was solved in Montgomery and not in Washington. This kind of locally based solution is clearly favored by the prevailing climate both locally and nationally.

2. *Is the policy compatible with important and enduring cultural values, particularly equity, fairness and justice?*

   Yes, at least on the surface. It appears that the tax burden mainly falls on employers who are in the best position to afford the cost, and while the workers' share increases temporarily, the workers will have more take-home pay when the fund reaches normal reserves. Of course, as we pointed out, any fringe benefit actually comes from the workers' pockets since it is ultimately a wage cost. From a populist perception, the new policy appears beneficial since it appears to shift the tax burden from the employees to the employers. Further, this policy change is evolutionary rather than revolutionary. Its essentially conservative nature will appeal to the values that support incremental change rather than to more radical ones.

3. *Is the policy compatible with social work's professional value and ethical system?*

   Here the answer is a qualified yes. The state chapter of the National Association of Social Workers took no public position on the issue.

Since there was no glaring problem that attracted their attention, it appears safe to assume that silence meant consent.

4. *Is the policy acceptable to those in formal decision-making positions?*

Yes. Preliminary work prevented any significant legislative struggle over the bill's passage. While Governor George Wallace offered no proposal of his own, he made it clear that he expected that an acceptable bill would be passed. Much has been written about George Wallace and this is not the place to engage in a long analysis of his role in either state or national politics. It does need to be said, however, that Governor Wallace is a more complicated man than he is often portrayed by the media. Whatever else one may think of him, Governor Wallace is a very effective politician. His support usually means that a proposal has a good chance of success, while his opposition is frequently fatal for a proposal. Given the cooperation of both governor and legislature on this policy change, there was no significant formal opposition.

5. *Does the policy satisfy relevant interest groups?*

Yes. The final bill was a result of extensive negotiations between government, business, and organized labor.[14] Representatives of all three groups spent a good deal of time hammering out the new law. Clearly labor won something—a lower direct tax on wages and a shifting of the tax to the employers, and higher benefits. The employers won, in that extremely marginal workers will no longer drain the system of benefits. The politicians can be satisfied, because they can take credit for acting like statesmen in a crisis. No special interest group appeared in opposition to the proposal.

6. *Is the policy based on knowledge that has been tested?*

Yes, to the extent that there were estimates made of the cost over time and, since the policy change was not very radical, it is perfectly rational to assume that the experience of the previous policy can be used as an adequate general guide to how the new policy would work.

7. *Is the policy workable in the real world?*

Yes. Again, this very incremental change will not appreciably increase any administrative costs and will not require any great change in the way things are done.

8. *Does the policy create few problems for both the public and the intended beneficiaries?*

This question must be answered carefully. The public interest is always served when governments find a relatively painless way to solve a problem. With an incremental reform such as this, nobody is apt to become severely discomfited by the minor changes that are involved. Clearly, the intended beneficiaries—those who are ordinarily employed—will be better off. The only person that is hurt is the very marginal worker. While one may believe that this is bad from a socially concerned point of view, it must be recognized that the program was not targeted at the part-time worker or the casual laborer. Given the aims of Unemployment Insurance—income maintenance for the regular work force—it is clear that the policy change creates the least problems for the fewest people.

9. *Is the policy effective?*

It should be. As of the moment that these words are written, it is too soon to tell. The Unemployment Compensation Trust Fund should be out of the woods by 1986. A very real crisis has been averted by what appears to be a constructive solution, given the economic conditions of the state.

10. *Will programs derived from the policy be efficient?*

Yes. Since the mechanism to collect the taxes and deliver the benefits is already in place, there is no reason to expect any reduction in efficiency. It appears that a more satisfactory benefit system will be delivered without any significant increase in cost. Of course, there may be problems that one cannot anticipate at this time, but it is reasonable to expect a successful future for this policy change.

There are a few comments that we would like to interject here. This policy change was passed and is in place. What features did it have that the more far-reaching proposal for change in Workers' Compensation lacked? As the application of our model shows, the Unemployment Insurance policy change can be shown to offer improvement over the previous policy in a number of areas at, at least, no harm in others. The UI policy change fit contemporary style, it challenged no important values either in society or for social workers, it was acceptable to the relevant decision makers, and it appears to be effective, efficient and easily workable. No sweeping changes in the program are required. No new technology for service delivery needs to be put in place. No powerful group rose in opposition. The working people of the state will get higher benefits when unemployed and the result is clearly beneficial with a minimum of pain to the public. This appears to be an unusually successful example of policy change. Unfortunately, in the next section of the chapter, a happy ending is not as likely, as we turn our attention to the major programs of the Social Security System—those programs known as the Old Age, Survivors, Disability, and Health Insurance.

Old Age, Survivors, Disability, and Health Insurance

What is generally called "social security" is more properly the federal social insurance programs that cover retirement, survivors, disability, and health insurance known as OASDHI (Old Age, Survivors, Disability, and Health

Insurance). These programs provide cash payments and medical benefits to retired and disabled members of the work force as well as benefits to the families of deceased workers. OASDHI benefits are paid from taxes on incomes. In the case of wage earners, the employer and the wage earner each pay one-half of the tax. Self-employed people pay a tax on their income that traditionally was not quite equal to the amount paid by an employer and an employee on a wage earner's income. Part of this tax goes to provide health insurance (Medicare), which we will discuss in Chapter 6 in connection with health and mental health policy.

The OASDHI program is vast, with over 90 percent of the American work force covered at a cost in excess of $150 billion. In the past, these have not been controversial programs, but since the early 1980s pressure for reform has been growing as difficulties built into the system began to come to the surface. Some of the issues are historic. One of these is the question of selectivity versus universality. That is, should social security be designed to provide benefits for those in need or should the benefits be for all citizens? The American pattern has been to take a middle line between extreme positions. Social security is selective insofar as the benefits apply only to those with an active connection to the work force. It is universal in that the benefits are available to all those who have a work record without regard for financial need. A second issue has to do with the adequacy of benefits. Should the benefits be based on one's "contributions" paid during working years or should they be based on some criterion of social adequacy? Although the initial benefit is based on one's prior income, subsequent adjustments are based on the Consumer Price Index. In recent years, this has meant that the actual benefits have moved in the direction of adequacy.

Alicia Munnell, an economist, has written a very prophetic evaluation of the retirement benefits under social security.[15] Two of her criticisms are pertinent. First, she suggests that social security may have a negative effect on saving, since workers may count too heavily on their retirement benefits. The second criticism is that the benefit structure overcompensates for inflation. In 1972, the Congress modified the benefit structure so that increases were tied to increases in the federal index of the cost of living. Munnell foresaw that the benefits would outstrip the tax income. She pointed out that since social security benefits are related to wages, today's workers' incomes would qualify them for extremely high benefits that would be hard to finance. In the first edition of this book, we noted that increases in the social security taxes that were passed in 1977 should have lessened the problem. In fact, we were quite wrong even though other changes were supposed to eliminate overindexing of incomes. By 1982, it became clear that what had been regarded as a benign and constructive program for taking care of older and disabled workers had become an economic disaster looking for a place to happen. We will return to this issue since it has become a major problem that certainly will not go away. However, we should briefly discuss an additional issue that has a bearing on this one—the effect of social security on poverty.

This is not a simple issue. Some believe that, although the current transfer systems are "considerably less than adequate," the social insurance programs have had an impact on poverty greater than those programs aimed especially at the poor. This impact has been greatest on the aged. In analyzing the problems of the public assistance programs, a presidential Commission on Income Maintenance Programs stated a few years ago that social insurance programs (OAS-DHI, Unemployment Insurance and Worker's Compensation) "do not provide adequate benefit levels for the very poor."[16] This is because the poor have irregular work records and low incomes that do not yield the same tax "contributions" of higher paid and more regularly paid workers. Since most social insurance benefits are work connected, programs that benefit persons who have spent years in the work force could not be expected to do very much for persons who have little or no connection to it. For those persons with substantial work records, particularly the aged, it is clear that the social insurances have meant the difference between poverty and adequacy in living standards. There is little question but that the OASDHI program has been successful in maintaining income for the work force, which is precisely what it was designed to do. The past success of the program should not blind us to the need for periodic reform. And reform—at least to some degree—is needed at the present time.

Let us begin by looking at the basic principles that have guided OASDHI up to the present. We believe that the program follows these guiding principles:

1. The program should be financed by specific taxes on employer and employee rather than from the general revenue.
2. Benefits ought to be work connected and based on earnings.
3. Everyone in the permanent work force ought to be covered.
4. Benefits ought to be independent of need.
5. Benefits ought to move in the direction of social adequacy.

Let us examine each of these points more closely.

1. The program is currently financed by taxes on both the employer and the employee. Part of the idea behind the OASDHI tax, as we said earlier, was to stress the idea that Social Security was a kind of insurance. If people believed that their money was going into something called a trust fund, they would be more accepting of the program. If workers were paying a portion of their wages into the system, they would feel that they had a personal stake in it. Accordingly, when the program started, each employee paid a tax of 2 percent of the first $1,500 in wages. This amount was matched by his or her employer, so that worker and employer each paid a maximum tax of $30 per year per worker. By 1960, the tax rate had risen to a rate of 3 percent on the first $4,800. In 1970, the first $7,800 was subject to a tax rate of 4.8 percent. The tax rate rose to 6.13 percent of the first $25,900 in 1980. The 1977 amendments to the Social Security Act provide for a tax rate increase to 7.65 for 1990 with the provision that the income base is to be adjusted to compensate

for increases in incomes. The reader should bear in mind that these rates are what the employee pays and it should be remembered that the employer is taxed a like amount per employee, so the actual figures must be doubled to reflect the total tax per employee.

Self-employed persons were added to the system in the 1950s. Their tax rates have been higher than those of employees. In 1960, the self-employed paid 4.5 percent on their first $4,800 of earnings. By 1970, the tax rate had risen to 6.9 percent on the first $7,800 and by 1980 it was 8.1 percent on the first $25,900. It is scheduled to rise to double the employee rate in the future.

Why have the taxes and the tax base been increased? Because Congress has steadily increased the benefits. Although the tax was first levied in 1936, no expenditures were made until 1940. For a number of years, the income exceeded the expenditure, but this situation eventually reversed itself, causing Congress to raise the taxes on current workers in order to insure that enough money was passing through the trust fund to pay current benefits. The problem came to a head in 1983, and we will discuss Congress' "quick fix" a little later in the chapter.

2. When one reaches retirement age and files for benefits, his or her initial benefit payment is based on a formula which is applied to past earnings. The higher one's income, the greater the benefit. After the initial year, however, one's benefit increase is calculated not on past earnings, but on a different basis. Up until 1984, the Consumer Price Index was used as the guideline for increases. This variation is a revision of the initial intent of the writers of the Social Security Act.

3. Initially, the Social Security program was devised with the industrial worker in mind. Over the years, more and more occupational groups have been included—farm laborers, domestic workers, physicians, attorneys and even, under certain circumstances, members of religious orders who have taken a vow of poverty. Although there are a few groups not covered, and a few groups of state employees who have left the system, the official policy is clearly in favor of compulsory and universal coverage. As we have explained above, part of the reason for extending the coverage is to include more taxpayers. The only problem with this is that the additional taxpayers in time become beneficiaries and the financial crunch is only delayed. *Newsweek* reported that "in 1945, for instance, a total of forty-two workers each paid a maximum of only $30 a year in payroll taxes to support one retiree . . . today each retiree is supported by just 3.2 active taxpayers, and by 2020, when the baby boom generation has dropped out of the work force, each increasingly long lived oldster will be supported by only two workers."[17]

4. Benefits are independent of need. This policy has so far been followed without compromise. The retiree with the necessary work history does in fact get the benefits when they are due. A person who has worked for years at minimum wages gets a benefit as does a corporation president

with a six-figure income. There has been a certain amount of disagreement about this policy over the years. A highly paid corporate executive probably doesn't need the money, say the critics of the policy, so why should he or she be eligible? Defenders of the policy argue that if one is not eligible on the basis of having been a "contributor" then social insurance becomes just another public assistance program and a fundamental purpose of the program is lost.

5. Benefits have moved in the direction of social adequacy. This is, however, a fuzzy point. Officially, Social Security is not committed to adequacy. The intent was and is to provide a basic economic floor for the wage earner below which he or she would not sink. The system was not designed to be the sole support of the retired worker. The Social Security Administration has always been very honest about this particular point. However, despite a lot of effort to convince the public that one should save and invest for the future, many working people have come to expect Social Security to be their major source of financial support during retirement. It appears that Congress has reinforced these feelings over the years. By increasing benefits as rapidly as has been done, Congress has raised the expectations of many older Americans. When President Reagan talked of reducing the growth in benefits—not cutting benefits, but simply slowing their growth—he was inundated with negative criticism.

This brings us to the crisis of 1983. It became obvious in January that there would not be enough money by July to pay benefits to retired and disabled people. Revenue was simply insufficient to pay the scheduled benefit increase. The problem was further complicated by the relatively high unemployment rate. During the previous year, President Reagan had appointed a bi-partisan commission, chaired by economist Alan Greenspan, to make recommendations for "saving" the Social Security System. Finally, the commission produced its recommendations. Basically, they involved delaying the benefit increases, raising the taxes on employers and employees, increasing the amount of salary and wages included in the tax base, bringing federal and self-employed workers into the system, and taxing some of the benefits.

When finally enacted by the Congress, the following provisions were added to Social Security:

1. Virtually all federal employees hired from 1984 on will be covered. Many current federal employees, including the President, Vice-President and the members of Congress, are also now part of the system.

2. All employees of non-profit organizations are now covered.

3. Groups of state and local governmental employees may no longer "opt out" of the system as they had done in the past.

4. The amount of wages subject to the Social Security tax has been increased from $35,700 to $37,800 with future increases dependent upon the economy. The tax rate was increased to 7 percent (14 percent when

the employer's amount is added in) for 1984. Effectively, the Congress simply moved up scheduled increases by one year. They cushioned this a little by allowing a tax credit which effectively reduced the Social Security tax rate to 6.7 for 1984, but after that, scheduled increases will resume.

5. If an individual's taxable income and half of his or her Social Security payment totals over $25,000 per year ($32,000 if a married couple), half of the social security income will be subject to federal income tax. This is a new departure, since Social Security benefits had been tax-free.

6. A provision was added that will hold the benefit increases down when the balance in the fund is low. If the trust funds fall below 15 percent (20 percent after 1989) of the expected outlay, the benefit increase will be figured on either the Consumer Price Index or the average wage increase, whichever is less. This may slow the growth of benefits.

7. The tax rate on self-employed persons was scheduled to rise over time to double the rate for individuals.

There are some other changes having to do with survivors' and divorced persons' benefits and for working people receiving federal pensions.

What will these changes do?   They will borrow time. They do not represent a permanent solution, but they may prolong the evil day of retribution for a number of years. A study of the demographics of the American population suggests that, given the low birth rates in the 1930s and the higher birth rates after World War II, the system will now correct itself in the short run. This is because there will be a relatively few retired people compared to the children of the "baby boom" that occurred between 1945 and 1962. The real crunch on the system may come when the baby boom generation begins to retire about twenty years after the turn of the next century. However, if Congress continues to raise benefits, the current reforms will not last beyond a few years.

Is there a permanent solution?   Clearly, unless workers of the future are willing to pay an increasing share of their income into the transfer programs that make up Social Security, something will have to be done before things get to a really critical point. A number of solutions have been devised. All of them involve slowing down the outgo in some way, e.g., increasing the age at which full benefits are paid, limiting the increases in benefits, or taxing the benefits. None of these solutions are popular among older Americans who see any change of this sort to be an attack on the system as a whole. Further, none of the solutions really represent a major shift in policy, but are merely ways of tinkering with the present system. We want to share with you a solution that is a departure from the present system.

Walter E. Williams is an economist who teaches at George Mason University. He has suggested making the social security system *private*.[18] This is not an original idea with Professor Williams, but his version is the most recent one to compete for attention. First of all, Professor Williams would have everybody under forty stop paying taxes into the system. Instead, they would be required to invest the money scheduled to be paid into Social Security in private Individual Retirement Accounts. Professor Williams would prefer that this not be a compulsory program, but is willing to compromise on this point because he wants to forestall critics that believe that people would not save for their old age unless they had to do so. People over forty would continue to pay into the Social Security system and would get benefits as they are presently scheduled. There would, of course, be a revenue shortfall when younger Americans stopped paying the tax. Professor Williams would fund the benefits by making up the shortfall out of the general revenue. At first, this would be very expensive, but the cost would diminish each year and after fifty or sixty years the expense would dwindle to nothing.

Eliminating the Social Security system would have been unthinkable a few years ago. Now, with the growth of company and industrial pension plans and the new laws permitting tax shelters for the average wage earner, it is possible to contemplate the possibility of alternate funding for old age and disability. Let us see how good an idea this is in terms of our policy analysis model.

1. *Is the policy under consideration compatible with contemporary "style"?*

   To this question, we must give a qualified yes, given the general climate. Certainly, supporters of the current administration would see the proposal as very much in the spirit of the prevailing conservatism. At the same time, there are large numbers of people for whom such a proposal would not be very appealing.

2. *Is the policy compatible with important and enduring cultural values, particularly equity, fairness and justice?*

   In line with what we said above, conservatives would find this proposal compatible with their interpretation of equity, fairness and justice. The policy would appeal to those who believe in the rights of the individual, self-reliance, a limited role for government and a success orientation. Liberals would not find this approach as palatable, because they believe in a positive role for government in the lives of its citizens. We would guess also that any serious attempt to institute a program of this sort would set off an intergenerational struggle that would have a lot to do with conflicting values between young and old.

3. *Is the policy compatible with social work's professional value and ethical system?*

   Few social workers would support the proposed approach. Certainly, the National Association of Social Workers would lobby against any attempt to end Social Security at this time. Although social work stresses the worth and dignity of the individual and the individual's right to make life choices, social workers also believe in the necessity of governmental intervention for the provision of basic social welfare programs and services. It would take a very long time to change the historic attitudes of social work as a whole.

4. *Is the policy acceptable to those in formal decision-making positions?*

Not at this time. Congress is committed to the preservation of Social Security. While there would be conservative support for this proposal, the conservatives do not command a majority on this issue.

5. *Does the policy satisfy relevant interest groups?*

If this proposal were seriously introduced, there would be a great deal of opposition from labor, many employee groups, and groups representing older Americans. Probably the only groups that would actively lobby for its enactment would be those considered extremely conservative. Our guess is that the opposition would be extremely active and vocal in defense of the present system.

6. *Is the policy based on knowledge that has been tested?*

Not really. It is true that the tax shelter idea has been around for some time, but until recent years, tax shelters have been mainly for the well-to-do. No society has ever made wide-scale use of tax shelters for the retirement savings of the bulk of its population and it is difficult to gauge the effect this policy would have on a mass society.

7. *Is the policy workable in the real world?*

Yes, it could be done with existing accounting technology. While Professor Williams' short article that we quoted above does not address how one would go about implementing this approach, we can visualize several ways in which it could be handled. Probably the simplest thing would be for the employer to pay the amount of money currently deducted for Social Security taxes into the Individual Retirement Account of the employee's choice. The employee could select a savings and loan, a bank, or a credit union if he or she wanted the maximum protection for the account, or could use a brokerage house or an insurance company if he or she were willing to take some additional risk. In making this suggestion, we are assuming, along with Professor Williams, that the system would have to be compulsory to meet the objections of those who believe that people would not save voluntarily. It would be more in keeping with the spirit of the proposal if the scheme were voluntary. The argument can be made that today's worker is, in general, more sophisticated about savings and investment than was true even twenty years ago. Further, it can be argued that the individual should have the right to plan for his or her own future even if he or she makes wrong decisions. The argument for this kind of a program obviously rests on an economically conservative base, but its workability is not really an issue.

8. *Does the policy create few problems for both the public and the intended beneficiaries?*

We can anticipate some problems. Undoubtedly, unless this program were compulsory, there would be some workers who would spend the money that had formerly gone to Social Security. Consequently, there would be people who would reach old age with no resources who would be forced to turn to relatives, public assistance, or the meager resources of the voluntary social agencies in the community. Second, this approach does not adequately cover the situation of the young worker who becomes disabled before accumulating a sizeable amount of money in his or her account. Before embarking on such a radical change, the whole question of what should be done for the disabled worker would need to be reviewed. There are other problems, but we will leave them for the student (see the Questions For Discussion at the end of the chapter) as an exercise. These two are serious enough to slow any momentum in the direction of the proposal.

9. *Is the policy effective?*

Given that the long-term goal is to maintain income for people who have retired, then this proposal would be highly effective if followed. Williams quotes a study which suggests that if a married person who began a career in 1980 put his or her social security money into a private fund paying a real return of 6 percent, the couple could retire on $28,000 a year and leave an estate of $500,000.[19] This remarkable phenomenon comes about because of the effect of compound interest. The catch is that the money would have to go in and not come out until retirement in order for this kind of a plan to be effective.

10. *Will the programs derived from the policy be efficient?*

Yes, probably. The technology is already in place. There are an infinite number of uses for the investment capital that would be generated by the plan. The only added expense would be the extra cost of mailing employee contributions to a variety of financial institutions. Of course, with modern tools, even this is not a big problem. Once set up, the whole process would run smoothly as long as the electricity was on!

It is clear that the readers do not have to hold their collective breath waiting for this policy. Although it could be done as a practical matter, and although it would probably be effective and efficient, it is unlikely that political support could be found for the idea. It is simply too radical a departure from the present practice. There are potential value clashes involved that would probably render the formal decision-making process powerless.

This is not to say that such a plan would never have a chance under any circumstances. Some years down the road, this may be an idea that will be eagerly embraced by a willing public. It is our opinion, however, that at the present time, the most likely reform will involve incremental changes in the current system. We will explain what we think is most likely to happen in the last chapter where we will make some forecasts on the future of the policy areas that we discuss in this and succeeding chapters.

REFERENCES

1. For a more extended discussion of the differences, see Claire Wilcox, *Toward Social Welfare* (Homewood, Ill.: Richard D. Irwin, 1969), p. 87.
2. Jack B. Hood and Benjamin A. Hardy, Jr., *Workers' Compensation and Employee Protection Laws in a Nutshell* (St. Paul, Minn.: West Publishing Co., 1984), p. 8.
3. James Robert Chelius, *Workplace Safety and Health* (Washington, D.C.: American Enterprise Institute for Public Policy Research, 1977), p. 17.
4. Hood and Hardy, *op. cit.,* pp. 1–2.
5. *Ibid.,* pp. 2–5.
6. Chelius, *op. cit.,* pp. 10–12.
7. *Ibid.,* p. 20.
8. Hood and Hardy, *op. cit.,* p. 31.
9. Chelius, *op. cit.,* p. 53.
10. *Ibid.,* p. 52–57.
11. *Ibid.,* p. 54.
12. Martin Feldstein, "The Economics of the New Unemployment," in David M. Gordon, ed., *Problems in Political Economy: An Urban Perspective*, 2nd ed. (Lexington, Mass.: D.C. Heath, 1977), p. 88.
13. The comments in this section are based on Tommy Stevenson, "How to Help Jobless Bone of Contention," *Tuscaloosa News,* February 6, 1983, Sec. A, p. 1, and Max Heine, "UA Prof Has Answer to Dilemma," *Tuscaloosa News,* February 6, 1983, Sec. A, p. 1.
14. Stevenson, *op. cit.,* p. 4A.
15. Alicia H. Munnell, *The Future of Social Security* (Washington, D.C.: The Brookings Institution, 1977), pp. 5–24.
16. The President's Commission on Income Maintenance Programs, "Federal Public Assistance Programs," in Gordon, *op. cit.,* p. 318.
17. Harry Anderson with Gloria Borger, Mary Hager and Howard Fineman, "The Social Security Crisis," *Newsweek,* January 24, 1983, p. 22.
18. Walter E. Williams, "A Skeptic's Challange," *Newsweek,* January 24, 1983, p. 26.
19. *Ibid.*

QUESTIONS FOR DISCUSSION

1. Do you believe that workers will be careless since they know that they are protected by Workers' Compensation?

2. Should workers be compensated for long-term chronic diseases (heart disease, for example) when the connection with work is uncertain?

3. Do you agree or disagree with the intent of the National Workers' Compensation Act?

4. Since unemployment is a national problem, do you think that the Unem-

ployment Insurance program should be operated by the federal government?

5. Should the structurally unemployed be retrained at public expense?

6. Unemployment Insurance benefits vary greatly from state to state. Is this all right? If it is not, how can it best be addressed?

7. What problems do you see in Professor Williams' proposal to shift Social Security to a private basis? What problems do you see, particularly for the public and the intended beneficiaries?

8. Should Social Security benefits be permanently tied to the amount of money that one earned in his or her working career, or should we continue to raise benefits according to the cost of living?

SUGGESTED PROJECTS

1. Find two or three persons who are beneficiaries of one of the social insurances. What is their evaluation of the program under which they are receiving benefits? What changes do they suggest?

2. Ask two or three employers about their beliefs about OASDHI. What are their evaluations of the program? Interview a self-employed person for his or her views.

3. Talk with, or write to, your member of the House of Representatives or your senator. What are his or her views on the future of social insurance in general and OASDHI in particular? Do his or her views differ from those of beneficiaries or employers?

4. Ask your local Social Security office about the current benefit levels for retired and disabled workers. Find out the current levels of unemployment benefits in your state. Check with an insurance firm, employer, or state official to find the current payment level in Workers' Compensation.

FOR FURTHER READING

James Robert Chelius. *Workplace Safety and Health.* Washington, D.C.: American Enterprise Institute for Public Policy Research, 1977. Good discussion of the background and development of Workers' Compensation.

Diana M. DiNitto and Thomas R. Dye. *Social Welfare: Politics and Public Policy.* Englewood Cliffs, N. J.: Prentice-Hall, 1983. An advanced and sophisticated text with broader coverage. Well written with lots of valuable detail.

William Haber and Merrill G. Murray. *Unemployment Insurance in the American Economy.* Homewood, Ill.: Richard D. Irwin, 1966. A comprehensive and scholarly analysis of the development of unemployment insurance in the United States.

Roy Lubove. *The Struggle for Social Security, 1900–1935.* Cambridge, Mass.: Harvard University Press, 1968. A history of the development of the social insurances by one of the most distinguished writers on the subject.

Charles I. Schottland. *The Social Security Program in the United States,* 2nd. ed. New York: Appleton-Century-Crofts, 1970. A thorough, well-written review of the history, development, and operations of the various social insurance programs in the United States. Even though dated, this book is valuable for its understanding of the major issues, which really haven't changed.

Edwin E. Witte. *The Development of the Social Security Act.* Madison, Wisc.: University of Wisconsin Press, 1963. A detailed account of the events leading to the passage of the Social Security Act by the executive director of the staff of the committee sponsoring the legislation.

5

Policies for Coping with Poverty

IN CHAPTER 4 WE DISCUSSED POLICIES and programs that focus on maintaining income, the assumption being that the citizen has some income to maintain. This assumption is invalid for a good number of people. What of those who have no regular income? The rules of the game are different. In this chapter, we will look at the major policies that address the question of poverty and then we will move on to a brief review of the major programs that flow from these policies. We will formulate an alternative approach and compare it with present policies using our policy analysis model.

What Is Poverty?

Poverty is a fascinating phenomenon. Everyone acknowledges that it exists, but there are disagreements about what the word "poverty" means and the numbers of people who are affected by it. The reason that poverty is such a mysterious concept is that there are different ways in which poverty is defined—and each definition conflicts with the other.

The most commonly used definition involves the notion of *absolute* poverty.[1] That is, a poverty line is drawn at a given income. The "official" poverty line in the United States is set by the Census Bureau. Originally, the poverty line was based on the amount of money required to purchase the food necessary to provide a minimally adequate diet, multiplied by three. The multiplication by three was chosen because a survey by the Department of Agriculture in 1955 suggested that families of three spent one-third of their income, after taxes, on food.[2] This figure is adjusted annually using the increase in the Consumer Price Index.

The second commonly used way to define poverty is the *relative* poverty approach. In this approach, poverty is considered to be relative to the standard of living enjoyed by most people in society. The relative poverty definition has never had any official status in the United States, so there are no actual guidelines on the matter. It has been suggested that a reasonable relative standard would be one-half the median national income. If this general approach were followed, about 20 percent of the citizens of the United States would be considered poor. The trouble with this kind of a formula is that a fairly sizeable number of Americans would always be poor no matter what happened since there will always be people relatively worse off than others.

The answer to the question, "How many Americans are poor?" rests, then, on one's definition. In a textbook that is revised every four or five years, it is difficult to maintain up-to-date figures. To complicate the issue further, the Census Bureau is in the process of changing the way that it identifies the poor.

Officially, the Bureau counts as the poor all whose cash income falls below the annual poverty line. Following this procedure, the Census Bureau reported that 15 percent of Americans were poor in 1982. However, in 1984 the Census Bureau responded to critics who argued that counting only cash income tends to overstate poverty. It published the latest of a series of technical reports that based estimates on poverty that included the value of non-cash benefits received by the poor—food stamps, school lunches, public housing and medical care. When the value of these non-cash benefits was included, the percentage of Americans below the poverty line was reduced to a range of between 10 and 13.7 percent, depending upon which of several alternative estimates were used.[3] As of this writing, there has been no official change to this new system of reporting. We speculate that both approaches will be used as the basis for published reports in the near future. It is not clear what effect the recession of the early 1980s has had on poverty, regardless of which measure is used, but a guess based on both press and official sources suggests that there has been an increase of at least 1 and perhaps 3 percent since 1982. This is still better than the approximately 20 percent in the 1960s and the nearly one-third who were poor during the Great Depression of the 1930s.

Of course, the poverty line, however drawn, continues to creep up with the general cost of living. As of the middle of the 1980s, a family of four can have a cash income in excess of $10,000 and remain officially poor.

Who Are the Poor?

There are several ways of looking at this question. We will briefly explore some of the more important factors. In order to be as current as possible, we have used a staff report done for the House Ways and Means Committee, published in late 1983, as the source for the data in the section.[4]

Age

Approximately 40 percent of the poor are children under eighteen. In effect, this means that about one child out of every five lives in a poor family. Older persons, those over sixty-five, used to be overrepresented among the poor, but because of various governmental transfer programs, this is no longer true. The proportion of older Americans who are among the poor is roughly equal to their proportion in the general population. That is, Americans over sixty-five make up about 11 percent of our population and about 11 percent of the poor are over sixty-five.

Ethnicity

About two-thirds of the poor are white. This is always a surprise to those who think that most of the poor are black, but this proportion has held steady for a number of years. It is true that blacks are overrepresented among the poor. Blacks make up about 12 percent of the U.S. population, but about 28 percent of the poor are black. People of Spanish origin (who may be of any race) are also overrepresented among the poor. Roughly 6 percent of the U.S. population are of Spanish origin, but they are almost 13 percent of the poor. Put another way, about 12 percent of whites, around 36 percent of blacks and nearly 29 percent of persons of Spanish origin are poor in the United States.

The "New" Poor

Although this is not strictly a demographic category, it needs to be discussed briefly. There are two types of people who are increasingly to be found in the ranks of the poor. First, there has been a dramatic increase in the number of young women and girls who have had children while unmarried. In 1950, approximately 4 percent of all children born in the United States were born to single women. By 1980, this percentage had increased to over 16 percent.[5] In effect, about one child out of six is born to an unmarried woman. The rates at which single women have given birth to children has increased by three times among blacks and nearly five times among whites. Since many of these mothers are quite young, this increase in births to single women is an added burden on the American welfare system. There does not appear to be any easy answer to this problem. Interestingly enough, the availability of family planning clinics and legal abortions has had little effect on the increase in births to young, unprepared women who now must find resources to support themselves and their children.

The second large segment of the "new" poor are those who are long-term unemployed workers and the technologically displaced. We will discuss their plight at greater length in a later section. The major point to be made is that a number of these people are not traditionally poor and are relative newcomers to the Food Stamp office. Many of them have held decent jobs for a number of years. For some of them, particularly the older workers, poverty—or at least severely reduced incomes—is a permanent condition.

Summary

This quick picture is obviously incomplete. We want to emphasize that poverty is a very complex phenomenon. It resists solution in part because many of the poor are children who have little power to affect their immediate circumstances. Certainly, ethnicity is a major factor for many. While old age is not as important as it used to be, there are still many older individuals for whom poverty is very real. Now, the addition of large numbers of single women with children and chronically unemployed workers can only complicate an already difficult problem. A simple, quick fix is highly unlikely and no one should indulge in wishful thinking about the future of the poor.

Our position is that, whatever the definition, the problem is extensive enough to warrant societal action. The reduction in the absolute numbers of the poor certainly appears to be progress. The general increase in productivity and the success of some of the income transfer programs have clearly had a beneficial effect.

However, there is another side to the question. More radical students of the problem, Lee Rainwater and David Gordon, for example, take the position that poverty should be viewed in relative terms and that there has been no real decline in poverty.[6] They argue that governmental transfers have had very little actual impact.

Because of the highly political nature of the definition of poverty, we doubt if the question can be settled readily. Coming to an agreement on a definition is not really relevant to our discussion. By any definition, there are millions of people who are poor. Our past and present welfare policy has not effectively eliminated the wretched conditions under which many Americans live. Any solution hinges, we think, on a major change in policy.

Current Policies

We can isolate several major policies that have historically guided social welfare programs for the poor in the United States. Although there have been shifts back and forth between liberal and conservative rule in the United States, these policies have remained more or less constant.

1. Work is the best anti-poverty policy. Therefore, the best thing that the government can do is to promote economic growth. Beyond this, there are some directly supportive things that can be done that will enable as many of the poor to work as is possible. These include:
   a. employment opportunities and job training.
   b. a minimum wage law.

2. For those who cannot work "through no fault of their own" a modest level of living should be provided if there is evidence of real need. Generally, this category includes older people with little income, the handicapped and the disabled. Benefits include:
   a. cash payments.
   b. non-cash benefits including food stamps, payment for medical care and low-cost housing.

3. For those who are not working because they have children, we should provide a relatively unattractive minimum level of support while encouraging them to prepare for work. The benefits include:
   a. relatively minimal cash benefits.
   b. food stamps, payment for medical care and low-cost housing.
   c. mandatory training and/or compulsory work as a condition of receiving benefits.

Other services are often suggested to the poor—family planning (where legally and morally acceptable) and counseling either at a family counseling center or mental health clinic—but these services are not specifically aimed at the poor. In this chapter, we will deal mainly with financial services for the poor. We will reserve discussion of medical services and housing for later chapters that specifically address these topics.

There is an obvious moral tone in American policies toward the poor. It is present when relatively liberal politics prevail and receives more emphasis when conservatives are in power. Much of this moral content centers around the accent on work. Many social workers have been critical of what is often called the "work ethic," and yet the value of work is central to American society as we pointed out in Chapter 2. It is unfair to say that only the poor are expected to work, since most middle-class people also expect it of themselves. Even those social workers who are most critical of work requirements in welfare work hard themselves and believe that their work is important and meaningful.

The work ethic as a moral concept is usually associated with the writings of Max Weber, primarily *The Protestant Ethic and the Spirit of Capitalism*. This, however, is not fair to Weber. He did not recommend the work ethic, he simply observed its effects. The two essays that make up *The Protestant Ethic* are Weber's attempt to deal with the place of moral thought in the development of modern capitalism. He concluded that economic and political factors were the most important elements in modern capitalism. He also observed that, in addition:

> One of the fundamental elements of the spirit of modern capitalism, and not only of that but of all modern culture: rational conduct on the basis of the idea of the calling, was born—that is what this discussion has sought to demonstrate—from the spirit of Christian asceticism.[7]

Weber's writing on the influence of puritan asceticism on modern capitalism does not seek to explain the importance of work as such, profit, or religion. Weber did not say that work was a value exclusive to Western economic life. Nor did he think that acquisitiveness was unique to capitalism:

> The impulse to acquisition, pursuit of gain, of money, or of the greatest possible amount of money, has in itself nothing to do with capitalism. This impulse exists and has existed among waiters, physicians, coachmen, artists, prostitutes, dishonest officials, soldiers, nobles, crusaders, gamblers, and beggars. One may say that it has been common to all sorts and conditions of men at all times and in all countries of the earth, wherever the objective possibilities of it is or has been given.[8]

Weber also tried to forestall criticism that he was saying that Luther and Calvin and their fellows were personally responsible for the Protestant ethic:

> But it is not to be understood that we expect to find any of the founders or representatives of these religious movements considering the promotion of what we have called the spirit of capitalism as in any sense the end of his life work. We cannot well maintain that the pursuits of worldly goods, conceived as an end in itself, was to any of them of positive ethical value.[9]

Weber's point was that Christian asceticism of the puritan sort elevated work to the level of a calling or a vocation. This kind of devotion to work, coupled with political stability, good markets, and a sound money and banking system, produced modern capitalism. Work and achievement, however, have been important in all human societies, even though few have pursued economic ends with the single-minded joylessness of those merchants and traders of the seventeenth and eighteenth centuries. All societies reward accomplishment and effort. While beggars have been tolerated and even revered in some cultures, they are never given political or economic power. The importance of work is such a deeply ingrained value in the world that it is unlikely that it will be readily discarded as a societal value. It should not be surprising that work is seen as the major remedy for poverty all over the world. It is not necessarily punitive to believe that work is important. It *is* punitive, however, to take the position that work is the only possible source of income when work is not actually available, when one is unable to perform it, when one is prohibited from getting it because of his or her race, sex, ethnicity, or religion, or when work is seen primarily as a morally redemptive activity.

We have made a major digression in our discussion of policy with respect to poverty. Only by bearing in mind the importance of work and achievement in human society can we understand the policies for dealing with poverty that have been developed in the United States. We will now turn to an examination of the policies that we summarized at the beginning of the chapter. Since most readers will be familiar with the major events in the history of social welfare and will know something about current social welfare programs, we will only need to focus on the broad outlines. Since the details change rapidly, the reader will need to check with local authorities for actual benefit levels and eligibility criteria.

Employment Opportunities and Job Training

The most conservative approach to employing the poor is to trust to the workings of the market. This has been the traditional approach and was American policy up through the Hoover administration. Theoretically, in a free market as new products are developed in response to demand, jobs are created. An economy that is growing tends to require more workers. The more people working, the less the level of poverty. Of course, under the most optimistic conditions, the conservatives admit, there will be those who are not able to take advantage of the opportunities provided by economic growth. However, so the argument goes, there should be only a limited number of these people who will suffer from "case poverty" (poverty idiosyncratic to the individual case) and these few cases can be given relief on the basis of demonstrated need. This traditional policy has been given new life by the Reagan administration. There is a certain amount of truth to this approach, at least in its general application. Like most economic theory, however, there are serious unfilled gaps. For instance, what about the structurally unemployed? Earlier, we remarked about the recent increase in poverty due to the economic troubles of the early 1980s. Some of the "new poor" are people who had formerly been workers in what have popularly become known as "smokestack" industries— steel and automobiles. Through a combination of circumstances including the inefficiencies of old plants and equipment and the stress of foreign competition, many workers in these industries will most likely be permanently laid off. From the standpoint of economic theory, these workers ought to be absorbed by other, more productive industries. In reality, many of these workers, particularly the older ones, will not be absorbed. Even if they do find work, it will not likely be at comparable salary levels. There is always a lag time during economic adjustments. That is, even if the numbers of workers formerly employed in automobile and steel production are eventually employed elsewhere, it will not necessarily be the same workers, but rather those from the next generation.

This will be an important enough point in the next few years so that we want to use a hypothetical example that will show the situation that the social worker and planner will face. Suppose that John Smith, aged fifty-five, is laid off from his job on the assembly line at Enormous Motor Company. Due to competition, the demand for Enormous automobiles is down. In response, Enormous Motors, at great capital investment cost, builds new production facilities that are automated and robotized. While this may restore EMC's competitive position, it also may mean that fewer workers are needed to run the new facilities. This is good for Enormous Motors, and, in the long run, will be good for the overall economy because people will be able to buy an Enormous product at a competitive price. But EMC will not likely recall John Smith to work in the newer facility. Theoretically, Mr. Smith is now free to work in some other field. Despite official antidiscrimination policies, Mr. Smith's age is against him. Further, he may not be considered a good candidate for retraining—not because of his age, but because of his potential number of years in the work force. While this is related to age, it is a slightly more subtle point. If it takes a year or two to retrain Mr. Smith, he will be fifty-seven before he can re-enter the work force in a more technologically appropriate role. Most training programs would prefer someone younger who would have a longer working career.

If Mr. Smith is lucky, he may be able to find work in the expanding service side of the economy. Generally, though, these jobs pay less than the automotive industry. At best, Mr. Smith will probably find that his standard of living has declined. If he is forced to work at a minimum wage job, even if it is full time, he will only make slightly less than $7,000 a year. If Mr. Smith is married and has two children at home—and if no one else is earning money— the family will be well below the poverty line. If Mr. Smith's children receive appropriate training, they may find work in the newer industries and move on to independent living. At that point, there will be more members of the family employed than was true before Mr. Smith got laid off from Enormous Motors. Further, it may be several years before the Smith children finish their training and leave the home. Even after the children leave home, unless Mr. Smith has gotten significant raises and Mrs. Smith finds a good job (assuming that she was not working before) the parents will still be relatively poorer than they were before Mr. Smith's initial layoff.

Although this is a purely fictional example, real-life versions of it are occurring in many heavy-industry towns in the Northeast and Midwest. Ultimately, the economic forces of the market may work to the benefit of the work force, but the short run prospect is often rather bleak.

A slightly altered version can be written that reflects the position of many of the "old" poor. Many people with limited skills find that it is entirely possible for them to be fully employed in hard and demanding jobs, but yet make so little that they cannot rise above poverty.

Prior to the Reagan years, high employment was sustained by governmental stimulation of the economy through public spending and a liberal increase periodically in the money supply. This approach is often attributed to the economic theories of John Maynard Keynes, although it is unlikely that Keynes would claim any credit for the way in which his ideas have been applied. In theory, Keynes suggested that government spending, even if it created some deficits, would stimulate the economy in times of economic depression. If money was available at low interest rates, business would be inclined to expand and hire more people. However, it must be noted that Keynes had only envisioned increased governmental spending during depressions—not as a matter of policy for normal times. A strict Keynesian would reduce governmental spending during times of economic growth and let market forces operate.

Over the short run, stimulating the economy works, but as we saw in the late 1970s, the easing of the money supply, easy credit and liberal governmental fiscal policies ultimately have an inflationary effect that does little for the poor—and for the non-poor, for that matter—in the long run.

Another conservative approach involves the provision of tax incentives for businesses that will hire the poor and the unemployed. The Work Incentive (WIN) program that was originally passed in 1967 provided a tax credit for persons who hired the poor. Few employers ever have participated in it or even know about it.[10] A similar approach has been suggested by the Reagan administration. The idea is to create what are called "Enterprise Zones." Businesses would be encouraged to develop plants in areas needing economic development. The owners would be given tax incentives that would make this an attractive proposition. A recent examination of this idea concludes that although this is a good idea as an experiment, only seventy-five zones are contemplated, leaving a great number of unemployed people untouched by this or any other program.[11]

Yet another approach is for the federal government to provide jobs. The United States successfully employed people during the Great Depression through the Works Project Administration and the Civilian Conservation Corps. More recently, during the Nixon administration, the Comprehensive Employment and Training Act of 1973 (CETA) provided public employment along with some training opportunities for a number of otherwise unemployed people. This Act superseded an earlier federal effort that was expressed in the

Manpower Development and Training Act (MDTA) of an earlier era, but it never quite succeeded. There were many negative evaluations of its effects and CETA did not get the public support that the programs of the Great Depression did. During his administration, President Carter proposed some programs reminiscent of the WPA and the CCC, but the proposals were never enacted into law. The WPA and the CCC have long been discarded and President Reagan has eliminated the CETA program. Current efforts to provide jobs at public expense are focused in the Job Training Partnership Act which is aimed at unemployed youth. Funding is not nearly enough to provide jobs and training for all who qualify.

The provision of employment services in all states is another attempt to employ the unemployed. Although these services are not specifically aimed at the poor, they are used primarily by the more marginally employed segments of the work force. The object of these services is to match the worker to the job through a program of testing, counseling and referral.

Another set of programs that have been used over the years involved training. The Economic Opportunity Act of 1964 contained a number of programs designed to prepare people, especially a number of youths, for employment.

Certainly any of these approaches will have some effect, however limited. However, they all run aground on several points. Many of the poor in this country are already working, but at minimum wages. As we showed in an earlier example, steady work at minimum wage will not lift the average-sized family out of official poverty. Approximately half of the poor currently receive some income from employment. A large number of the poor in this country are dubious candidates for regular employment since they are under eighteen, over sixty-five, or parents of pre-school children. Current approaches, then, will only provide answers for some of the poor some of the time.

Employment of the poor is also partially addressed by a number of indirect policies. The policy of economic development of certain areas of the country has been used with some success in the past. One example is the Tennessee Valley Authority, which provides relatively cheap power for large parts of the Southeast. Employment opportunities have increased in the region with a significant reduction in poverty over pre-TVA days.

The Minimum Wage and the Poor

The payment of a minimum wage is seen by many as an attractive weapon against poverty. Since many of the poor are employed, it would appear that the minimum wage would have been their salvation. England and some of the Commonwealth nations enacted minimum wage laws around the turn of the century. Some states in this country enacted minimum wage laws for women early in the twentieth century. After a stormy legal history, states now have minimum wage laws that apply to both men and women. However, the coverage of state laws is limited to local businesses.

The Fair Labor Standards Act of 1938 and its subsequent amendments govern the wages for the bulk of the jobs in the country under the constitutional power of Congress to regulate interstate commerce. Technically, only a few types of employment are not covered. There is a minimum wage for farm labor and a slightly higher rate for nonfarm labor.

The minimum wage law has raised the income of those who are paid according to its provisions, but as we have pointed out above, it will not be enough to lift the poor out of poverty. Further, evasions are not uncommon. Policing is difficult, especially in small businesses.

A number of economists consider the minimum wage a mixed blessing. Because an employer must pay the minimum wage, he or she may lack the capital to start a new business or expand a present one. Professor Walter E. Williams has been widely quoted on his opposition to minimum wage laws. In a recent book, he argues (among other things) that minimum wage laws have had an effect on the high unemployment rate of youth in general and black youth in particular. He cites Bureau of Labor Statistics figures which show that the employment rate among black youth was approximately the same as that of white youth in the late 1940s, but that now black youth participation in the labor force is only about 60 percent that of white youth.[12] While the minimum wage law may raise the wages of those who are employed, argues Williams further, it also means that fewer people can be hired.

While many have taken issue with Professor Williams' position, his argument is persuasive enough to take seriously. The minimum wage law might just be an example of a social policy that had a noble purpose but in practice causes as many problems as it solves.

Other Social Services

Some social casework service has always been available to the poor. In the early days, this often had a moralistic tone. However, counseling has not always been actively sought or offered. In 1962 the Social Security Act was amended to provide a federal contribution of $75 for each $25 of state funds committed to the provision of rehabilitative social services to those receiving public assistance. There is no evidence to suggest that these additional services have had a positive effect on reducing poverty. Even when counseling services are divorced from the administration of grants and rendered by skilled social workers from a voluntary agency, there is little evidence of great benefit.[13] This should not be surprising. Even if social workers were able to relieve all of the emotional conflicts and family problems of poor people, it is unlikely that poverty would be ended. People are not necessarily poor because they have a disorganized personal life. It is more likely that poverty creates conflict and poor social functioning. While some individuals are undoubtedly helped, casework without the provision of an adequate income from some source can only be a Band-aid approach.

The most recent program innovations regarding social services are embodied in Title XX of the Social Security Act, passed in 1975. While Title XX continued the emphasis on rehabilitation and self-support (which was not a new policy), states were expected to develop comprehensive services and were expected to provide for citizen participation in the service planning process. Delegating planning responsibility to the states is a "new" policy move, although of course, prior to the Social Security Act, states had the responsibility for social welfare planning. Title XX was not a return to the old nineteenth-century policy of neglect, however. Some services were required under the Act, but the people of a state theoretically had a good deal of freedom to select and design services that were considered important. Federal guidelines and federal funding, as well as a provision for showing accountability, were supposed to provide for quality control. In the beginning, states did design some innovative programs, particularly for older citizens. Subsequent funding cuts have reduced the impact of Title XX services, and it has not produced the service revolution that many had hoped would ensue.

Family Planning Services

Family planning is a highly controversial approach to the problem of poverty. Some people are wary of family planning and believe that it must involve artificial means of birth control. In reality, family planning does not require artificial means of birth control, but instead only involves people in methods that their consciences will allow. Some blacks have argued that family planning is a thinly disguised approach to the reduction of the black population. There seems to be little objection to voluntary family planning by individuals for private reasons, but there is considerable objection to family planning of any kind as public social welfare policy.

Even in cultures where there is governmental support for family planning, it is hard to see that it has had a profound effect on poverty. Many of the poor are indifferent or opposed. Men, particularly, seem reluctant to change their attitudes about sex and engage in family planning even where there is no moral objection to it.

There is another stubborn fact that complicates the situation. Most poor families are small. Of course, there are occasional examples of large poor families, but the *Statistical Abstract of the United States* for any given year shows that families receiving AFDC average between three and four members.[14] This is only about one more member, on the average, than American families in general. Of course, to have even one less child would be of economic help to both the poor family and the taxpayer. And, in those cases where poor people can be assisted in avoiding large families that they do not want and cannot afford, family planning can be of value. The point is, however, that we are not talking about millions of families with twenty children each. Most of the poor families that receive AFDC consist of a mother and one or two children. They are poor despite the size of the family. They will continue to be poor even if there are no more children. Family planning may prevent those women and children from being worse off, but it will not prevent them from being as poor as they already are.

It appears that the most effective family planning has been done voluntarily as a by-product of upward social mobility. As people earn more money (the one thing that most poor people are ill-equipped to do), they control their family size and raise their standard of living. This phenomenon tends to support the argument that economic development is the most effective tool for the reduction of family size. With upward social mobility, value changes occur. Family planning is not successful without such a change. It is probably incorrect to blame large families (when they do occur) on ignorance or on the lack of availability of contraceptive information. People know about contraceptive methods and instruction about appropriate means of pregnancy control is readily available and has been for years. People simply do not hold the avoidance of pregnancy as important until they see some benefit in it. When there is some point to it, people find contraceptive information and use it. Without a change in values, family planning policy will fall short of the expectations of its supporters.

Legal Services

It was widely recognized in the 1960s that the poor had little legal protection. It was also recognized that the poor were a politically impotent group. Therefore, the War on Poverty legislation of the Johnson administration provided for legal aid and community organization on behalf of the poor. At times there seemed to be more rhetoric than progress, but these programs did provide some access to both the law and the political process. The provision of legal aid to the poor has had some very grave funding difficulties in recent years. Legal aid services now operate in a much more restrictive arena. Reduced funding has also taken most of the steam out of community action programs. The poor seem to be more aware of their rights than was true thirty years ago, and some are politically active. It is clear, however, that the poor are on the fringes of the legal and political process and that this is unlikely to change dramatically in the near future.

Cash vs. Non-Cash (In-Kind) Benefits

The poor laws of England have provided the prototypes for American social welfare policy. The Elizabethan Poor Law of 1601 (43 Elizabeth) provided for the local relief of the poor according to a categorical definition of eligibility. The "impotent" or helpless poor received relief while the able-bodied were punished if they refused to work. Work was available in workhouses for those unable to find it elsewhere. Relief was meager because it depended upon local citizens' willingness to tax themselves. Relief by category remains a central policy today, although there has been some modification.

A second policy was borrowed from the English Law of Settlement of 1662. This law said that one could only receive relief in his or her own parish. The parish could refuse relief to those who did not have legal rights of "settlement" and could order the poor to depart the parish. The concept of "settlement" gave way to "residence" in this country and these laws were still in use until struck down by the Supreme Court in 1968.

The English "reform" of 1834 was not so much a change in welfare policy to assist the poor as it was a change to help the business classes who felt burdened by the poor. The major policy to come out of the reforms of 1834 was the "doctrine of lesser eligibility." This is the notion that the poor should not receive as much in relief as the lowest going rate for employed labor. The object, of course, was to make welfare unappealing—a job that hardly needed doing. From a policy point of view, it is interesting to consider that the doctrine of lesser eligibility ascribes great rationality to the poor. It assumes that the poor will pursue a rational decision to maximize their cash flow regardless of any other value. Therefore, welfare payments must be set low or the poor will make a conscious economic choice to accept them. This is at odds with another belief about the poor—that they are emotional children and are incapable of making rational decisions.

At the heart of English welfare policy (and American policy too) there have been choices. First, if the poor are going to be given relief, should it be in the form of cash or should it be "in-kind"? Second, should relief be given "indoors" through some kind of workhouse or poorhouse system or should it be given "outdoors," allowing the poor to remain in their own homes? Having tried it both ways, American and British policy has gradually become one of cash relief (with some important exceptions) on an "outdoor" basis.

American social welfare historically was based on the principle of local relief and private charity. Both "indoor" and "outdoor" approaches have been prominent at various times. Residence (or settlement) was required, and the benefits have been governed by the policy that the poor should be forced into work by the difficulty of living on what was provided. It is the placing of work in this context that gives rise to the criticism that Americans are "hung up" on the work ethic. It is one thing to believe that work is good, fulfilling, and meaningful and that one ought to do it because there are tasks of importance to be done. It is quite another thing to structure a welfare program in such a way that work is regarded as punishment rather than as a useful way of reaching personal and social goals.

The Social Security Act of 1935 responded primarily to the needs of those who would normally be employed by providing the income maintenance features that we discussed in Chapter 4. As a secondary concern, there were provisions for public assistance for those who were not ordinarily expected to be part of the labor force. Originally, the public assistance provisions of the act provided for federal participation in state-operated programs for the old, the blind, and dependent children. Benefits for the permanently and totally disabled were added in 1950. We might note that these latter benefits were primarily intended to cover persons who were not eligible for benefits under

Workers' Compensation and OASDHI. The option of participating was up to the state. The state could elect to participate in any or all of the public assistance programs under the Social Security Act. States did, in fact, selectively adopt programs, although all states finally came around to adopting programs for the old, the blind, and dependent children. The federal government sold the programs to the states by providing a good deal of the money through the now familiar device of the matching formula. Over time, the federal contributions have increased. In order to qualify for federal funds, a state program had to meet certain criteria. These criteria still apply to Aid to Families with Dependent Children (AFDC):

> (The federal government) requires that the program be in operation in every county in the state; that the state itself contribute to its costs; that it be supervised by a single agency; that the employees of this agency be protected by a merit system; that benefits be available to all citizens; that they not be denied by imposing unduly restrictive residence requirements; that assistance be given only those who are in need; and that applicants be assured fair hearing, the right of appeal, and prompt determination of their claims.[15]

These categorical programs were supplemented in a number of states by a General Assistance program (GA), which functions to cover gaps in the public assistance program. The financing is from state and/or local funds. Some states pay cash benefits while others use a voucher system, and still others use a combination of both.

Some changes were made in January 1974 when the Supplemental Security Income (SSI) program replaced the public assistance categorical aid program of Aid to the Blind, Old-Age Assistance, and Aid to the Permanently and Totally Disabled. SSI is now federally funded and administered, but states may make supplemental grants from state funds. Less than half the states actually pay supplements. Eligibility is standardized, and SSI now looks more like the income maintenance programs. This is more than a cosmetic change. As a policy matter, the connection with the Social Security Administration makes some change in the status of the beneficiary by easing the stigma attached to public assistance. Second, the shift from categorical aid to SSI represents a relaxation of the notion that these people are unworthy. The lack of public criticism of the SSI program suggests that there is greater acceptance of it than was true of the previous program. Slightly over 4 million people currently receive benefits from SSI. When these categorical aid programs were begun in the 1930s, there was the assumption that eventually they would dry up. The thinking was that, as OASI (and later OASDI) expanded, virtually everybody would be eligible for work-connected benefits. This has not happened and SSI continues to provide a financial resource for those who either do not qualify for the work-connected social programs or whose benefits are so small that the individual remains in poverty.

AFDC continues in its old status as a federal/state categorical program. General assistance, in the states that have it, is also not affected. Both offer wide differences in benefits from state to state.

Food Stamps. An interesting anachronism in welfare administration remains in the federal food stamp program. Although the program is financed by the federal government, application is made through the local offices of the state welfare department. Persons meeting a needs test may receive coupons that are redeemable for food. The amount of food coupons one receives depends upon one's income and family size. The use of redeemable coupons is only one step removed from providing "in-kind" relief. The food stamp program replaced an older system of distributing food products that had been bought up by the federal government as a means of sustaining farm prices. In the 1980s there has been a resurgence of the direct distribution of surplus butter and cheese which is reminiscent of the old practice of queueing up at the county welfare office once a month to get surplus farm commodities.

Low-Cost Housing. Since the 1930s the federal government has been involved with local authorities in providing low-cost housing for people with small incomes. This will be discussed more fully in Chapter 7. It is enough here to note that low-cost housing is available in many localities with rents based on income. To ensure that such housing will only be occupied by low-income tenants, an income limit is fixed. When one's income exceeds the limit, he or she must move into nonsubsidized housing.

An Alternative to the Present Policy

The present programs for the control of poverty are broad without being comprehensive. They are based on emotional values rather than on reason or knowledge. Society's misconceptions of the poor and their potentialities have so infected policy decisions that programs are irrational. The main criticism that can be made of them is that they simply have not worked. Even the most staunch liberal must admit that the major force in reducing poverty has been the market.

In our brief review, we can see some change in the basic American policy of coerced work or stigmatized discomfort. Certainly the transfer of three categorical aid programs to the Social Security Administration is a progressive step, since the aged, the blind, and the disabled will be seen as beneficiaries rather than recipients. While SSI is not the same as OASDHI, it will increasingly be identified with social insurance because it is administered by the same agency. Regarding people as beneficiaries is an important symbolic change.

Those whose problem is plain, uncomplicated poverty still face an uncertain future. What alternatives to coerced work and stigmatized discomfort are possible? After all, these policies have been around for a long time and fit comfortably into a number of contemporary American values. Because the present policies have a certain appeal for many people, it has been possible to ignore the simple truth that they do not work. Coerced work and stigmatized discomfort have had a fair trial. If in nearly 400 years these policies have failed to eliminate poverty, it would seem reasonable that either we ought to accept the fact of poverty as a permanent condition and plan accordingly or we ought to try a new approach.

The problem, it seems to us, has been the inability or unwillingness of policy makers to be realistic about work when they are talking about the poor. To some extent, we must plan to accept that poverty is a fairly permanent condition for some individuals, and there is little that can be done about it. There are poor people whose health will not permit strenuous or prolonged work. No amount of motivation will alter the situation of people who are disabled and beyond the reach of rehabilitation as we know it. Further, some of the poor are fragile, elderly people. No program will make them young and vigorous again. The bulk of the poor are under eighteen, and although they may someday be earners, there will always be more children to take their place. Many persons simply are not employable and any policy change will have to recognize the limits of what can actually be done. What we can do is employ those who are genuinely able to work, but who may have been displaced by technological changes. We can also enable those to work who are currently unprepared because of a lack of skill, training, or good work habits. There may also be some things that can be done to upgrade the marginally employed and those who work but are unable to earn enough to rise above the poverty line.

There are several points to be made here about effective social welfare policy. The first point is that some of what needs to be done involves the economy at large and is beyond the direct control of people in the social welfare enterprise.

The Need for a Stable Economic Policy. A healthy economy creates jobs. Social workers should support those economic policies that are identified with growth in employment and low inflation. The advent of Reaganomics has had a number of consequences. One of the positive ones is that it has made more Americans aware of some elementary economic theory. It is now clearly recognized that there are things that can be done to promote economic growth with a minimum of painful side effects. First, it is now clear to everybody that there must be restraint in the rate of growth of governmental spending. Huge deficits, from any source, are ultimately harmful. At some point, the government must not be allowed to soak up all the available credit. This will cause a rise in interest rates and slow down economic expansion. Second, taxation should be fair and at a level that encourages saving and investment. Third, it is now clear that Professor Milton Friedman is essentially correct in his insistence that there should be restraint in monetary growth. While there is justification for deficit spending during periods of stagnation, there is no justification for deficit spending, at least on the present scale, during periods of growth.

Clearly, leaders of both political parties now recognize that there are limits to what government can do and that there is little enthusiasm in the United States for increasingly higher taxes. A stable economy that continues to grow reasonably will create jobs for many people. However, this will not, in all probability, cure poverty by itself. There will still be people who will need something more aggressive in the way of policy if poverty is to be reduced to a minimum.

Effective policy in this area should do several things. First, it should ultimately provide the poor with more money. Second, effective policy should reduce the stigma of being poor as much as is possible. Third, good policy should not have a paternalistic flavor, but should help the poor achieve as much independence as is possible. Fourth, good policy should be uncomplicated and easy to administer.

Before making a concrete proposal, we need to establish a few things first.

1. We think that it is necessary to continue Supplemental Security Income benefits in their present form. As we remarked above, there are people who are old and unable to work and there are disabled people who cannot achieve sufficient rehabilitation to qualify them for employment. We should continue to provide direct federal supplements to the income of these people based on their need as determined by a fair and equitable procedure. There is nothing inherently wrong about a needs test if it is fairly applied and done with due regard for human dignity.[16] Providing these benefits through the Social Security Administration is, as we have said before, a major step toward the elimination of the stigma of poverty for those who are beneficiaries of this program.

2. We think that it will be necessary to continue the present AFDC and GA programs at least for the near future. We cannot do without an emergency grant system to handle short-term needs. Our proposal, which we will present a little later, would eliminate need for a good many people, but there would still be emergency situations. There will always be a few people with limited capability for whom some form of public welfare is the only realistic alternative. However, we think that these situations would be greatly reduced if the following proposals were adopted.

1. *Make work as attractive to the poor—and as realistically available—as is possible.*

   There is nothing wrong with the general expectation that members of a society ought to find fulfillment in work and that work is important. As we have argued earlier, a stable economy will help many people. For those who still face unemployment, we propose that the federal government get back into the business of providing employment for those who cannot or do not find employment in the private sector. This is not a new remedy, but we do have a few wrinkles that have not been used before.

   During the Great Depression of the 1930s, we created jobs in two large categories, public service and the environment. The Works Project Administration provided many public service jobs ranging from street repair to the building of public buildings. The Civilian Conservation Corps engaged unemployed young men in a number of conservation projects of direct benefit to the public. As a by-product, many of those young men learned valuable skills including typing, operating a bulldozer, and forestry.

Our proposal would basically resurrect the WPA and the CCC, although it would probably be a good idea to give the proposed agencies some new names.

There are two important differences between our proposal and the Depression era agencies. First, we propose that these agencies be set up as independent agencies of the federal government and made as permanent as it is possible to make them. One of the problems with previous governmental work programs is their clearly emergency flavor. Second, we propose that as many career positions as possible be filled by the currently unemployed and the poor as they qualify themselves to bear such responsibility. This answers a second problem with previous governmental work programs—they had no realistic future. They provided temporary work that led nowhere. We think that if the agencies were permanent and if there was a career ladder which one could aspire to climb, that many of the poor and the hard-core unemployed could have more positive expectations for the future and would be encouraged to better themselves.

What would these people do? First, there are a number of things that could be done around environmental concerns. A variety of jobs can be created ranging from simple tasks, including picking up the trash along public roads, to the operation of heavy equipment in reclaiming old strip mine land. There is room for a number of people to be employed as clerks, typists, timekeepers, mechanics, guards, laborers, and administrative personnel. Some of these jobs can be created in urban places while others would be in remote rural areas. A number of jobs, ranging from very simple to very complex, could be created in cities. Here again, there is a lot of room for entry level labor jobs and fairly complex administrative and planning roles.

Under our proposal, one might indeed start at the bottom doing very much the same kind of thing that has been done in other governmental programs, but there would be the real possibility of promotion and salary increases if one worked hard and were good at the job. Of course, there are people who would be content to remain at a simple task as long as it was steady work and use the improved standard of living for other activities. There is no reason why one could not do that. But if the worker were ambitious for added responsibility or more complex work, it would be available through promotion.

We think that it might even be possible to employ most of the recipients of public welfare benefits in time. It is entirely practical to think of employing many handicapped people. Many older people might very well choose to work if they were able. Creating public service and environmental jobs would add to the quality of both urban and rural life.

The governmental work force could be expanded or contracted as economic conditions warrant. During times of high economic activity, many people would probably choose to leave the public service for private industry. In this country, private industry will always be more attractive because of the variety of opportunities available, the fringe benefits, and the perquisites. Because the work in private industry is apt to be considered more desirable for most people, salaries are higher, so industry should not suffer from a lack of employees because of governmental employment. The important thing is for the public service employment structure to remain in place on a permanent basis so that the jobs are always there when they are needed or wanted. There are a number of people who work for various levels of government now. Sometimes they leave governmental service for private opportunities. There are also people who cross over from private business to governmental service. The problem is that many of these people are at fairly complex levels and their reasons are usually political or personal. What our proposal does is to make this possible for people at lower skill and economic levels as a matter of public policy. There is a second part of our proposal which over time could blur these differences.

2. *Provide realistic training opportunities.*

Previous schemes involving governmental employment usually included some kind of training. Most of these efforts have been notoriously unsuccessful. One gets the impression that many of these training opportunities were very makeshift operations that were basically efforts in grantsmanship. The WIN program required that AFDC recipients accept training as a condition for receiving the grant. The problem in some localities has been that the training was for jobs which the recipients already had experience in doing or which required no real training.

We see no point in resurrecting these failed efforts. What we do recommend is that successful workers in the public service and environmental agency should receive some educational benefits. In today's world, technical schools, colleges, universities and other bona fide institutions are already in place and could be used to provide the training. We do not propose sending unqualified persons to Ivy League schools in droves. What we do think is practical is tuition and text materials grants to qualified and ambitious persons at the nearest properly accredited institution of the appropriate type. We would hope that a fair number of people would take the opportunity to improve their ability to compete for more complex and higher paying jobs.

What Would This Approach Do?

We think that the above policies would produce upward social mobility for many of the poor and the unemployed. These policies would also provide personnel for jobs that need doing at various levels of competence. They would provide employment and educational opportunities for youth in a more effective way than previous programs. They would also reduce the stigma of welfare over time by gradually reducing the number of people on the rolls and by changing the character of the recipients. Our guess is that most capable people would opt for employment and training, leaving as the majority of recipients those who would be seen with more sympathy by the public. In simpler terms, those left on the rolls would largely be persons that clearly need public support and would be seen as legitimate members of the "truly needy."

The reforms that we propose would not produce the perfect society. There will continue to be antisocial people. There are always going to be people who engage in criminal behavior for a variety of reasons—but these people occur at all levels of society. We do think that if human needs are met, those antisocial acts that are really attributable to poverty will be reduced. We doubt the notion that the poor are more dishonest than other people (although they probably are just as dishonest). We think that they are as interested in improving their state as is anyone else. The paternalistic and negative values with which we have approached poverty have hampered us in dealing with the problem.

What Would Be the Role of the Social Services under This Proposal?

We think that counseling services ought to be voluntary and separate from any benefit program. We would leave services, including family planning services, to the option of the counselee. We do not think that citizens should be coerced into use of social services unless their behavior is clearly harmful to themselves or others. Protective services for adults and children, mental health services, and correctional services will still have to be maintained for the involuntary client who does harmful things. Steady work and increased training opportunities will not cure all human pathology, but there may be some noticeable effect on abuse, neglect and some kinds of antisocial behavior.

If counseling services were voluntary, who would pay for them? Services are better used when the consumer pays for them. Employed persons could pay a fee for services on a prepayment system as is now used in health insurance. Persons receiving a social insurance benefit or recipients of welfare payments could pay for their services using a voucher system as with Medicaid. We will deal with questions of social service delivery in a later chapter since these matters are outside the scope of the present chapter.

Analysis

We have generated these new policies for analytical purposes. We will now examine our work and training proposal as an alternative to the existing policy of coerced work and stigmatized discomfort.

1. *Is the policy compatible with contemporary "style"?*

    No. The current climate in the country is not encouraging to large national programs. Conservative administrations tend to value local control in social welfare programs. Even liberal administrations cannot be expected to endorse massive governmental programs in the current climate in the United States. If the proposal could be organized on a state level, it would have a much better chance of satisfying this criterion. On the other hand, this proposal might have a certain popular appeal, since the idea of education as a means of achieving personal advancement and satisfaction is very much a part of the American way of life. This might generate some public support, but given the current conservative style that seems to pervade officialdom, we doubt if any current national administration would embrace our proposal and make it the centerpiece of its program of welfare reform.

2. *Is the policy compatible with important and enduring cultural values, particularly equity, fairness and justice?*

    We think so. The current Public Assistance Program of Aid to Families with Dependent Children is not a marvel of equity and fairness. There are widely varying benefits from state to state. The work requirement is basically punitive as it is now organized. The present policy blames the victims of poverty. Consider the example of the father of a child born to a single woman. Although he is legally responsible, the law is virtually unenforceable. It is the woman who is left with the bills. She will be the one to apply for welfare. Little stigma is attached to the man. In fact, having left a woman pregnant may be a source of pride in some circles. Since the woman should have "known better" (men are apparently not expected to "know better") she alone becomes the financial victim. While women are less discriminated against on moral grounds than was true years ago, they are still left with the responsibility for the child and the financial obligation. Valid employment and training opportunities would help these women build their own futures. Our proposal would be uniform throughout the country and would reduce the wide variation in benefits. Federal minimum wage rates would apply for entry level jobs, and appropriate pay scales could be developed just as is done for other federal employees.

3. *Is the policy compatible with social work's professional value and ethical system?*

    The present policy of coerced work and stigmatized discomfort is unpopular among social workers. It is much more in line with social work values to provide opportunities for self-fulfillment. It is also better to provide attractive resources than to coerce the use of unappealing services. Social workers know, more intimately than anyone besides the victims, the debilitating effect of poverty. While our proposal is a very modest one, it is not incompatible with social work values. Some would argue that the proposal does not go far enough, so we would not expect unanimity among social workers.

4. *Is the policy acceptable to those in formal decision-making positions?*

Probably not. A similar proposal during the Carter administration did not reach the floor of Congress, but this was primarily because of the cost. With a fairly conservative Senate, this proposal probably doesn't stand a chance. Congress usually passes work *requirement* provisions. It would be hard for them to understand a program that is focused on work and training opportunities, but that has no requirements as such. On the other hand, work and training programs often pass. However, only during the Great Depression has anything on this scale been tried. In the absence of a really severe economic downturn, it is unlikely that Congress would look in this direction.

5. *Does the policy satisfy relevant interest groups?*

This is a tough question. The proposed policy could conceivably receive support from interest groups that have been identified with a mainstream concern for the poor. Interest groups on the near right could probably accept the proposed policy if they believed that it would reduce the welfare system. Groups on the far right would probably reject the proposal as they have rejected most governmental programs that would cost money. Groups on the far left would not like the proposal because they would perceive it as pandering to the capitalist system and failing to deal with the real problem of redistribution. It is doubtful if there would be enthusiastic support across the board.

6. *Is the policy based on knowledge that has been tested?*

Yes, in a way. The programs of the Great Depression, as we have said, embodied some of these characteristics as far as the work programs are concerned. In other words, we have provided work for large numbers of people before and it would not be an impossible task to find the jobs and set up a bureaucracy to hire and assign people to them. The educational benefit provisions of the proposal are similar to the several G.I. bills that have provided training for veterans of the armed services. Clearly, the country could draw on a reservoir of experience in putting these proposals into operation.

7. *Is the policy workable in the real world?*

Certainly. As we noted in the previous paragraph, there is historical precedent in both cases. No new technology needs to be invented, and we know that these kinds of programs can be operated with success.

8. *Does the policy create few problems for both the public and the intended beneficiaries?*

The poor would have nothing to lose. Since they would be no worse off if they did not accept work or training, they would not be exposed to any risk. If the program reduced poverty, the public would clearly be better off. Not only would some important jobs get done, but poverty would be reduced.

Current programs designed to assist the poor have not really done much to open up the opportunity structure. While the provision of cash benefits to eligible persons does enable them to survive, nothing much is done to positively improve their life chances. We cannot see where this proposal would create any great human problems either for the public or the intended beneficiaries.

9. *Is the policy effective?*

Obviously, it would have to be tried out in some pilot projects. We know that these programs worked at one time or another in the past. Poverty was reduced during the Great Depression. People have improved their economic conditions through education and training in the past. We can see no reason why the proposed reforms wouldn't work, beyond the obvious "glitches" that plague any large program.

10. *Will programs derived from the policy be efficient?*

This, too, needs experimentation. There is nothing in the proposal that could not be done efficiently over time. The major problem is the cost. It is difficult to predict how many people would accept the opportunities that would be presented. We know that there are approximately 3 million caretakers currently receiving AFDC and we have around 3 million or so more who have been unemployed for over fifteen weeks, and another nearly 3 million who are currently listed as "unable to work."[17] It is unlikely that the program would be deluged with 9 million people since not all AFDC caretakers are able to work, some of the unemployed will find other work, and those unable to work may still be unable despite increased opportunity. Our best intuitive guess is that not over 2 million people would be likely candidates for our proposed program. Our rough calculations (which are not scientific enough to expose to public scrutiny) suggest that it would cost a minimum of 20 billion to deliver this program for one year. If it caught on, there would be an escalation of costs for education and training, although if people left the public service for private employment, the costs would tend to level off over time. Of course, a few pilot projects would not cost a prohibitive amount. It would make sense to try these proposals in a few states in order to see if they were genuinely worthwhile. We think that they should be given a try.

Summary

Is there any real likelihood that innovations of this sort will be tried in the near future? No. Although there are no programs for the long-term unemployed and the AFDC program satisfies very few people, there is little real impetus for this profound a change in approach to the reduction of poverty. The present policy of coerced work or stigmatized discomfort is deeply ingrained in the Anglo-Saxon mind. It is compatible with a number of moral social values including external conformity, racism, and sexism. It is not compatible with humanitarianism, equity, freedom, democracy, and the worth of the individual. Our proposed policy takes into account work and achievement, as most Americans see those things for themselves. Our proposal stresses the human aim of mutual aid. We are willing to take the position that most people want to grow and to become self-reliant, provided that there is a viable opportunity structure. In short, we think that our policy reflects what most Americans would want for themselves if they were in the same position as the poor. However, most Americans have jobs, get training and education, and live comparatively well. They are not likely to be willing to pay the cost that proposals of this sort involve. It is our opinion that this is a bad time for welfare reform. We will discuss what we think is apt to happen in the next few years in the last chapter, but the reader must not expect anything very dramatic.

Why Have We Presented This Proposal?

It is legitimate to wonder why the authors have presented a proposal that they believe to be such an obvious "non-starter." There are some points that we want to make and this example will help us make them.

It is entirely possible to devise a perfectly rational policy that would probably work and have nothing come of it. Here we have a policy that, to our way of thinking, would reduce poverty and improve the general level of living of the public. Further, the policies that we have discussed have even been tried and found successful in the past. It should be clear to the reader that proposals that are not compatible with contemporary style, are politically unpopular, are contrary to the prevailing value system, and are expensive will not likely be put into effect even if they might work and would improve the quality of life. We do not live in a world where rationality prevails. As we have approached poverty, we have used a combination of the "naive priorities" and the "naive criteria" approach in arriving at our proposal. We did not tailor our notions to the prevailing social, political, or economic climate so our analysis process yielded disappointing results. We really need to go "back to the drawing board" and draft a new proposal while we keep in mind the various questions that have to have satisfactory answers before real reform can take place. We wanted to use this kind of an example primarily to dramatize that well-intentioned people often produce neat proposals that are unrealistic in the real world.

We hope that we have energized the reader's critical apparatus with respect to the problem of a new proposal for the reduction of poverty. We seriously believe that any proposal must be carefully thought out from the angles that we have used and must satisfy the criteria that we have proposed. Perhaps one of you who read this will be able to devise a more effective proposal. We are sure that there will be plenty of poor and unemployed people around who need something better than the present inadequate system.

REFERENCES

1. For a more technical discussion, see David M. Gordon, ed., *Problems in Political Economy: An Urban Perspective*, 2nd ed. (Lexington, Mass.: D.C. Heath, 1977), pp. 272–276, 293–300.
2. U.S. Congress, House. Committee on Ways and Means, *Background Material on Poverty*, 98th Congress, 1st Session, 1983, pp. 1–4.
3. Actually, there are currently a number of ways of drawing poverty lines, depending upon family size. See U.S. Bureau of the Census Technical Paper 51, *Estimates of Poverty Including the Value of Noncash Benefits: 1979–1982*, (U.S. Government Printing Office, Washington, D.C., 1984.)
4. U.S. Congress, *op. cit.*, pp. 10–24.
5. U.S. Bureau of the Census, *Statistical Abstract of the United States: 1982–83*, 103rd edition (Washington, D.C., 1982), p. 66.
6. See Gordon, *op. cit.*, pp. 295–300 and Lee Rainwater, "Perceptions of Poverty and Economic Equality," *ibid.*, pp. 285–293.
7. Max Weber, *The Protestant Ethic and the Spirit of Capitalism*, trans. by Talcott Parsons (London: George Allen & Unwin, Ltd., 1930), p. 180.
8. *Ibid.*, p. 17.
9. *Ibid.*, p. 89.
10. See Marilyn Flynn, "Poverty and Income Security," Ch. 7 in Donald Brieland, Lela B. Costin and Charles R. Atherton, eds., *Contemporary Social Work* (New York: McGraw-Hill, 1975), p. 104.
11. Marc Bendick, Jr., "Employment, Training, and Economic Development," in John L. Palmer and Isabel V. Sawhill, eds., *The Reagan Experiment* (Washington, D.C.: The Urban Institute Press, 1982.)
12. Walter E. Williams, *The State Against Blacks*, (New York: McGraw-Hill, 1982), Ch. 3.
13. See, for instance, Edward J. Mullen, Robert M. Chazin, and David M. Gelstein, *Preventing Chronic Dependence—an Evaluation of Public-Private Collaborative Intervention with First-Time Public Assistance Families* (New York: Institute of Welfare Research, Community Service Society of New York, 1970).
14. See the most recent edition of U.S. Census Bureau, *Statistical Abstract of the United States.*
15. Claire Wilcox, *Toward Social Welfare* (Homewood, Ill.: Richard D. Irwin, 1969), p. 230.
16. Neil Gilbert and Harry Specht, *Dimensions of Social Welfare Policy* (Englewood Cliffs, N.J.: Prentice-Hall, 1974), p. 64 ff.
17. U.S. Bureau of the Census, *op. cit.*, p. 375.

QUESTIONS FOR DISCUSSION

1. Pamela Roby has written: "The lives of the poor are shaped less by much-heralded poverty programs than by those factors in the U.S. economy that cause some to be poor and others to be rich in the first place." Do you agree or disagree: What factors in our economy do you think she is referring to?

2. Several years ago, the notion of a guaranteed annual income plan was discussed at some length. This approach has not been seriously mentioned for ten years. Do you think it likely that any plan based on this approach will be recommended in the next ten years?

3. Why might the lower middle and working classes be critical of the policy change that we examined in this chapter?

4. What are some of the pros and cons of the federal government serving as the employer of the poor and unemployed?

5. Youth is now to be exempt from the minimum wage law, at least for summer jobs. How do you think this proposal will work?

6. Casework counseling with welfare poor has been a popular policy in this country over the past century. Do you agree or disagree with the authors' contention that it is not likely to make a difference without some additional programs?

SUGGESTED PROJECTS

1. Discuss with a friend or relative his or her views on poverty and welfare. Does he or she perceive poverty as an individual failure or an economic problem? What would he or she do about the problem?

2. Examine newsmagazines and newspapers for a period of time and read the articles and editorials on some aspect of poverty, welfare, unemployment, or a related issue. Do these seem like controversial topics in the press? Can you detect any consensus? Are conservatives or liberals doing most of the writing?

3. Find out how much money a family of four receives from AFDC. Do the same for an aged couple receiving SSI. Ask about the amount each gets in food stamps.

FOR FURTHER READING

Winifred Bell. *Contemporary Social Welfare.* New York: Macmillan, 1983. A contemporary review of American social welfare policy from one of its most intelligent students.

Eli Ginsberg and Robert M. Solow, eds. *The Great Society: Lessons for the Future.* New York: Basic Books, 1974. A series of articles by prominent economists, political scientists, attorneys, and educators assessing the War on Poverty and projecting future trends. Interesting reading from the perspective of 1984 and beyond.

John L. Palmer and Isabel V. Sawhill, eds. *The Reagan Experiment.* Washington, D.C.: The Urban Institute Press, 1982. A good review of various social programs in the United States and the impact of the Reagan administration's policies on them.

Frances Fox Piven and Richard A. Cloward. *The New Class War.* New York: Pantheon, 1982. A sequel to their *Regulating the Poor,* this book argues that the struggle between economic classes will be expressed politically in the future. Current social welfare programs have a broad constituency and American society is more democratic, they say, so the Reagan administration's attempt to de-emphasize social programs was doomed to fail from the start.

Mildred Rein. *Dilemmas of Welfare Policy*. New York: Praeger, 1982. A sophisticated analysis of the failure of work requirements to actually add welfare recipients to the work force.

Harrell R. Rogers, Jr. *The Cost of Human Neglect*. Armonk, N.Y.: M. E. Sharpe, 1982. A biting analysis of American welfare programs, which Rogers generally considers a failure. The book includes a basically liberal proposal for reform.

Nathan Glazer. "The Social Policy of the Reagan Administration: a Review." *The Public Interest*, Spring 1984, pp. 76–98. A sympathetic analysis of the conservative approach to welfare problems. Glazer seems to think that Reagan's successors will not make an early return to social engineering (in terms of specific programs targeted on identified problems) because the American public is no longer supportive of novel social progams, primarily because they did not produce dramatic results.

Major Policy Problems in Health and Mental Health Systems

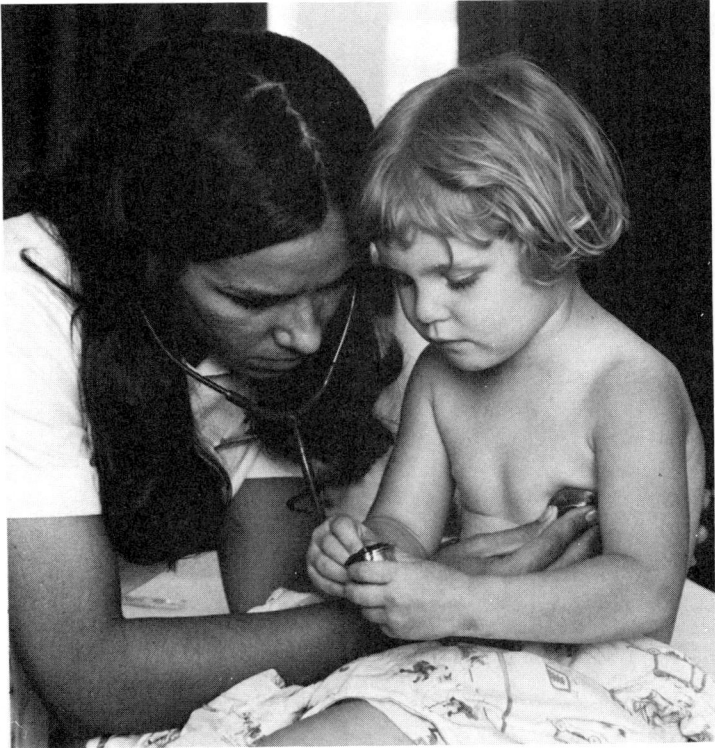

IN THIS CHAPTER WE WILL DISCUSS four major public policy issues in the field of health including mental health. All four have serious implications for social work practice and social welfare policy. Of course, there are other important issues in the health field, but in our judgment these are the most important from the standpoint of the social work practitioner.

The issues that we have chosen generate a great deal of discussion from those who are involved in them. While there is a certain amount of agreement on what the problems are, there is little general agreement on the solutions. We must tell you that this is a highly volatile area in public policy and new proposals are brought out with such rapidity that this material could well be out of date by the time the book is off the press!

Three of the issues are in the area of general health care. As Marmor and Christianson identify them, they are: the price of health care; the uneven geographical distribution of health resources; and the difference in the consumption of services between the poor and the non-poor.[1] There is considerable interrelation among these issues and certainly the price of health care is the issue that receives the most attention, so we will devote more space to it than the others. The fourth issue to be discussed is in the specific area of mental health and goes by the rather long name of deinstitutionalization. This is the policy of discharging the patient into the community as early as possible on the theory that the mental patient has a better chance of reaching a state of maximum functioning when in familiar surroundings.

Frequently, writers treat questions relating to health care and mental health separately. There are good reasons for doing it that way, but we have chosen instead to deal with them in one chapter because we want to avoid the fallacy of separating mind from body. The care of those with emotional and psychological problems is, after all, a part of the larger health care system and the issue of deinstitutionalization is related to some of the general issues of health care as we will show.

The Price of Health Care

It is usual to speak of the *cost* of health care but we will follow Christianson and Marmor's lead and discuss the *price*. The difference is more than an academic one. While we often interchange the two in popular speech, economically they are different. Cost refers to the amount of economic good that goes into the production of an item or service. Price is what the consumer pays and includes any surplus that accrues to the provider or manufacturer as profit. Although some health providers are non-profit organizations, they still may earn an amount of money beyond their costs even though it does not become payable to an owner or any stockholders. In short, health care providers calculate their costs and then set a price for us to pay.

While there has been an increase in the price of nearly everything, few things have increased as dramatically as health care. In 1950, citizens of the United States spent a total of 12.7 billion dollars on health care, but by 1982 this figure had risen to 322.4 billion.[2] Another way of understanding the increase in price is to look at the per capita figures. In 1950, Americans paid an average of eighty-two dollars for health care, while by 1982 the per capita price had risen to $1,365.[3] Still another way of describing the increase in the price of health care is to say that the price increased from 4.4 percent of the gross national product in 1950 to 10.5 percent by 1982.[4] In other words, between ten and eleven cents out of every dollar spent for goods and services in the United States goes to some part of the health care enterprise. Almost as much is spent for medical care in the U.S. as is spent for food. To add one more perspective, in 1984 it was reported that Chrysler Corporation paid $5,700 per year in health benefits for every employee and that this added $550 to the price of every car.[5] Clearly, the price of health care is a major social issue.

Why the High Price?

There are a number of reasons for the high price of health care and they are interrelated to the point that it is hard to tease them apart. Further, different writers, depending on their values, assign different weights to the identifiable factors.

First, let us identify the major source of the price increase. Contrary to what one might think, it is not primarily in doctor's fees, although they have risen steadily over the years. While the dollar cost of physicians' services has risen from around 14 billion dollars in 1970 to nearly 62 billion in 1982, the doctors' share of the health care dollar has remained constant at about 20 percent.[6] That is, twenty cents of every dollar paid for health care in 1970 went to the doctor. He or she got the same share in 1982. Other health care prices have remained fairly constant on a relative basis (although there have been declines in the shares of the health care dollar going to research and construction) with the exception of the price of hospital care. In 1970, hospital care accounted for a little over $.37 of every health care dollar, but by 1982 the hospital's share had climbed to $.42. Thus, while all health care prices have increased sharply, it is the price of hospital care that has led the way. It is for this reason that most attempts to deal with health care prices have centered on the hospital. To give some perspective, it may help to interject some small-scale data. In the 1950s, in the Midwest, the daily charge for room and board in an acute illness hospital was around $25. Today, the use of that same bed would be priced at nearly $200. (Other charges are added on, making the total charge for a day in the hospital much more than this). Of course, prices were—and are—higher on both coasts and in some other parts of the country, but the principle is much the same.

Comparing the basic room and board rate is somewhat deceptive. An experienced hospital administrator informed us that hospitals try to keep basic room and board charges as low as possible because that is what patients look at when they shop for a hospital. Administrators will increase the price of everything else first and only increase the basic charge as a last resort. Since hospital charges beyond room and board are now so complex, it is nearly impossible for anyone without an accounting degree to make sense of the actual bill even if it is itemized. Therefore, it is difficult for the consumer to make informed decisions.

Now that we have at least a loose grip on the problem, let us return to the original question. The short answer is that health care prices have shot up because there is no real incentive to limit them. While this answer is correct as far as it goes, it needs a great deal of explication.

First of all, health care costs would be reduced if more Americans took better care of their health. A significant amount of illness would be avoided if people ate a healthy diet, avoided smoking, exercised, drank in moderation, got enough sleep and avoided the abuse of both legal and illegal drugs. This is the one factor in reducing health costs that is agreed upon universally. While good health habits would not eliminate all illness, that is no excuse for not doing what we can to control those illnesses for which these actions are helpful. All of this sounds preachy, we know, and yet it is evident that good health is not by itself enough of an incentive. After all, if we get sick, there is always the health care system.

The major problem with the health care system is that the patient does not, in most cases, pay directly for his or her care. The main culprit here is the third party payment. In simple words, someone else—an insurance company or the government—is paying the bill for most Americans. Up until recently, this has not been a problem and the major sources of payment have been willing to pay physicians' and hospitals' "reasonable and customary" fees. Of course, ultimately the consumer pays the bill, but that has not been an obvious burden until the last few years.

This, too, is a simplistic answer and there is a good deal more to the problem. A specific reason for the increased price that governments and insurance companies are asked to pay has to do with the increase in medical technology. In 1950, there were no transplants (beyond corneas and some experimental efforts), no CAT scanners, no laser surgery and no ambulatory dialysis. Although health care was not primitive, it was not as technological as it is today. All these innovations—and others—are expensive to develop and to use. To complicate this point, today's hospitals all seem to want to have a higher level of equipment then their neighbors and there is a great deal of money and effort invested in attempts to stay ahead of the competition even if the technology involved is not economically a good idea. The duplication of costly services has had some part in driving up the price of health care.

Along with the more sophisticated equipment comes the need for more sophisticated personnel. The modern hospital employs technicians and specialists in fields that did not exist thirty years ago.

Construction costs are higher. Further, construction is more complicated. New hospitals have oxygen and vacuum lines piped to every room. This increases the cost of electrical wiring and plumbing. Further, hospitals are overbuilt. Following World War II there was a shortage of hospital beds and an expanding population. Congress passed the Hospital Safety and Construction Act in 1946, more commonly known as the Hill-Burton Act. This act encouraged the renovation and construction of hospitals by providing federal matching funds. Communities took advantage of these funds and built and remodeled to the point that the United States now has an excess hospital room capacity. A number of hospitals have had to close wings and lay off personnel, but certain fixed costs must still be paid even for vacant rooms.

Yet another factor has to do with patient demand. Patients want color television in the room and varied menus. Few would want the forty-bed wards and starchy mass cookery of an earlier day. The better amenities add to the cost and therefore, the price.

In summary, health care prices have increased because standards of care have risen. Equipment, buildings, expertise, and comfort cost more than they used to. Mainly, it appears that prices have increased because the money was there. At the heart of this situation is the problem with which we started. There is no effective control over the price of health care. There is a great deal of concern over the problem. Employers have found that their costs continue to rise for the health insurance that they provide for their employees. Taxpayers are increasingly reluctant to pay the cost of governmental programs in health care. As a consequence, it appears that the country is in the process of changing profoundly the way in which health care prices are handled. We will now turn to a look at this process.

What Can Be Done?

There have been three broad strategies followed in the United States.[7] Unfortunately, they have not been tried separately but more or less at the same time, so it is difficult to sort them out. The first approach was to find ways to pay the bill. The second approach was to regulate the hospitals. The third was to regulate the way doctors used the hospital.

Pay the bill. Traditionally, people were expected to pay their medical bills directly. Many hospitals in the United States were and are operated by Catholic religious orders, or sponsored by both Jewish and mainline Protestant bodies. Some are operated by non-sectarian foundations, municipalities, universities, and other governmental bodies. A growing number are operated by profit-making organizations. In our grandparents' time, patient fees, gifts, endowments and, in the case of those operated by some level of government, a small tax, was enough to support the hospital. People also paid their doctor bills directly. Those who could afford it paid cash. Others bartered produce or labor to pay the doctor's bill. Many doctors treated indigent persons at no charge and hospitals were usually able to absorb the cost of the indigent patients that they admitted. This summary has a charming, old-fashioned sound, and it is true up to a point. First, in those days, health care did not involve so much expensive technology. Secondly, a lot of poor people did not get very much in the way of medical care unless a physician and a hospital were willing to give it.

The increasing price of medical care began to pinch the ordinary citizen during the 1930s. Fortunately, a group of teachers had formed a prepayment plan for hospital costs in the late 1920s, so a model was available that could be pressed into general use. Soon, the idea known as the Blue Cross Plan spread. In the late 1930s, the companion Blue Shield Plan was developed to prepay physician's charges.

Today, many companies, educational institutions, and governmental units pay the premiums for their employees. Others use plans marketed by a number of insurance companies. Nearly 200 million Americans now have some coverage. The trouble is that the coverage is uneven. Some plans will pay for virtually every expense, while others have serious limitations. Further, a sizeable number of Americans have no coverage of any kind.

In order to assure quality health care for all Americans, there has been a good deal of support for some form of national health insurance. Although the idea has been around since early in the century, it first came to national prominence during the Great Depression of the 1930s. There was some support for inclusion of a form of national health insurance in the Social Security Act of 1935, but this was successfully opposed by, among others, the American Medical Association.

In 1960, Congress passed a bill known as the Kerr-Mills Act which provided payment for health care for older Americans who were receiving public assistance. While this was of some help to the older poor, there were still large numbers of underserved people. Finally, as a part of the War on Poverty programs of the Johnson administration, Congress passed two amendments to the Social Security Act in 1965. These amendments created Medicare and Medicaid.

Medicare. Title XVIII of the Social Security Act is a program that pays some of the cost of hospital and nursing home care for persons over sixty-five who receive OASDHI benefits. There are actually two parts to the Medicare program. Part A is financed by a portion of the Social Security taxes on employees and employers. It is the "HI" in OASDHI. In 1966, when the first taxes were collected, the employee paid .35 percent of the first $6,600 of salary and his or her employer paid a like amount. Self-employed persons were taxed a like amount. In dollars, the maximum tax that each employed and self-employed person paid was $23.10. As of 1984, the tax rate has risen to 1.3 percent of the first $37,800 or $491.40 per year for each taxpayer. Employers are assessed a similar amount for each employee. Self-employed persons are scheduled to pay 2.6 percent, or double the tax paid by a person who is employed by others.

Medicare does not cover everything, nor does it cover the whole bill for hospital or nursing home care. There is a deductible and there are limits on the number of days that will be paid. Initially, the beneficiary paid the first forty dollars. As the cost of the program has increased, the deductible has been raised. Since this figure changes annually (it was $400 in 1984), the student will find that one of the projects at the end of the chapter is to obtain the current figure (along with some others) and present them to the class. The point is that the proportion that the patient must pay has steadily risen. As a consequence, many older people have purchased additional insurance to cover what Medicare does not. One of the things often cited as a major shortcoming is that Medicare does not cover the cost of drugs. For the older patient, this can be a sizeable part of the health care bill.

Part B of Medicare is voluntary. It provides for the collection of a premium for the payment of physicians' services through a deduction from the OASDHI benefit payment. Originally, the cost of the premium to the beneficiary was three dollars a month. This amount has been increased to a current amount of $15.50 (which may have increased again by the time you read this) which is supplemented by a direct appropriation from Congress.

Medicare has provided health care to a segment of the population that, it is generally agreed, was medically underserved. However, it has also added to the health care cost inflation. This is because Medicare in the past has been an open-ended appropriation item in the federal budget. While there were limits on the number of days that one could receive benefits, there was no limit on the number of patients, nor the charges made during the time of eligibility. The limitation on the number of days coverage did not really constitute an effective brake on prices since most hospitalizations are for less than thirty days.[8] Within the time limits, there was nothing to stop physicians from filling the hospitals and ordering a whole battery of expensive tests. There was also nothing to stop hospitals from charging a great deal of money for those tests. Fortunately, medical professionals and hospital administrators were not systematically avaricious and the hospitals were not absolutely stuffed with unnecessary patients. Doctors have, on the other hand, ordered tests and procedures that have the primary function of protecting them against malpractice suits. It has recently been reported that these procedures have cost more than 15 billion dollars a year and are occasioned by the sharp increase in lawsuits from less than 3.5 claims per hundred physicians before 1978 to eight per hundred today.[9]

Medicaid. Title XIX of the Social Security Act, popularly known as Medicaid, was also passed by Congress in 1965. This program pays health care costs of persons who meet a means test. Since this is a Public Assistance program, both the definition of need and the benefits vary from state to state. As a general rule, benefits are paid to vendors of medical services on behalf of recipients of AFDC, SSI, and those who have enough to live on but would be impoverished by any significant medical expenses. Since this is a program in which the state sets the guidelines, it is possible, in theory at least, to hold down the cost. The state can simply take the position that it will pay X dollars for a given procedure. If the physician or other provider charges more than X, the patient must make up the difference or the provider must settle for what he or she gets from Medicaid. Because Medicaid does not pay the provider's "reasonable and customary" charges, many doctors will not accept Medicaid patients, nor can they be compelled to do so under present rules. Ironically, the Medicare program has been relatively free of scandal while the Medicaid program, which has a limit on payments, has figured prominently in the news chiefly because of charges for undelivered services.

Both Medicare and Medicaid have been extremely expensive attempts to solve the problem of the price of health care. The costs of both now exceed 70 billion dollars a year. They are classic examples of how a solution can actually become part of the problem. Designed to pay the rising costs of medical care to the elderly and the poor, they were not designed to control the prices. The difficulty is that the programs' well-intentioned authors did not take into account the greed of some providers or the empire-building propensities of others. Health care providers could simply adjust upward their definitions of "reasonable and customary" and the federal government, up until recently, was willing to shower them with money. Clearly, paying the bill has proven to be an insufficient policy. Accordingly, a second alternative was available.

Regulate the hospital.   Following the passage of Medicare and Medicaid, Congress attempted to work on the other end of the problem. In the middle 1960s, the Comprehensive Health Planning Act was passed along with several related acts. The idea behind them was to encourage voluntary health planning that would restrain unneeded growth and unnecessary duplication of services. These acts had no effective teeth and were never well funded, so the effects were negligible.

In 1974, Congress passed the National Health Planning and Resources Development act. The act authorized the formation of a system of agencies to identify health needs and to plan for the development of resources to meet them. The infusion of federal funds made it possible to develop a system of both local and state planning agencies that could be designated as official Health Systems Agencies (HSAs) under the provisions of the legislation. Each official planning body was expected to form a board that had representation from both health care providers and consumers. An important function was the limitation of new construction to instances where need was clearly evident. If need was clearly established, the HSA could issue a "certificate of need" (CON). Certificates of need had been issued under the previous policies, but were not successful in preventing unneeded construction. This time, there was supposed to be enough federal clout to deny funds to hospitals that built without a certificate. It did not take hospitals long to find the way around the intent of the law. Non-federal money could be devoted to construction and equipment leaving the federal funds to pay for other things or, budget items specifically for construction could be eliminated and creatively spread over the other parts of the budget. The point is that the attempts to regulate hospital spending were largely ineffective. Although Hill-Burton funds were dried up by Congress, and HSAs were in place, supposedly armed with the ability to deny certain kinds of funds, the hospitals continued to build and duplicate equipment. Clearly, the federal attempt to deal with rising costs by regulating the hospitals has not been effective. However, as the events described in this section were going on, attempts were being made on another front.

Regulate the doctors. As a result of Medicare and Medicaid, hospitals were required to have utilization review committees. A committee of doctors reviewed cases that other doctors had admitted to see if treatment was necessary. This review process did very little to restrain hospital use, and therefore had little effect on prices. In 1974, the Social Security Act was amended to require the establishment of a network of Professional Standards Review Organizations (PSRO). These were composed of practicing physicians. In each community, the PSRO was charged with the review of Medicare, Medicaid, and other federally financed medical care with a view toward the prevention of overutilization of health care services. Since the members of the PSRO were colleagues of those whom they were supposed to regulate, the results were less than spectacular.

Why have Medicare and Medicaid been the focus of regulatory attempts? The attention is due to their size and the fact that they are programs that the federal government can tinker with, without the difficulty involved in regulating non-governmental medicine. There have been non-governmental attempts to reduce the cost of health care also. In recent years, corporations and insurance companies have begun to bargain with providers for lower rates. The way this often works is for a company to contract with a provider for a set fee. The company then recommends that its employees use the provider's services. If the employee chooses to use other health care providers, he or she is free to do so, but the company will only reimburse the expenses at the set fee and the employee must make up the difference. It appears that this aggressive stance works.[10]

The most recent federal attempt to regulate the use of medical care is the requirement by the Department of Health and Human Services that each state designate a Peer Review Organization (PRO). The PRO must review non-emergency Medicare admissions before the patient is admitted to the hospital. If the PRO does not agree with the patient's physician, Medicare will not reimburse the expenses.

Further, the Department of Health and Human Services has recently adopted another policy which will be phased in over three years. Medicare will pay hospitals a flat rate for all patients in a given diagnostic category. All illnesses have been classified into 467 "diagnosis-related groups" (DRGs). The idea is for the hospital to keep the charges at or below the level of reimbursement. If a given hospitalization costs less than the allowed amount, the hospital keeps the difference. If it costs more, the hospital must absorb the loss. The idea is to force the hospital to economize.

Will the new policies work?   In the short run, these policies may have an effect, but the long-run predictions are gloomy. In a speech to the National Association of Social Workers' National Health Conference, Henry Aaron (a senior fellow of the Brookings Institution, a Washington, D.C. "think tank") identified a serious problem. Aaron pointed out that the DRG approach limits the cost per admission, but does not deal with the problem of total cost. There is nothing to stop providers of health care from admitting an increasing number of people. Further, Aaron points out that health care providers will probably argue that the categories are not precise enough and that more will be needed. The new categories will require higher reimbursement and this in turn will complicate the system.[11]

A recent study reported in the prestigious *New England Journal of Medicine* suggests that there is little agreement among doctors about when hospitalization is needed for a given patient.[12] Therefore, hospitals may cater to physicians with "more lucrative practice styles." In short, the study echoes Aaron's conclusion that there is really nothing to stop hospitals and doctors from simply admitting more patients if the hospital is in financial trouble. The authors of the study argue that if the DRG system is to work, more must be done to control the hospitalization rate.

Will Regulation Work?

Along with others, we are not enthusiastic about the use of governmental regulation as an overall policy for controlling health care costs. The fundamental problem is that the regulators are themselves involved in the activities to be regulated. This brings up the general point of regulation as a process. Since it has a great impact on health care we will discuss it in that context, but it should be clear that the discussion has wider applications.

Who Should Regulate Health Care?

On the one hand, it can be argued that only another physician has the necessary technical skill to understand when a doctor has followed good practice and done all the appropriate things in a given case. On the other hand, when a member of the profession to be regulated takes on the role of regulator, it can be claimed that it is like hiring a fox to guard the chickens! This dilemma is there whether one is talking about health care, electric power, or social work practice. So far as we know, no one has been able to resolve the question to the satisfaction of all concerned. One popular approach to the general problem involves some form of public representation on regulatory boards. There are three problems with this approach. All are serious.

First of all, ordinary citizens usually lack expertise in the activity to be regulated. This leads to the second problem. Because community representatives lack expertise, they may lean on the "experts." Over time, this can lead to the capture of the community representatives by the experts. One often hears of a person who runs for a seat on a regulatory board ostensibly to represent the public interest. As time passes, the individual comes around to the point of view of the regulated. Sometimes, the person leaves the regulatory board to take a position in the industry that he or she previously regulated. Why should we expect regulation in the health care industry to be different?

The third problem is that there is no standard way of assuring that citizen participation is genuinely representative. While in some cases there are elections, it is not uncommon for citizen representatives to be appointed by a public official or to be selected from a pool of volunteers by the existing members of the board. Persons seeking appointment may have agendas of their own that may or may not reflect the positions of the public.

We are forced to conclude that the only viable regulator is the informed consumer. While this is an uncertain alternative, it may well be the only one that is ultimately successful.

The "Health Maintenance Organization"

One of the ways of involving consumers, including employers who pay health care costs for employees, in the containment of health care costs is the Health Maintenance Organization (HMO). This is not a brand new idea, but it is increasingly hailed as the most viable solution to the problem. The idea is simple. Instead of using either the fee-for-service approach or buying health insurance, the consumer or the employer bargains directly with a firm of health care providers and pays a flat monthly fee for health care services that include physicians' care and hospitalization.

The HMO idea has its roots in the nineteenth century when companies hired physicians to treat their employees.[13] A number of HMOs have become well known, including the Ross-Loos organization, Kaiser-Permanente in California and the Health Insurance Plan of Greater New York. In order to encourage the formation of additional HMOs, Congress in 1973 appropriated funds to be used for start-up costs. These are being phased out. The current trend is to use private capital for start-up costs and avoid the constraints inherent in governmental financing.

There are other proposals for cost containment that do not involve regulation. Among them are proposals to increase deductibles for Medicare beneficiaries and members of insurance plans and a proposal to encourage individuals to save for medical costs through tax-deferred savings. However, the HMO appears to be the idea that is clearly in the ascendant.

The HMO approach is not without problems. We will analyze the HMO and in the process of that analysis, the problems will be discussed.

1. *Is the policy under consideration compatible with contemporary "style"?*

   Perhaps the best answer to this question is, "not quite yet." A relatively few Americans use HMOs for their health care. On the other hand, there has been a dramatic increase in HMO membership. *Business Week* reported that membership in HMOs increased from 5.6 million members in 1975 to 13.6 million as of December 1983.[14] While HMOs are not yet the preferred mode of marketing health care, they are clearly a growing part of the industry. It is yet too soon to tell if the HMO approach will have broad appeal. Certainly there is nothing that suggests that HMOs are inherently incompatible with contemporary American style, although there is some opposition as we shall see later.

2. *Is the policy compatible with important and enduring cultural values, particularly equity, fairness and justice?*

   We think that the HMO approach can be equitable, fair, and just. Of course, provision will have to be made for the poor, the chronically ill, and those who face catastrophic illnesses. Further, there has to be an element of choice. We do not think that Americans would accept the idea of being assigned to an HMO any more than they would accept assignment to any other form of health care delivery. Consumers should be able to "shop around" since this is an important factor in quality control.

3. *Is the policy compatible with social work's professional value and ethical system?*

   As of this writing, the National Association of Social Workers has not taken a position on the issue. However, we can see no problem providing that any widespread use of the HMO is equitable, fair, and just. Should the HMO concept be used in a discriminatory way towards any minority or high risk group, we would expect NASW to take note of it and raise issues of conscience.

4. *Is the policy acceptable to those in formal decision-making positions?*

   As we noted above, Congress supported the HMO concept in 1973 by providing start-up funds. Although the federal role has not expanded to large-scale support, there is no evidence of official hostility. There is some support for using Medicare funds to purchase HMO membership for older Americans, but this is far from a general movement as of this writing. The administration's position is not unfavorable, so more may come from Washington before too long.

5. *Does the policy satisfy relevant interest groups?*

   Again, we must give a tentative answer. It is best to say that the HMO principle does not seem to have gravely offended any important interest group. There is opposition from some physicians. There are those who want to continue the present fee-for-service system. Some have formed "preferred provider organizations" (PPOs) which offer discounts to companies and groups, but do not deal in prepayment contracts.[15] Most consumer organizations seem to have taken a "wait and see" position.

6. *Is the policy based on knowledge that has been tested?*

Yes. As we noted, HMOs have been around for a long time. It is clear that this approach can be used to deliver health care services.

7. *Is the policy workable in the real world?*

In this case, the answer is the same as in Number 6. The HMO has proven itself in "real world" applications for over forty years.

8. *Does the policy create few problems for both the public and the intended beneficiaries?*

We have not been able to note any problems inherent in the HMO approach. Of course, no delivery system is proof against just plain bad medicine. Poor quality service will not be made better just because one pays for it in advance. On the other hand, since the HMO involves a group of physicians, there is a certain amount of hope that they will have an interest in quality control on the basis of their own self-interest if nothing else.

9. *Is the policy effective?*

The whole point of the HMO approach is whether or not it reduces costs. On the basis of current research, it appears that the HMO is very effective in cost reduction. The preliminary studies suggested this conclusion, but they were cautionary because most HMOs had selective patient caseloads. Most customers were the employees of a given company, or were health conscious persons who had joined an independent plan. In 1984, a study using a random assignment of patients strongly suggested that the HMO will be effective in general use.[16] The study found that the HMO approach reduced the use of hospital admissions by 40 percent and cut overall prices by 25 percent. Support was given to previous studies that had indicated that the style of practice in the HMO approach was less "hospital intensive."

It appears that HMOs tend to practice more preventive medicine and use outpatient facilities for more diagnostic tests and treatment. This style of medical practice tends to reduce prices because, as the reader will recall, hospital costs are the most significant factor in the escalation of health care costs.

10. *Will programs derived from the policy be efficient?*

Since the effectiveness of this policy has to do with efficiency, this question is not really separate from Number Nine.

Some Additional Comments

On the basis of the information currently available, it appears that there is some real hope for controlling the increase in health care costs. There are, of course, certain problems that must be faced. We have noted that there will need to be a way to deal with the problems of the poor, the chronically ill, and the elderly. Further, there must be competition among HMOs in order to keep prices down. It is quite likely that there will be detailed proposals forthcoming that will involve governmental purchase of care on behalf of economically disadvantaged groups. We may see something involving the use of "Doctor Stamps" or vouchers that can be used to purchase HMO membership by the poor. It is also possible that some form of governmental assumption of responsibility for catastrophic illness can be grafted onto the HMO system in order to prevent imbalances in prices that would be caused if a given HMO suddenly found itself with a large proportion of patients with extremely expensive conditions. We can conclude that there is some potential for improvement in the future.

There is another cause for hope. The doctor shortage appears to be over. The number of active physicians in the United States has nearly doubled since 1960 and the supply is increasing. There are signs that the increased supply may have an effect on prices. For many years, physicians set their prices as they chose. Because there was a shortage of physicians and because people in pain do not have time to bargain, there was no pressure to keep prices down. Now, as deductible amounts rise and companies try to keep their costs down on health care fringe benefits, consumers are exerting pressure. *Business Week* reports a drop in the average net income of physicians by 3 percent for the period of April through September of 1983.[17] (There is no need to begin taking up a collection. The average physician would still clear around $105,000 on an annual basis after expenses.) Whether the surplus of physicians and the activity of consumers will have a sustained effect is not yet clear.

In any case, there are signs that the dramatic rise in health care prices may moderate in the near future. Let us now turn to a second problem.

The Uneven Geographical Distribution of Health Resources

Although this problem may be as serious as that of prices, it will take much less space to discuss. The difficulty is that most health care resources are in urban places. In a way, this is appropriate since most of the population is in urban places. However, the problem is a little more complicated than this.

When America was more rural and the citizenry were more thinly spread on the land, each little town had at least one doctor. The physician could carry almost everything that he needed in his buggy—or later, in his business coupe. However, house calls take a lot more of the physician's time than do office calls. Further, as medicine has gotten more complicated, the physician uses equipment that no longer is portable. Modern health care demands expensive technology. Small towns and rural places cannot afford to provide the technology and few doctors want to practice without the support of a modern outpatient clinic and hospital. Consequently, most physicians are attracted to communities where the facilities are. In addition to the technology, physicians are generally attracted to what they believe are the superior cultural amenities of larger places. Therefore, rural Americans have lost their doctors. Even small towns that have good basic hospitals are not much better off, since these small hospitals cannot afford the expensive equipment that is available in larger cities.

Congress has tried to solve this problem in several ways. A large number of medical students have financed their education with governmentally guaranteed loans. Congress passed a plan in 1965 that wrote off the loans of those physicians willing to practice in rural areas. Many doctors paid off their loans rather than remain in rural practice. Medical schools receiving federal money are supposed to reserve places for students who indicate a preference for practicing in medically underserved areas, but there has been no effective way to guarantee that the graduates will actually locate in rural areas.

Probably the most effective way has been to recruit rural people to go into medicine. The available research suggests that most doctors that stay in rural areas are persons who originally came from the country themselves. However, this approach has not yet answered the problem. Rural America remains a medically underserved area and will probably remain so for the near future. We will attempt no policy analysis, since we can find no policy with enough promise at this time to justify analysis. There is some discussion that the HMO concept may have some promise, if the rural physician is linked to a group in a nearby city, but this idea has not received an adequate test.

The Uneven Distribution of Health Care

We have already touched on this issue in the discussion of price. In its simplest form, the problem is that those who can afford it get more (but not necessarily better) health care services than those who cannot. Some of this difference is probably not very important. For instance, people with money may choose to have expensive cosmetic surgery that the poor cannot afford. Other kinds of "fashionable" treatment may also be denied the poor with little harmful effect. There is a point, however, where the uneven distribution of health care begins to make an important difference in the quality of life.

In the past, as we have pointed out earlier in the chapter, the health care of the poor was largely provided through the charity of those health care providers that were inclined to give it. While charitable health care is better than no health care at all, it is not a very satisfactory large-scale answer to the problem. It is certainly insufficient in an era when people have been led to have higher expectations. At best, charity is uneven. One cannot count on doctors and hospitals to be consistently charitable. Further, many people believe that charity is demeaning.

These considerations led, in part at least, to the passage of Medicare and Medicaid. While Medicare tends toward universality in coverage, Medicaid is specifically targeted toward the poor. This has led to the charge that the United States has a two-tier system of medical care. The non-poor can pay, use insurance or Medicare (when they are older), while the poor are left to use a Medicaid program that pays on a fee schedule set by the state and is not accepted by many of the nation's health care providers. One response to this situation has been a reawakening of interest in the idea of a national health insurance. Although all national health insurance schemes would apply to all social classes, they are usually defended by the argument that they would improve the health care of the poor.

There have been a number of national health insurance plans put before the public over the last several years. Basically, they fall into four categories:[18]

1. *The "tax credit" approach.*

   The American Medical Association advanced a plan in the 1970s which would give tax credits to people who purchased health insurance from private carriers. Lower income people would get a larger credit than would higher income people. Medicaid would pay the premiums for those with no earned income.

2. *Catastrophic insurance.*

   In this approach, federal insurance would only cover the cost of major medical catastrophes after a large deductible had been satisfied. Martin Feldstein, President Reagan's former financial advisor, has advanced one of the best known approaches of this type.

3. *Semi-comprehensive coverage.*

   Proposals of this sort offer a great deal of coverage, but share the cost with the patient through moderate deductibles. Of course, the tax necessary to support a plan of this kind would add substantially to the current rates. The Kennedy-Mills proposal is probably the best-known scheme of this sort.

4. *Comprehensive coverage.*

   The Kennedy-Corman proposal, for example, would provide extremely comprehensive coverage with no deductibles and very few limitations. While the tax on individuals would not be very great, the burden on employers would be sharply increased. Further, the magnitude of this scheme requires that the amount of money raised through payroll taxation be matched by funds from the general revenue.

While there is still considerable interest in some kind of national health insurance, the idea seems to have been overshadowed by other concerns. One of the major problems with the latter two approaches is the cost. Opponents have argued that either of these plans would cost a great deal more than their supporters have claimed. The current problems in financing Medicare and Medicaid would seem to preclude embarking on a national health insurance if there were a strong possibility that the price would increase dramatically as a consequence.

Essentially, the various plans for a national health insurance simply extend Medicare to all ages of the non-poor and leave Medicaid in place for the poor. They vary in how much they cover and in the amount paid by the consumer, of course, but there is great similarity. It appears to us that they do not represent any great change *in principle* from the present system. They all would retain the present two-tiered system and one cannot easily see how the poor would be better off and how medical resources would be redistributed.

An Analysis of a Proposal for National Health Insurance

Since there are a number of plans with wide benefit and tax differences, it is impractical to analyze "national health insurance" as if there were one monolithic proposal. We are hesitant to analyze any of the existing plans, since we would guess that some changes will be made in them before any appear before Congress again. Accordingly, we have devised our own version of national health insurance. Our proposal is the extreme case. As far as we can find, no one has seriously advanced any plan with all these features. We present this plan strictly for the purposes of this exercise and we do not endorse it. Here are the details:

1. *Benefits*

   All physicians' services, hospitalization, prescription drugs, eyeglasses, nursing home care, and rehabilitation services. In other words, full coverage for diagnosis, treatment, and aftercare.

2. *Eligibility*

   All citizens of the United States, all resident aliens, and every visitor with an official visa.

3. *Deductibles*

   No deductibles. Everything is covered.

4. *Administration*

   It will be necessary to form a federal agency to operate this scheme. The simplest way to deal with the problem is to restructure the network that handles Medicare, although since the federal government will handle all claims, there is no need to interface with any private health insurance companies.

5. *Financing*

   This scheme would be financed by an 11 percent tax on all income from whatever source. (This amount is based on the current cost of medical care from all sources.) Of course, the tax would increase if medical prices increased. For wage earners, the tax would be collected by the employer in the same way in which other federal taxes are deducted from one's check. For persons whose earned income is from investments, business, or a profession, the income would be taxed through the same mechanism used to collect the income tax. All taxes would flow to the federal agency set up to operate the health scheme and would be disbursed directly to health care providers upon receipt of a bill.

6. *Special provisions*

In order to keep the costs from rising too quickly, the DRG approach would be used for all beneficiaries. Additionally, *all* nonemergency hospital admissions (not just those for Medicare) would be screened by a Peer Review Organization. Unlike other proposals, there is no special provision for the poor. True, as in other proposals, the persons with income actually pay the costs of health care for the poor since the money comes from incomes. However, since there is no co-payment or financial payment directly from the patient, everyone will be treated alike at the point of service delivery and the poor would not be identifiable as Medicaid patients since there would be no Medicaid forms—just the same reimbursement form for everybody. Persons would still be free to choose their own medical practitioners under this scheme. Doctors would still be free to reject patients if their patient loads were too high, provided that there was no discrimination on a racial, sexual, ethnic, or age bias.

As we said in the beginning, this is a rather extreme proposal. It would certainly change the character of health care in the United States. Let us see how it stands up to an analysis and if it will solve the problem of the distribution of health care resources.

1. *Is the policy under consideration compatible with contemporary "style"?*

No. Contemporary style does not favor large federal programs with this wide a sweep. Certainly, this approach is not compatible with the general style of the national government. Existing national health insurance schemes fall far short of the scope of this one.

2. *Is the policy compatible with important and enduring cultural values, particularly equity, fairness and justice?*

Any system's ends and means can be perverted if one works hard enough at it. However, this approach would appear to be equitable, just, and fair. Plainly, it runs counter to other important values. There is some dissonance with notions of individualism, achievement and success, and many individual notions of group superiority. Many Americans consider the level of health care that they enjoy to be a benefit they have earned, and while they are willing to provide a certain level of health care for the poor, they are unwilling to advocate a system in which there was no recognition of social differences.

3. *Is the policy compatible with social work's professional value and ethical system?*

We think that this approach would be compatible with the public stand taken by NASW, although that organization has not endorsed anything quite this extreme.

4. *Is the policy acceptable to those in formal decision-making positions?*

Clearly, no. Nothing this extreme has been proposed to Congress. Even the most conservative proposal has not gotten much support let alone anything this radical. The formal decision makers seem to favor the present system, but they do engage in some adjustments to it, as evidenced by the DRG and PRO provisions that have been added to current federal programs.

5. *Does the policy satisfy relevant interest groups?*

Certainly most of the health care industry would oppose this proposal. In the lead would be the health insurance industry. Virtually every conservative organization in the country would gear up to defeat such an extreme proposal. Although this proposal does not require that health care professionals be employed by the federal government, or that health care facilities be confiscated, most Americans would be easily led to believe that this was "socialized medicine." We doubt if political liberals would embrace this proposal either. It simply goes too far beyond the current agenda of most American interest groups.

6. *Is the policy based on knowledge that has been tested?*

In a limited way, some nations of Western Europe have schemes that are not too different. In Britain, although everybody has to pay for the National Health Service, neither providers nor patients have to use it. Patients may elect to be treated on a private basis, but then they must work out their own financial arrangements. Our proposal makes no provision for any purely private arrangement, because we wanted to put everybody on the same basis insofar as that was possible.

7. *Is the policy workable in the real world?*

Theoretically, with computerized records and billing systems, this approach is technically feasible. However, since computers are loaded by humans, there would undoubtedly be problems in individual cases.

8. *Does the policy create few problems for both the public and the intended beneficiaries?*

This is hard to answer definitely. Certainly the value problems are formidable. "Socialized medicine" is not a popular concept. Even people who propose these schemes prefer to consult old fashioned fee-for-service physicians when they themselves have serious medical problems. It would be hard for patients to make the emotional adjustment to what essentially would be a voucher system for everybody. Again, theoretically, it should solve some cost problems with the additions of the DRG provisions and peer review of nonemergency admissions. The most serious problem is that the questions of cost containment are not addressed by any superior mechanism over what we have now. Further, there is no allowance for competition or for consumer control. We suspect that a system like this would not ultimately keep costs down or improve the quality of care. It would, in short, simply be a modern version of the "pay the bill" approach and unscrupulous providers would have a field day milking the system. While this proposal stops far short of actual "government medicine" as it is practiced in the Soviet bloc, it would be unfavorably compared to that kind of system everytime anyone made either a medical or an accounting error.

9. *Is the policy effective?*

The picture here is mixed. Again, only a theoretical answer can be given. While everyone could pay for his or her medical care, there is no competitive advantage for anyone and no improvement in quality control over the present system. True, one would be free to change doctors and hospitals, and providers could still refuse patients, but it is quite probable that a deadly sameness would descend on the health care industry.

10. *Will programs derived from the policy be efficient?*

Given what we know about large governmental programs, it is unlikely that many would believe that the system would be efficient even if it were proven so. It would be the accounting nightmare of Medicare on a grand scale. The individual would be as helpless as he or she is when dealing with the telephone company or the power company!

Summary

The reader will notice that, at bottom, all the objections are really translatable into value problems. While a national health insurance has a theoretical advantage in redistributing health care through a one-tiered system, the value problems are so great that any technical superiority is buried. It is doubtful if the poor, who ostensibly would be the major beneficiaries, would be happy, given the American character. It is also obvious that we have become biased in favor of some form of HMO because we tend to favor policies that maximize consumer control and maintain some form of competition as a cost control measure. We think that most Americans will reach the same conclusion. (See Question 2 in the "Questions for Discussion" at the end of the chapter.)

Deinstitutionalization

We now turn to the final issue to be examined in this chapter. The history of the problem will probably be familiar, so our review of it will be brief.

The background of mental health care in the United States is quite different from that of health care in general. From the beginning, the persons who behaved "differently" were cared for at public expense when they became a burden to the family, either in the almshouse, jail, or hospital. This care, such as it was, was the responsibility of the local community and later the state government. Of course, mild cases would be treated by one's physician or spiritual adviser, if treated at all. Individual quirks of a common sort were seen as things which one could change through an act of will or through prayer. It was only in the nineteenth century that the notion that aberrations in one's behavior might be due to an illness began to take hold. By then, the principle of state responsibility had become ingrained. While there was a smattering of privately financed facilities for treatment of mental disorders, the bulk of care was provided by state hospitals. In the United States, the level of care in virtually all of them left much to be desired. Dorothea Dix spent many years of her life as an activist on behalf of the mentally ill, and many states improved their systems of care as a result of her efforts. She successfully lobbied a bill through Congress that would have provided federal land grants to the states for the purpose of supporting an improved mental health system, only to have it vetoed by President Pierce. The federal government remained largely aloof from the concerns of the mentally ill until after World War II (except for combat psychiatry and care of veterans).

Although improved since the nineteenth century, the state mental hospitals were seen as primarily a system for removing annoying people from the community. Many of them were located in small towns far removed from major population centers. It was relatively easy to commit troublesome people to these remote institutions and to forget that they were there. In this manner, the mental hospitals grew larger and were invested with their own mystique as either grim fortresses (some were Gothic in appearance) or as "funny farms" or "giggle factories." These latter terms probably stem from the early days when mental patients were exhibited as objects of entertainment for the "normal" populace who visited the places of confinement as one visits a zoo.

There were, however, physicians who became interested in the mentally ill and the speciality of psychiatry gradually developed during the nineteenth century. The names of Pinel, Charcot, Breur, Freud, Adler, and Jung in Europe and Sullivan and Horney in the United States are now familiar to us. Although much of Freudian psychology is out of vogue now, it cannot be denied that his work was more influential than any other in creating a public awareness of mental problems and the need for specialized study of them.

Certainly the modern treatment of the mentally ill was dramatically enhanced with the discovery of that family of drugs known collectively as the "tranquilizers." When the phenothiazines came into general use after 1956, the large mental hospitals began to empty. As other drugs were developed, it became possible for the first time to contemplate the possibility of shorter treatment periods and more frequent recovery from a number of serious mental illnesses.

The development of more scientific psychiatry and the invention of effective drug therapies provide an important stage in the development of the idea that mental disorders were not all chronic and permanently disabling. It became practical to take down the iron fences and to open most of the wards. It also became feasible to think of mental disorders as problems that could be better treated in the community and avoid the "warehousing" (to borrow Erving Goffman's term) of the mentally ill in the old grim fortresses of the nineteenth century.

Federal involvement in the revolution in mental health care actually began with the National Mental Health Act of 1946. This act funded research and professional training through the National Institute for Mental Health. It also provided some limited funds to states for the development of outpatient services. However, the doors were really opened with the Community Mental Health Act of 1963. This act provided federal funds to support the development of comprehensive community mental health centers. A local, privately supported mental health clinic (of which there were a fair number) could qualify for federal funds if it provided the following services:

1. a consultation and education service to the community that was designed to help reduce the incidence of serious mental illness.
2. a twenty-four hour emergency service.
3. an outpatient service, including follow-up care for patients discharged from state hospitals.
4. a partial hospitalization service for persons not needing full hospitalization (usually a day hospital program).
5. inpatient care (usually made available in a psychiatric ward of a local hospital).

Later, other required services, including transitional facilities, were mandated as a condition of receiving federal funds. Communities that lacked a mental health clinic soon developed one in order to qualify for federal funds, and the coverage has become nearly uniform throughout the country, except for remote areas.

These centers were looked upon as the major providers of mental health services for the public. As a direct consequence of the Community Mental Health Act of 1963 and its more recent revisions, the accent is on local treatment for the mentally ill. More local hospitals now have psychiatric wards for short-term care. Fewer people are sent to large public hospitals, and many states have closed down some of their older institutions in favor of smaller decentralized treatment centers that do not have the forbidding institutional aspects of the older hospitals.

There is another trend that leads to the overall policy of deinstitutionalization. In a class action suit originally known as Wyatt vs. Stickney, Judge Frank Johnson, of the Federal Fifth Judicial Circuit, laid down the principle that mental patients are entitled to treatment and not just confinement. Further, treatment should be given in the least restrictive atmosphere. Although Judge Johnson's decision was not binding on cases outside the federal judicial circuit in which it was announced, it has certainly been the basis for a great deal of reform of the conditions under which treatment is conducted.

There is one more factor that supports a policy of deinstitutionalization.

The old mental hospital system was getting costly. Very few health insurance plans paid any of the bills, so the burden fell on the taxpayers. Increasingly, legislatures were reluctant to find the money, and since insurance plans do not cover care in a public institution, it was not possible to shift the burden onto patients' families, even in those states that require some financial participation from responsible relatives.

The Result

It is our contention that all these various factors combined to produce the general social policy of deinstitutionalization. Better psychiatry and the psychotropic drugs made long-term treatment less necessary for most patients. The community mental health center movement increased the availability of treatment in the local community. Changes in the law discouraged unnecessary restrictions in patient movement, and the costs became prohibitive anyway. The end result is that many people who in former years would have been "stored" in large mental hospitals are no longer confined. As is the case with most changes in human affairs, there is both a good and a bad side to the policy of deinstitutionalization.

The good side is that most mental health treatment is short-term and most (but not all) patients can be returned to productive living in a short time. The bad side is that the community is not always ready to receive the patient back again. For many former patients, deinstitutionalization has not meant a return to a warm, supportive environment. Although there is supposed to be a system of follow-up care through the community mental health centers, the patient does not always follow through. Many of the released mental patients end up as "street people" because there has not been the network of financial and support services that were envisioned by the policy makers who have emptied the institutions. Over ten years ago, Scott Briar expressed the concern in a way on which we cannot improve:

> Bad institutions are harmful to persons, but it does not follow, as some would have it, that all institutions—the good ones as well as the bad—are harmful and should be abolished.[19]

We will do a brief analysis of this policy because there are some points to be made through such an analysis.

1. *Is the policy compatible with contemporary "style"?*

   Yes. Conservatives want to keep the costs down. Civil libertarians oppose institutions almost in principle since institutions deprive people of liberty.

2. *Is the policy compatible with important and enduring cultural values, particularly equity, fairness and justice?*

   Yes and no. Certainly deinstitutionalization is consistent with notions of individualism and civil liberty. As far as we know, most institutions have tried to be equitable and just in their dealings with patients, and they have taken seriously the notions of individual treatment plans and treatment in the least restrictive atmosphere. However, we are not sure that it is just and fair to turn people out into the street without adequate support systems that enable them to survive with dignity. In recent years, many states have provided halfway houses and shelter care facilities, but there are still too many people living in firetrap hotels and on the street.

3. *Is the policy compatible with social work's professional value and ethical system?*

   Yes. Social workers support better and more effective treatment. They oppose the "warehousing" of people and support civil liberties. They have been pioneers in the community mental health movement and have tried hard to make it work. At the same time, as Briar's editorial shows, they are concerned about the negative impact of this essentially humane and libertarian policy.

4. *Is the policy acceptable to those in formal decision-making positions?*

   Evidently, yes. It appears that Congress has washed its hands of the matter, believing that it has made sufficient provision through the existing social welfare programs and the community mental health legislation. Street people do not vote and are usually quite harmless to others. They are sufficiently isolated and powerless, so they are of limited attractiveness as a cause.

5. *Does the policy satisfy relevant interest groups?*

   Again, the answer evidently is yes. The only group that seems to have been bothered about the unsuccessfully deinstitutionalized person includes the social workers that have to try to stretch inadequate funds. No powerful interest group has taken up the struggle for those who have been lost in the shuffle.

6. *Is the policy based on knowledge that has been tested?*

   This is discussed in the next question.

7. *Is the policy workable in the real world?*

   One of the flaws that remains in our policy analysis scheme is that sometimes one or more of the questions turn out to be duplicates. This is one of those times and the reader will have noticed one or two others. Our original purpose in having two questions usually makes sense. There are times when one wants to know whether or not a proposed policy has some basis on tested theoretical grounds and/or whether a policy (or something similar) has any practical "real world" test. In the case of long-standing policies (and deinstitutionalization has been a policy for nearly twenty years) these two questions often get hopelessly entangled. We know that certain aspects of the situation have had some empirical test. We know, for instance, that the tranquilizing drugs work both in the laboratory and in the real world. It is also clear that a great many persons with mental disorders can expect to have their symptoms abated in a relatively short time. Further, it is clear that long-term hospitalization tends to "institutionalize" most patients and make them dependent on the institution. Clearly, deinstitutionalization has worked for the benefit of many people who have access to adequate supports. On the other hand, it is equally clear that some people's disorders are such that long-term care is the only humane solution.

8. *Does the policy create few problems for both the public and the intended beneficiaries?*

The public in general clearly benefits from deinstitutionalization. Fewer people are dependent upon long-term care and there is less likelihood that anyone will be incarcerated without some reason for long periods of time. Patients benefit, in the main, from improved drug therapy and better treatment. The increased protection for the patient's civil rights is also a major plus. The only people for whom the policy creates problems are those discharged patients who do not have adequate support following discharge.

9. *Is the policy effective?*

As we have argued above, the policy has been effective in reducing unneeded long-term care.

10. *Is the policy efficient?*

This has been a very efficient policy in terms of its goals. The mental health inpatient population has been reduced dramatically and most people receive treatment for their mental disorders at outpatient clinics in their community. Most hospitals have short-term psychiatric wards, and there are fewer chronic cases needing long-term care.

Summary

On balance, the policy of deinstitutionalization has been highly successful for everybody concerned, patients, professionals, and taxpayers. But this is a good example of a policy that is fundamentally sound and yet seriously flawed. It seems to be based, ultimately, on the generalization that institutionalization is bad for everyone and should only be considered as a last resort. It is fairly typical of American social policy to find that an essentially good and well-motivated policy is applied universally when it ought to be followed selectively. Gradually, the mental health enterprise has come to recognize that institutions are not bad by definition, but in fact are useful treatment resources when well run. In fact, it should be clear to the reader that under the wrong circumstances, deinstitutionalization is a bad policy.

Conclusion

This has been another long, complicated chapter. We think that it accurately reflects the controversies that plague these difficult issues. There are no easy answers, and one of the important lessons to be learned is that simplistic solutions will not be found to these problems. There are always some unattractive outcomes that are usually unintended. The supporters of deinstitutionalization, to use the last issue discussed, did not intend to leave helpless people adrift in the street. They have come around to a more realistic use of institutional care where the money and the law will permit. But it does not get any easier to formulate successful social welfare programs.

REFERENCES

1. Theodore R. Marmor and John B. Christianson, *Health Care Policy* (Beverly Hills, Cal.: Sage Publications, Inc., 1982), p. 13.
2. U.S. Bureau of the Census. *Statistical Abstract of the United States: 1984,* 104th edition (Washington, D.C., 1984), p. 102.
3. *Ibid.*
4. *Ibid.*
5. "Health Care Costs and Auto Prices," *Birmingham Post-Herald,* April 23, 1984, p. A–4.
6. U.S. Bureau of the Census, *op. cit.,* p. 103.
7. We have loosely followed the approach of T. R. Marmor, Andrew Dunham, and Julie Greenberg, "The Politics of Health" in David Mechanic, ed., *Handbook of Health, Health Care, and the Health Professions* (New York: Free Press, 1983), pp. 67–80.
8. U.S. Bureau of the Census, *op. cit.,* p. 115.
9. *Birmingham Post-Herald,* July 11, 1984, p. E6.
10. "The Corporate Rx for Medical Costs," *Business Week,* October 15, 1984, pp. 138–146.
11. "No Easy Answer for Rising Health Costs," *NASW News,* Vol. 29, No. 7 (July 1984), p. 11.
12. John E. Wennberg, Klim McPherson and Philip Caper, "Will Payment Based on Diagnostic-Related Groups Control Hospital Costs?" *New England Journal of Medicine,* Vol. 311, No. 5, pp. 295–300.
13. Howard S. Luft, "Health Maintenance Organizations," in Mechanic, *op. cit.,* pp. 319–320.
14. "Doctors are Entering a Brave New World of Competition," *Business Week,* July 16, 1984, p. 59.
15. *Ibid.*
16. Willard G. Manning, et al., "A Controlled Trial of the Effect of Prepaid Group Practice on the Use of Services," *New England Journal of Medicine,* Vol. 310, No. 23, pp. 1505–1510.
17. *Business Week,* p. 56.
18. For a longer description, see Marmor and Christianson, *op. cit.,* pp. 90 ff.
19. Scott Briar, "Prisons Without Walls," *Social Work,* Vol. 20, No. 1 (January 1975), editorial page.

QUESTIONS FOR DISCUSSION

1. What do you think of the chances for some form of national health insurance under the current administration?

2. Look again at the analysis of national health insurance in this chapter. Did the authors lose their objectivity? Is this a fair analysis?

3. What new policy might succeed in effecting some geographical redistribution of health care services?

4. Some argue that any form of consumer co-payment of health care charges discriminates against those least able to afford it. Others argue that co-payment is needed to keep costs down by forcing consumers to pay some of the bill. What do you think?

5. In many cases, there are relatively inexpensive alternative treatments that get results similar to those in more expensive treatments. Do you think that Congress should require physicians to select the most inexpensive alternative when treating patients who receive either Medicare or Medicaid?

6. As a consumer, what do you think are the most important problems in health care policy?

7. If you were a member of Congress, which general approach to national health insurance would you favor if you were inclined toward this policy?

8. Should mental health care be handled within the same framework as is general health care? Why or why not?

SUGGESTED PROJECTS

1. Find out the current level of deductibles, consumer co-payments, and benefits for Medicare.

2. For any given health condition of your choice, find out how payment would be handled under the Medicaid program of your state. What are the eligibility criteria? How much would be paid?

3. Visit your local hospital and talk to the business manager. What does he or she see as the cause of high hospital costs? What remedies does he or she suggest? How does the person feel about national health insurance?

4. Visit your local community mental health facility. Ask about funding patterns, services, and costs. How much does a patient pay for services? How does the facility study the mental health needs of the community? What roles do social workers play in the operation of the agency?

5. Design a model health care system for the United States that would provide good quality health care for everybody at a reasonable cost.

FOR FURTHER READING

American Enterprise Institute for Public Policy Research. *National Health Insurance Proposals.* Washington, D.C.: American Enterprise Institute. 1974. Since national health insurance has been on "hold" for some years, this is still a useful summary of a number of proposals. Costs have risen, of course, but otherwise this is still worth looking at.

Roger M. Battistella and Thomas G. Rundall, eds. *Health Care Policy.* Berkeley, Cal.: McCutchan Publishing Co. 1978. Although the figures and the program descriptions are limited by its age, this volume contains lots of detail on health care policy issues and is a good source of background information.

Theodore R. Marmor and John B. Christianson. *Health Care Policy.* Beverly Hills, Cal.: Sage Publications. 1982. Marmor is a long-time student of American health policy. He and his associates can be counted on for aggressive and critical analyses of any aspect of health care policy that they address.

David Mechanic, ed. *Handbook of Health, Health Care and the Health Care Professions.* New York: Free Press. 1983. A huge volume with contributions on virtually every aspect of health care policy. The book has an enormous amount of information, particularly on the history of current policy, the operation of an HMO, and national health financing schemes including Medicare and Medicaid.

Because health care is such a volatile area, one must update his or her knowledge quite often. We have found that *Business Week* is a dependable source for balanced reporting on the economic aspects of health care. *The New England Journal of Medicine*, which we have quoted several times in the chapter, is an outstanding source of information on health care policy and innovations in service delivery.

7

Policies for Problems
in Living Space

IN THIS CHAPTER WE WANT TO look at some problems in the conditions under which some people live. Principally, we will focus on housing, but living space includes the neighborhood, transportation facilities, and other amenities that are desirable to full human living. This topic may be seen by some as outside the mainstream of social welfare policy. Indeed, it is primarily the province of others who may have a larger stake in it than do social workers and social welfare planners. Nevertheless, this problem has an impact on areas for which social workers are responsible, though other groups may have more to say about the policies, programs, and delivery systems for products and services.

We cannot exhaustively discuss all the problems in living conditions in a single chapter. What we will do is review some central issues of particular concern to social welfare and examine these issues in terms of their impact on social welfare clientele. It is at these points of impact that social workers will find opportunities for intervention.

We discussed social welfare policy and poverty in Chapter 5 where our discussion centered on money. But lack of money is not the only thing that impoverishes the human being.

> The quality of the environment in which people live, work, and play influences to no small degree the quality of life itself. The environment can be satisfying and attractive and provide scope for individual development or it can be poisonous, irritating and stunting.[1]

Whether the conditions under which people live, work, and play are satisfying and attractive or poisonous, irritating, and stunting is not accidental. The quality of human life is a matter of policy—choices made on the basis of knowledge and values which result in a line of decisions over time. That some people live in substandard housing, walk unsafe streets, attend poor schools, and lack humanizing amenities are outcomes of policy choices that have alternatives.

It's not that we lack the technology to produce other outcomes. There is no technological reason why all Americans cannot live a decent life, so far as the country's ability to provide the basic necessities of life goes. One must look, as we shall see later on, at political, economic, and social values for insights into the reasons for policy being what it is.

We do not want to rest our case for concern about living space on the basis that "bad" living conditions cause "bad" people. The naivete of this position is seen easily when one considers the number of "good" people who have come from very difficult backgrounds and the "bad" people who were born into privilege. Chester Hartman provides a much less emotional basis for concern:

While good housing can provide a supportive environment for change, it is unlikely that basic problems of employment, education, and crime will be swept away by moving into a good home in a nice neighborhood . . . The country's serious need for improved housing cannot rest exclusively on arguments of health and safety or social pathology.

A sufficient basis for concern and action with regard to housing is that most people feel that their living conditions are central to their lives, and millions of American families deem their current living conditions as onerous and unacceptable in view of what the society offers to the rest of its people.[2]

Hartman's position is compatible with our position that human survival is dependent upon mutual aid. We ought to be concerned that people live under onerous and unacceptable conditions simply because "they" are part of "us." We would reject an argument which says that we should be concerned because "they" live in a way that is a threat or an affront to "us."

The Federal Government and the Housing Industry

It can be said that most people in the United States live in better circumstances than members of any other society, although some people still live in squalid and substandard conditions. The present policies work for most people. In regard to housing, the current major policy is that the federal government guarantees the payment of a large number of mortgages and provides for the liquidity of capital in the investment market. This policy makes it possible for many more people to have housing than would be the case otherwise. The primary beneficiaries of the federal effort are the lending institutions, the housing industry, and the realtors. There is virtually no opposition from the political right to the policy of loan guarantees given that the federal government massively intervenes in the housing marketplace.

The role of government in the mortgage field is quite complex. Probably the feature best known to the general public is the function of the Federal Housing Administration (FHA). The FHA was established during the Great Depression. It insures lenders against default on mortgages. Ordinarily, lending institutions will loan a buyer 60 to 80 percent of the value of a house, requiring repayment to be made over fifteen to twenty years. Most home purchasers are unable to come up with down payments of 20 to 40 percent of the purchase price of a house. If one has good credit, he or she may apply for an FHA-guaranteed loan which permits the purchaser to make a down payment of 5 to 10 percent and pay off the balance over thirty or even forty years. Of course, the home purchaser with an FHA-guaranteed loan ends up paying a great deal more for the same house than does a purchaser with a "conventional" mortgage. Although the monthly payments may be lower for the FHA-guaranteed loan, lending institutions figure interest in such a way that for half of the life of the loan, the purchaser is paying mostly toward the interest. And, of course, one is making payments for a longer period because of the smaller down payment. While the new variable-rate mortgages complicate this matter somewhat, the basic principle remains the same. On the positive side, FHA has made home ownership possible for millions who would otherwise not be able to afford it.

A second form of federal intervention is the provision of a system that guarantes availability of capital to the lending industry. There are a number of federal supports to the mortgage market.

> To back up the primary mortgage market, the federal government has a byzantine array of agencies and programs, many of which date from the collapse of the housing credit system in the 1930's. These include the Federal Home Loan Bank Board and its twelve regional banks, a central banking system for home-loan banks analogous to the Federal Reserve System for commercial banks, insurance agencies, the Federal Deposit Insurance Corporation and the Federal Savings and Loan Insurance Corporation, to protect depositors in various types of savings institutions; and a secondary mortgage market, which permits mortgage investors to sell mortgages in their portfolios or convert them into securities acceptable to other segments of the investing public.[3]

The point is that the federal government is, heart and soul, committed to the success of the development of housing through its intervention in the housing market. All this activity is beneficial to the steadily employed classes, but the federal government has failed in its efforts to have a positive effect on poor families.

The Federal Government and the Low Income Individual

Federal involvement with the poor has had a very disappointing history with respect to the housing problem. In order to get a really good grip on the difficulties, it is necessary to review some of the background.

Urban Renewal and Public Housing

Slum living has never been as charming as those who have been able to leave it have sometimes nostalgically described. Hartman summarizes the problems:

> Among the more notable hazards of slum living are a higher incidence of fires, related to poor heating equipment and wiring; higher rates of home accidents from broken stairs and other structural defects; rat bites . . . and hazards to personal safety resulting from poor lighting, inadequate locks, and the like.[4]

Hartman also lists the dangers of carbon monoxide poisoning from faulty heaters and lead poisoning from paint in old houses.

One of the most readable accounts of the development of federal attempts to deal with slum living conditions is by Ashley A. Foard and Hilbert Feffernan.[5] We have drawn heavily on their summary of federal legislation through 1960 in the discussion of the early federal attempts to provide housing for the poor.

The earliest that national attention was focused on housing and living conditions (aside from journalistic accounts and fiction) was the President's Conference on Home Building and Home Ownership in 1931. No legislation grew out of the work of the conference, and the United States had no national policy on housing until the Housing Act of 1937 (although some public housing was built under the National Recovery Act of 1933). The 1937 act's title is descriptive of its aims: "An Act to provide financial assistance to the States and political subdivisions thereof for the elimination of unsafe and unsanitary housing conditions, for the eradication of slums, for the provision of decent, safe and sanitary dwellings for families of low income, and for the reduction of unemployment and the stimulation of business activity, to create a United States Housing Authority and for other purposes." Foard and Feffernan say that the 1937 act was "intended to help clear slums through federal loans and annual contributions for the provision of low rent housing."[6] It is also clear that the act would benefit idle construction workers and the companies that employed them.[7] What seemed to be a sensible blend of altruism and practicality in 1937 gave way to a different purpose in the Housing Act of 1949.

The Act of 1949 had a stormy history. As one might suspect, the idea of clearing slums and replacing them with federally subsidized housing looked better in the Depression than it did after World War II. The chief provisions of the Act of 1949 included federal money for slum clearance and some public housing (which was the most controversial part of the bill) but focused on urban redevelopment which was broader in scope than just providing housing for low-income people. In essence, the bill provided for localities to generate a plan for urban redevelopment. With federal help, a local community could acquire slum land, clear it, and sell or lease it—but it was not committed to replace whatever was cleared with low income housing. The act only required that new construction be "predominantly residential," which was taken to mean one-half. The federal government undertook to underwrite up to two-thirds of the loss that a locality might incur as the difference between what purchase and demolition cost and the sales price or lease value. The locality would have to underwrite one-sixth of any loss in cash, but could count as its other one-sixth of the cost anything that it paid for in parks, streets, and other improvements. In effect then, the relatively benevolent Act of 1937, which was designed to provide low income housing and put the unemployed back to work, was changed into a policy to encourage urban redevelopment, which included the sale of land for purposes other than housing.

Another milestone was the Housing Act of 1954. This act reflected a further shift. First, the idea of urban redevelopment changed to "urban renewal." Second, the local planning body had to present a "workable program" for eliminating blight and for doing overall community development if it was to obtain federal assistance. FHA mortgage insurance was made available for private residential construction with the Federal National Mortgage Association (which is related to the federal government in a similar way as the United States Postal Service) standing by to purchase any mortgages not taken up by private investors. The FNMA makes a market in mortgages, another helpful backup to the housing industry provided by the federal government. Another important provision of interest to us here was the removal of the requirement that an urban renewal area had to be rebuilt as "predominantly residential."

With the passage of the 1949 and 1954 acts, the way was cleared for cities to condemn slums, sell or lease the land more freely, and avoid public housing. Foard and Feffernan note that:

> The additional low-rent public housing units authorized by the 1954 Act were made available only for meeting the needs of families displaced by government activities in a community where an urban redevelopment or urban renewal project was being carried out.[8]

While this latter provision was repealed in 1955, the policy's intent was clearly opposed to further public housing. Hartman is more pungent on the subject of urban renewal:

> This program (urban renewal) was introduced in the 1949 Housing Act as "slum clearance" but was taken over at the local level by those who wished to reclaim urban land occupied by the poor for commercial, industrial, civic, and upper-income residential uses. Over half a million households, two-thirds of them non-white and virtually all in the lower income categories, have been forcibly uprooted. A substantial percentage of these persons were moved to substandard and overcrowded conditions and into areas scheduled for future clearance, at a cost of considerable personal and social disruption.[9]

The 1949 act was a turning point and public housing has been used more sparingly since. Congress failed to appropriate enough money for the amount of housing authorized until the Kennedy administration, and even then the best that was done was 100,000 units in 1961. There was a modest upswing in public housing during the Johnson administration. Some innovations came in 1968.

The Housing Act of 1968 contained two provisions that were novel. Section 235 provided for the purchase of a home by low-income people. The purchaser was supposed to pay only 20 percent of his or her income in monthly payments which included property taxes and insurance on the property. The federal government, through the FHA, guaranteed the loan and paid all but 1 percent of the interest. This made very low payments on the principal possible. Most of the homes were bought by relatively low-income families, but the very poor were not affected. Even though the down payments were only about $200, the very poor could not afford them.

Section 236 of the act made it possible for rental units to be built using private capital. The federal government subsidized the interest. Since interest makes up a good part of the total payment on housing loans, the federal subsidy made it possible, in theory, to rent to low-income people at a price that they could afford. The catch was that it was still necessary for the local Housing Authority or the nonprofit sponsoring body (both alternatives were used) to collect rents sufficient to pay the mortgage principal and the upkeep, so it was never financially realistic to admit tenants who were too poor. Most of the tenants were, therefore, from the upper end of the eligibility range.

There was some public housing constructed in the late 1960s. One innovation was the so-called "turnkey" approach. Formerly, most local housing authorities acquired the land and hired a contractor, maintaining a supervisory role over the project. In the turnkey approach, "a builder arranges to construct or rehabilitate a development to housing authority specifications and turns the completed units over to the authority at a prenegotiated price."[10] This approach proved to be popular, since it provided the private builder a guaranteed return on the product.

Since 1965, the practice of leasing units became part of federal programming. This approach did not build new housing; it leased standard housing units from existing stock and rented them to low-income tenants for a fixed proportion of their income. The Local Housing Authority, using federal funds, covered the difference between the tenant's payments and the market value of the housing.

The 235 and 236 programs ran into problems. Simply put, it appears that too many builders cut too many corners. The 235 housing was often shoddily built, but the builder got his money just the same. It was not uncommon for a family to purchase a house under the 235 plan and simply walk away when they needed to move. They had built up little or no equity, so there was little incentive to bother to sell the house. They could only lose their very modest down payment. A number of housing tracts built under the 235 provisions fell into disrepair simply because the tenants were unable or unmotivated to fix their houses. Since foreclosure takes time, the houses often deteriorated. The 235 program was revised and aimed at primarily lower-middle income people. The 236 program has not always worked out well either. In one such operation, which is fairly typical, a private non-profit corporation built a very attractive set of townhouses for rental to low-income families. Although the federal subsidy kept the monthly payments low, there were still substantial payments to be made on the principal and upkeep. Poor tenants did not pay regularly despite vigorous attempts to collect, so the operation was continually on the edge of financial failure and reversion to the ownership of the Department of Housing and Urban Development. The pressure was on to rent to dependable tenants with as high an income as possible.

By 1973, when the Nixon administration declared a moratorium on federal housing programs and any new subsidized housing, defaults from 235 and 236 programs were costing HUD some $2 billion annually.[11]

The difficulties came to a head in the early seventies because of the so-called Brooke amendments (sponsored by Senator Edward Brooke of Massachusetts) which increased governmental subsidies, but limited the amount that the poor were expected to pay for housing to a maximum of 25 percent of their income. The Office of Management and Budget stalled on implementing the Brooke amendments and the provision of housing for the poor slowed to a crawl.

Current policy, while continuing federal participation in the existing programs, has been mainly based on the Housing Act of 1974. Subsequent legislation has not made any profound change in policy, although there have been shifts in emphasis.

Basically the Act of 1974 contained two fresh approaches. The first involved combining a number of HUD categorical grant programs, including those for waterworks, sewer systems and urban renewal, into block grants for community development. The idea was to give the local community more flexibility in setting priorities. At the same time, the total amount of money going to the community was cut when the several grants were combined.

The second emphasis was embodied in Section 8. Briefly, Section 8 provided for government subsidization of rent payments either in newly built apartments (built either by public or private developers) or in existing housing stock. Under the current version of this program, tenants who meet the income criteria pay 30 percent of their income toward the rent and the federal government pays the difference. During the Reagan administration, the tendency has been to emphasize renting from existing stock because it is cheaper than renting new apartments. Consequently, there is little new construction aimed at Section 8 consumers at this time.

The idea behind Section 8 was to encourage private developers to build low-cost housing. In such cases, the building remains in the hands of private individuals who have contracted with the federal government to rent the property to low-income persons for a period of between fifteen and forty years, depending on the contract. Over time, the aim was to replace public housing eventually, leaving privately operated housing to take up the slack, as the government gradually got out of the housing business.

The Reagan administration has been promoting a new approach. It has, of course, been against the building of any new public housing, so very few new units have been built except a few for the elderly and handicapped. The administration wants to use a voucher system to replace both the declining stock of public housing and the Section 8 subsidies. Essentially, the Reagan administration has proposed to give the poor vouchers which they could use to rent the housing of their choice.

Interestingly enough, this idea has been researched. In 1970, HUD funded an extensive Experimental Housing Allowance Program (EHAP). EHAP was actually three experiments conducted by private contractors which began in 1973 and produced its final reports in 1982. The success of the experiments depends upon whom one reads. The contributors to Friedman and Weinberg's review of the experiment generally agree that a housing allowance is much cheaper than constructing new housing and has no inflationary pressure on the housing market.[12] Mary K. Nenno is representative of the critics. She points out that "family housing allowances . . . do nothing substantial either to generate new housing or to improve housing or neighborhood conditions."[13]

Currently, the older public housing units are still available, although less money is forthcoming for their upkeep and they are getting older. Section 235 is no longer realistically a resource for the poor. Some Section 236 units still exist, but one is hard pressed to find any new construction under this program. Section 8 payments for the rental of existing stock still have congressional approval, and the Reagan voucher system has so far been rejected. There are some units being built for the handicapped and the elderly under Section 202 of the Housing Act of 1937, but these are few. There is little in the way of government-subsidized new construction on the horizon.

What Went Wrong with Public Housing?

Up through the 1960s federally financed public housing units were the major weapons in the war against substandard housing. Then, as we detailed above, there was a shift actually beginning with the Housing Act of 1949, and the momentum was gradually lost in favor of some form of subsidy. Why did this happen? A number of critics have tried to answer this question. Martin Anderson in his book *The Federal Bulldozer,* published in 1964, gave an answer that has remained popular.[14] Although the specific demon that Anderson felt compelled to fight was urban renewal as a whole, he made several points concerning the 1949 Housing Act that apply to some of the subsequent legislation. In essence, Anderson noted that urban renewal was tearing down about four times as many homes as it built. Further, the homes built on urban renewal lands rented for much more than the original tenants could pay. Therefore, most of the poor were forced to move into neighborhoods of about the same quality as they moved from—and often at higher rents.

In another article, Anderson raised constitutional issues.[15] Slum clearance is done under the constitutional doctrine of "eminent domain." This rests on a phrase in the Fifth Amendment of the Constitution which says, "nor shall private property be taken for public use without just compensation." It was Anderson's position that the condemnation of private property, which is then resold to private developers after it has been cleared, is not public use but is clearly private use. Robert Groberg, one of Anderson's critics, maintains that public use is equivalent to public benefit and that it has been of public benefit to rid the communities of slums.[16] While this is not the place to argue the constitutional merits of the case (the Supreme Court having already ruled in favor of urban renewal), Anderson's main point remains that urban renewal has not been a very effective tool in providing housing for the poor, but it has been a boon to the real estate developer.

Bellush and Hausknecht make a slightly different argument.[17] In their view, Americans have taken seriously Jefferson's idea of "the virtues of the yeoman farmer and the sterling pioneer" and have made of home ownership a symbol of success and achievement. Public housing runs counter to this symbolism. It also runs afoul of the interests of powerful groups in real estate and home building. This American attitude contrasts with that of Britain where public housing has been relatively well accepted and continues to be built.

Other writers have mentioned that public housing is barren, lacks the character of neighborhoods that it replaces, and has a stigmatizing effect on its inhabitants. Still others emphasize a point that we made earlier—that public housing has failed to serve the very people that it supposedly sought to serve. Since the payments on the principal and upkeep costs must be made, local housing authorities tend to give preference to families and individuals at the upper end of the income range of eligibility. For instance, in public housing there is an income limit. Let us say that in a given project, one's family income must be less than $12,000. Most local housing authorities prefer to rent to those making as close to $12,000 as they can and tend to discourage the very poor from renting simply because they know that there is a better chance of getting the rent from those with some income.

Further, public housing has not been well received by the tenants. The classic case is that of Pruitt-Igoe in St. Louis. Built in 1954, this housing complex was a model of its kind and won design awards. However, when Lee Rainwater wrote about it in 1967, the complex had a vacancy rate of 20 percent.[18] It had become unsafe and unsatisfactory. Whites had moved out and the only blacks who would move in were those who were desperate for housing. The residents had become discouraged and alienated. Rainwater's suggestion was to provide more income to the lower economic class and to discard the idea of ancillary services that he believed had been predicated on the notion that the poor would remain poor. Though he did not say so, one would presume that if the income of the poor was raised, the poor would find their own housing and services on the private market. All Pruitt-Igoe units were torn down after heroic attempts to salvage the complex. It did not fail because it was governmentally financed housing. Other housing units, particularly those for the old and the handicapped, have been well accepted. Our conclusion is that Pruitt-Igoe failed because it was too big and too different from the surrounding city.[19] The eleven-story Chicago-type complex had 2,800 units in thirty-three buildings. There were also a number of management problems which did not help. The junior author of this book was an occasional visitor to St. Louis during the middle 1960s while Pruitt-Igoe was still standing. It was his impression at the time that the project would have been better suited to a condominium for young professionals. It would have been an ideal setting for mobile people whose personal and professional interests would not have required the same sense of community that are apparently of more importance to permanent residents. If Pruitt-Igoe had been the usual urban condominium, it might have been successful. As a replacement for housing, no matter how dilapidated, for people who knew each other and had worked out personal survival systems that worked, it was a failure. This, we would argue, is the general problem with public housing as a social resource. It violates the sense of community that long-term residents have by placing them under the control of outsiders. Public housing works for the elderly and the handicapped because it is more supportively administered and the residents find the amenities advantageous.

In any case, the idea of building new housing for the poor is not popular. It is clear that federal policy is opposed to it and has been opposed to it for some decades. The only time that there was active governmental support appears to have been during the 1930s when unemployment of skilled people was high, construction was down, and the poor included the temporary poor of the Great Depression.

The present federal position is clearly in favor of the subsidization of rentals from existing housing stock. There is one source of pressure that could conceivably change the federal position. High interest rates and the increasing cost of land and materials (but not labor costs which have not risen as fast as these other factors) are slowly driving the price of single-family dwellings out of the range of many Americans. The citizen who can pay for it can still buy comfortable housing. The higher cost of buying a house will have its major effect on the young who are or who will be entering the housing market. This situation could possibly trigger some renewed interest in direct governmental participation in the housing market if a housing shortage should develop, but we consider this a fairly unlikely possibility.

Other Concerns in Living Space

We have written primarily about housing so far. This is because housing is such a primary concern to most Americans, both poor and non-poor. Hartman claims that the poor consider housing their first or second most important problem. Certainly we can all agree that housing is also a crucial factor in the lives of the non-poor as well, given the amount that Americans spend on grass, lawnmowers, furniture, and home entertainment packages. Among the more privileged classes, one risks losing out in the status game if he or she does not have a microwave oven, a video-recorder, and a small computer in the home! But while the home is a primary concern, it is not the only problem that one faces in his or her living space.

The surroundings have a great deal to do with whether or not the quality of life is considered high. For most Americans, the environment is satisfactory. In addition to comfortable housing, most Americans own serviceable automobiles and have access to a wide array of places to shop. Most Americans can go outdoors at night without great fear—although this is not as certain as it once was. Most American children attend schools that may not be distinguished, but are at least adequate for the purpose. And most Americans are able to find reasonably satisfying work that pays a salary that allows a modicum of personal luxury.

It is true that air pollution, acid rain, water pollution, dangerous chemicals, energy problems, and political corruption plague the citizens of the United States, but by and large these problems, although they may get our attention from time to time, seem remote from daily life. Besides, the citizen can tell himself or herself that someone is working on these problems. The rest of life is rewarding enough to keep our minds busy and our bodies comfortable.

For the poor, too, most of these problems are remote. This is not because the poor are too comfortable to care. We have already cited some of the problems that the poor have with housing. We should also mention that the poor, as a consequence of their lack of economic power, put up with a good deal more frustration in their living space. The poor often do not have access to dependable transportation. The myth of the welfare Cadillac is well entrenched in our society. Actually, the Cadillac Motor Car Division of General

Motors manufactures only around 300,000 units per year while there are around 3 million families that are recipients of AFDC. It is impossible for all welfare families to own new Cadillacs, but we do not think that the facts will destroy the myth. The poor, when they own cars, usually own poorly maintained older vehicles. Often they have to depend upon friends or today's generally outdated public transportation systems. Consequently, they often find it difficult to take advantage of the benefits of comparison shopping. Thus, they often pay too much for merchandise simply because they lack practical alternatives.

Residents of many poor neighborhoods fear to leave their homes in daylight, let alone after dark. The children of the poor generally attend schools for whom the taxpayers are taking less and less financial responsibility. There is little need to detail all the miseries that impinge on the living space of the poor since that has been done at great length in a number of places. The reader will find Claude Brown's *Manchild in the Promised Land* listed in the "Suggestions for Further Reading" at the end of the chapter. There is little charm in Brown's neighborhood, and his description of growing up is still a reality for far too many Americans.

What Can Be Done About the Problems in Living Space?

First of all, it must be acknowledged that American housing in general is getting better largely due to consumer demand. The consumer has been helped by the federal policies that assure both loan and capital protection. The Census Bureau uses the presence of plumbing facilities as a rough indicator of the condition of housing. In 1940, it was reported that approximately 45 percent of U.S. homes lacked indoor plumbing. By the last census in 1980, this figure was around 3 percent. While this indicator probably underestimates the condition of houses, it is a useful tool since houses with indoor plumbing usually also have other amenities.

Second, it appears that building codes have also had a beneficial effect in increasing the general quality of housing. While there are still a number of unsafe homes in use, the home builders of America have been encouraged to build better houses and to upgrade older properties when renovations are done. There are, of course, landlords who do not upgrade rental units until forced to do so. We have had acquaintances who owned rental property in low-income areas. One of these individuals claimed, to give one example, that his property was extremely profitable because he never spent any money on it unless he absolutely had to. He defended this practice by saying that the kind of tenants he had probably would not take care of the place if he did keep it up aggressively. This is not an unusual approach to rental property in low-income areas.

Third, although we have only mentioned it briefly, governmental action has provided safe and satisfactory housing for older people and the handicapped both in public housing and through Section 8 subsidy programs. We see no reason to quarrel with what works. Few Americans, excepting ideologues of the extreme right and the extreme left, would want to tamper drastically with either the FHA loan program and its attendant support systems or the guarantees on savings that encourage capital savings. There is also little support for the discontinuance of the tax benefits to home owners. Most Americans, we suspect, support reasonable zoning laws and building codes. We also think that most Americans can accept governmental intervention on behalf of older Americans and the handicapped and their housing needs. The most controversial and the least settled problem is the housing of the younger poor family, particularly those with children.

A number of solutions have been proposed. One of the most radical has been suggested by Emily Paradise Achtenberg and Peter Marcuse who recommend what they call the "decommodification" of housing.[20] They believe that the major reason that there are housing problems in the United States is that housing is treated as a commodity which can be traded at a profit. They argue that governmental intervention has primarily helped reinforce the benefits to the capitalist establishment. They recommend an increase in what they call the "social ownership" of housing "under public, collective, community, or resident ownership that is operated solely for resident benefit and subject to resident control, with resale for profit prohibited."[21] Ultimately, Achtenberg and Marcuse would progressively tax the private sector to pay for housing that would be equitably distributed according to need and subject to social ownership and community control.

A less extreme answer to the housing problems of the poor is suggested by Raymond J. Struyk of the Urban Institute who would continue the provisions of Section 8 that subsidize rents of existing and newly built housing, but who would also make an aggressive attempt to save public housing.[22] Arguing that present federal assistance is calculated in a way that really fails to reward good management, Struyk would replace the current federal categories with a single subsidy as is done under Section 8. He would also vigorously upgrade the quality of the management at the local level and maintain quality through a selective evaluation focused on those housing authorities that had problems.

We have already alluded to a third approach. President Reagan has proposed a voucher system which has the support of the research done by the Experimental Housing Assistance Project. This approach would give the subsidy directly to the poor and let them shop for housing on the private market.

We thus have three proposals (there are, of course, others) that have been advanced. We will now examine them using our criteria to see if any one has a pronounced superiority over the others. For convenience, we will refer to the Achtenberg-Marcuse proposal as the collective approach; the Struyk proposal as the public housing approach (although it admittedly includes the continuation of Section 8 subsidies to owners of existing structures and builders of new ones); and the third will simply be called the voucher system.

1. *Is the policy under consideration compatible with contemporary "style"?*

    Clearly, the collective approach is not. No American president of either party would recommend it. Home ownership and the desire to sell one's house at a profit are deeply held values and it is quite outside current public style to actively support such an idea. The public housing approach is clearly not popular either with the Administration or the public. Since President Reagan has pushed the voucher system, it is obvious that he supports it. The notion that people should have a maximum of control over their consumer habits is certainly in line with popular style, but it is uncertain that the public is willing to accord the poor this much freedom to act. The current policy, which relies heavily on the use of Section 8 subsidies of housing from the current stock, seems to be the fashion, at least in the short run. One might reasonably expect that the voucher system might get a trial in the near future, however. It is not really a new idea, since it was one of the alternatives considered during the debates over the Housing Act of 1937. The major objection was that the poor do not have the savvy to negotiate for themselves and many people still feel that way. Of the three alternatives, the voucher system would appear to have the best chance, but the current policy still has a lot going for it right now.

2. *Is the policy compatible with important and enduring cultural values, particularly equity, fairness and justice?*

Here again, the unsuitability of the collective approach is obvious. We are sure that our friends on the left would disagree with our evaluation and would argue that their proposal is eminently equitable, fair and just because it would be responsive to personal need instead of market forces and the profit motive. The trouble is that the collective approach is not compatible with the general American *understanding* of equity, fairness and justice. Few Americans find fault with the notion of differential rewards based on achievement. In other words, if you make a lot of money and have worked for it, most Americans believe that it is fair, equitable and just that you have a nice house. Home ownership is tied to notions of success and achievement. It is what people want for themselves. Most disgruntled Americans do not want the system of home ownership changed radically—they do want it to operate in their favor, though. The public housing approach involves the least social change. The problem is that, as we have pointed out above, public housing is not really acceptable to most Americans. Making it more efficient will not make it more acceptable to the values of most Americans. The voucher approach shares some of the potential problems with other voucher programs, food stamps for example. As we have noted before, the big concern is whether or not the poor can be trusted to act in their own best interests and whether or not they can survive in the rental marketplace. EHAP results suggest that minority groups may need some advocacy assistance when market conditions are tight.[23] Other than this conditional exception, which strongly appears to be related to racism rather than poverty, the poor can negotiate for themselves. The present emphasis on Section 8 probably is more acceptable to the prevailing values of most Americans, since the subsidies go to landlords and cannot be usurped for some purpose that would be seen as nonconforming to the prevailing ethical posture of public morality.

While the Section 8 approach will probably prevail for a time, we think that the case can be made for the voucher system on the grounds that it is what most Americans would want for themselves were they in the position of the poor. Again, our support for the voucher system is predicated on a somewhat naive hope that it is possible to convince the American public to abandon their paternalism toward the poor and allow them the political right to control their own lives.

3. *Is the policy compatible with social work's professional value and ethical system?*

This is a tough question to answer. Some social workers are far enough to the political left to accept the collective approach. We believe this to be a minority of social workers in general, but a sizeable number within the subset of social workers who are policy activists. Most social workers would accept the public housing approach (remember that the public housing approach is really a mix with Section 8 and other current programs) because it is well within the twentieth century liberal mainstream where most social workers' values lie.

Few of the liberal social workers see that this position is basically paternalistic. We have always been fascinated by this aspect of most of our colleagues, particularly the therapeutically oriented. Virtually all social workers who teach or practice some form of treatment believe wholeheartedly in the rights of clients to grow and change in ways that lead to independence. At the same time, these same therapists will often rationalize certain policies that are paternalistic. Public housing is one of these entities. It would be difficult for some of our colleagues to endorse a voucher system that seems to us to be more in keeping with social work values relating to freedom of choice, independence, and the exercise of personal rights.

In all fairness, it must be said that social workers are usually willing for their clients to have all the rights available to everyone else except the right to fail. That the paternalism of many Americans may stem from kind motives does not really help. Obviously, we think the voucher system is more in keeping with major social work values. It is just as clear to us that most social workers will not favor the voucher system, especially if it is recognized as having the endorsement of the Reagan administration. On this issue, we believe that the conservative answer is actually closer to traditional social work values than most social workers will want to admit.

4. *Is the policy acceptable to those in formal decision-making positions?*

Here is a question for which the answer can be relatively short. The collective approach is not acceptable. So far, the public housing approach has not been acceptable. Congress rejected President Reagan's request for a trial run of the voucher system and cut it out of the 1984 budget. The formal decision makers have opted for a program that will primarily fund rental subsidies under the Section 8 provision which relates to the rental of existing housing. While there are funds for maintenance of existing public housing, it is clear that this is not popular. Any form of new construction for the poor is not popular among the formal decision makers.

5. *Does the policy satisfy relevant interest groups?*

The collective approach would only satisfy those who are identified with the left. This is not a large body in contemporary America. The public housing solution has some limited liberal appeal and will satisfy mainstream groups who ordinarily side with the public housing establishment. The voucher approach will gain some conservative support. None of these approaches will appeal to the arch-conservatives of the extreme right. There are cries for reform, often from tenant organizations, but there is no current movement of the magnitude of the rent strikes in St. Louis in the 1960s, for example.

6. *Is the policy based on knowledge that has been tested?*

The collective approach has been used in socialist countries for some years. It has not produced a satisfactory supply of quality housing. The public housing approach has been used in most of Western Europe. A great deal of public housing was built in Britain while Sir Harold MacMillan was Minister of Housing in the second Churchill premiership in the 1950s. MacMillan, a conservative, was an exponent of a "middle way" between conservatism and socialism. His ministry became heavily involved in building "council houses" (the British term for public housing built by local county councils) because of the severe housing shortages caused by World War II. Although many Western welfare states have built public housing, they have not espoused a complete change to publicly owned housing and have preserved the private ownership of most housing. The idea of social ownership espoused by Achtenberg and Marcuse goes well beyond the actualities in most Western countries. Further, public housing in Europe is not complicated by the problem of racial and cultural discrimination that is such a large factor in the United States. Our point is that public housing has only been tested on a large scale in relatively culturally homogeneous societies where there is a fairly long tradition of government involvement in housing. This does not seem to us to provide a test directly relevant to the American experience.

The public housing approach—in the form in which Struyk envisions it—has not been tested, but there is some justification for the management procedures on which it is based. Of course, the Section 8 program has been in operation for a number of years and it undoubtedly works.

EHAP has tested the voucher system, but there have been no trials beyond the selected sites. Of the three alternatives to the present system, EHAP is the only one with useable evidence that could guide policy.

7. *Is the policy workable in the real world?*

   There are no outstanding workability problems in any of these approaches except for the legal complications that would probably arise in the collective approach. Obviously, if the political will were favorable, these could be gotten over, but there would have to be a major overhaul of the pricing system of housing. For instance, there would have to be an agreement on the fixing of housing prices. Given the proclivity of the American public to defeat prior attempts to freeze prices, we would expect that the workability problem would be formidable. The other approaches would have no such complications.

8. *Does the policy create few problems for both the public and the intended beneficiaries?*

   A lot of what has been said before applies to this question. The collective approach would involve a major restructuring of American society because the implications radiate beyond just the question of housing. The decommodification of housing would create a major realignment of social and economic relationships that most Americans would find hard to accept. For many people of limited means, property is their only significant capital investment. Given the emotional and financial investment that most Americans have in their homes, we would not want to be the functionaries charged with the responsibility of explaining that one could no longer sell his or her house at a profit and that the property was to be subject to some form of community control!

   The public housing approach would not appear to create any new problems for the public or for the beneficiaries. No major social adjustment would be required because this proposal simply calls for internal reorganization of existing programs.

   A voucher system would also create few problems—with the possible exception that there may indeed be some who cannot effectively negotiate their way in the rental market. Undoubtedly, there would be unscrupulous people who would try to victimize poor individuals who lacked sophistication about shopping for the best deal, and the legal implications of various leases. However, we think that the victims would be a small minority and that they would find sources of help which would ensure their eventual success. This is not the world of the 1920s any more (which ought to be obvious), and it is getting harder to victimize the poor, particularly the minority poor. There has been too much done by a whole host of organizations for extensive victimization to be very effective. We think that if the poor actually had the choice of renting from A as opposed to B they could do quite well. One of the major problems as we see it is that the poor have not operated in social situations where they had many choices. We think that if the poor had more choices they would make them pretty well—or would soon learn to do so. At least, we are willing to risk it, and we think that most of the poor are willing to do so, too.

9. *Is the policy effective?*

We know that the present policy works to provide a certain level of housing. However, most public housing projects have waiting lists and there are people hoping for more Section 8 funds so that they can move into something better than they have now. The major problem is money. As we have pointed out above, there is little interest in new housing on the part of Congress. Most federal money is directed toward Section 8—subsidizing existing housing rental by paying the landlord the difference between what the tenant can pay and the fair market rental of the apartment. This program would be effective enough, provided that the money was forthcoming.

In our view, the collective approach would not be effective in the United States, given the problems we have outlined. If American values were radically different from what they are, conceivably the collective approach would be effective. However, nothing short of armed insurrection would bring about a situation in which Americans would allow the collective approach to be effective.

The public housing approach would probably be effective, especially since it would be combined with existing Section 8 programs. The present deterioration in public housing could be halted, and more money and better administration would certainly make a difference.

We think that the voucher system would be effective, too. Simply by giving the poor more purchasing power, some of their housing problems would be solved, particularly if the additional funds were given as a voucher that would have to be used for housing.

10. *Will programs derived from the policy be efficient?*

The policy that would procure the most housing for the tax dollar is the voucher system. There is no disagreement about this point in any of the literature that we consulted. Even its opponents do not disagree.

The collective approach would probably be the most expensive to put in motion. Of course, once housing was collectivized, it might be efficiently operated, but the cost and the legal problems that would be encountered in making a radical change in the society would take years to pay off.

The public housing approach would cost more than the present system, since it involves continuing current programs and increasing the amount of money that is invested in public housing in order to bring all of it up to a higher standard of repair and comfort.

The problem with giving a really good answer to this question is that housing can cost whatever a society is willing to pay in order to satisfy a demand. If Americans would be satisfied with a house the size of the standard two-car garage, then it would be possible to house everyone at a cost of about $20,000 per family exclusive of the lot and whatever amenities were desired. This is neither practical nor desirable.

Summary of the Analysis

We have tried to keep this analysis as brief as we could, but it still is not very neat. We have summarized our analysis in Table 7.1.

Table 7.1 ANALYSIS OF THREE PROPOSALS TO SOLVE HOUSING PROBLEMS

	Policy		
	Collective	Public housing	Voucher
Style	no	no	yes
Cultural values	no	no	limited
Social work values	few	yes	few
Decision makers' approval	no	no	no
Interest group approval	few	few	few
Tested knowledge	limited	yes	yes
Workability	hard	yes	easy
Few problems	no	yes	yes
Effectiveness	no	yes	yes
Efficiency	no	fair	yes

It would seem to us that the voucher system is the best alternative to the present set of policies. However, there is not enough clear superiority in the minds of the public, interest groups, or formal decision makers to suggest that any change is imminent. Readers of our first edition will recall that we examined a slightly different set of alternative housing policies, but that our conclusion was the same—that some kind of direct subsidy to the consumer would be the best alternative. We cited Solomon's arguments for changing to a more consumer-oriented strategy.[24]

1. Twice as many families can be moved into decent standard housing for any given federal dollar commitment.
2. Short of bulldozing and rebuilding (which has already proved itself politically, morally, and financially unacceptable), it is the only strategy designed to stabilize and modestly upgrade declining inner-city neighborhoods.
3. Tying the subsidy to the family rather than the dwelling permits a flexible response to changing local market conditions and programmatic needs.
4. Direct subsidies to consumers offer the most practical means for dispersing low-income households outside impacted, blighted areas.
5. Using the existing supply of older housing minimizes vertical and horizontal inequities.
6. The choice of housing type, structure, and location is placed in the hands of the tenants themselves rather than the government.

We find these arguments still convincing. We are surprised to find that the Reagan administration agrees with us. It is possible that, while we are in favor of the same policy, we may be so for different reasons. Our guess is that the relatively cheaper cost is the thing that primarily makes a voucher system attractive to the administration. While we also like the efficiency of getting more housing for the tax dollar, the major appeal of the voucher system for us lies in its consumer orientation.

Concluding Comments

Our conclusion, then, is that Americans would be best served with a combination of the present provision of insured mortgages and federal supports to the money market coupled with the provision of a housing allowance for those who are in need. As we have said, the federal programs that assist the working and middle class home buyer work reasonably well. It appears that housing subsidies work for the poor, but we think that they would work better if the subsidy went directly to the poor individuals instead of to the vendor.

Since we do have many public housing units that are still useable, we also think that attention should be given to Struyk's proposals for upgrading them and improving their administration. There is no sense letting these units go to waste. Ultimately, a successful voucher system would allow their replacement with more consumer-oriented housing.

If there is an overall direction in our policy, it is toward the principle of consumerism. We believe that the best remedy for poverty involves mechanisms that will allow the poor to develop consumer skills rather than to remain the recipients of a paternalistic welfare system's benefits. The most effective war on poverty will involve ways to assist the poor to achieve increased participation in the society as a whole.

REFERENCES

1. Harvey S. Perloff, "Preface" in Harvey S. Perloff, ed., *The Quality of the Urban Environment* (Washington, D.C.: Resources for the Future, 1969), p. v.
2. Chester W. Hartman, *Housing and Social Policy* (Englewood Cliffs, N.J.: Prentice-Hall, 1975), pp. 2–3.
3. *Ibid.*, p. 29.
4. *Ibid.*, p. 2.
5. Ashley A. Foard and Hilbert Feffernan, "Federal Urban Renewal Legislation," in James Q. Wilson, ed., *Urban Renewal: The Record and the Controversy* (Cambridge, Mass.: The MIT Press, 1966), pp. 71–125.
6. *Ibid.*, pp. 78–79.
7. Lawrence Friedman argues that this was the only motive. See Lawrence Friedman, "Public Housing and the Poor," in John Pynoos, Robert Schafer, and Chester Hartman, eds., *Housing Urban America* (Chicago: Aldine, 1973), pp. 449–450.
8. Foard and Feffernan, *op. cit.*, p. 99.
9. Hartman, *op. cit.*, p. 107.

10. *Ibid.*, p. 120.
11. *Ibid.*, p. 145.
12. Joseph Friedman and Daniel H. Weinberg, *The Great Housing Experiment* (Beverly Hills, Cal.: Sage, 1983).
13. Mary K. Nenno, "Housing Allowances are Not Enough," *Society,* Vol. 21, No. 3 (March/April 1984), pp. 54–57.
14. Martin Anderson, *The Federal Bulldozer* (Cambridge, Mass.: The MIT Press, 1964).
15. Martin Anderson, "The Sophistry that Made Urban Renewal Possible," in Jewel Bellush and Murray Hausknecht, eds., *Urban Renewal: People, Politics, and Planning* (Garden City, N.Y.: Doubleday, 1967), pp. 52–66.
16. Robert P. Groberg, "Urban Renewal Realistically Reappraised," in Bellush and Hausknecht, *op. cit.,* pp. 67–73.
17. Jewel Bellush and Murray Hausknecht, "Public Housing: The Contexts of Failure," in Bellush and Hausknecht, *op. cit.,* pp. 451–461.
18. Lee Rainwater, "The Lessons of Pruitt-Igoe," in Pynoos, Schafer, and Hartman, *op. cit.,* pp. 548–555.
19. A view shared by Thomas Costello and Anita Miller, "Beyond the Rent Strike at Pruitt-Igoe," in Richard Plunz, ed., *Housing Form and Public Policy in the United States* (New York: Praeger, 1980), pp. 1–6.
20. Emily Paradise Achtenberg and Peter Marcuse, "Towards the Decommodification of Housing: A Political Analysis and a Progressive Program," in Chester Hartman, ed., *America's Housing Crisis* (Boston: Routledge and Kegan Paul, 1983), pp. 202–231.
21. *Ibid.*, p. 221.
22. Raymond J. Struyk, *A New System for Public Housing* (Washington, D.C.: The Urban Institute, 1980).
23. James P. Zais, "Administering Housing Allowances," Chapter 10 in Raymond J. Struyk and Marc Bendick, Jr., eds., *Housing Vouchers for the Poor* (Washington, D.C.: The Urban Institute, 1981), p. 253 ff.
24. Arthur P. Solomon, *Housing the Urban Poor* (Cambridge, Mass.: The MIT Press, 1974), pp. 182–183.

QUESTIONS FOR DISCUSSION

1. Do you agree or disagree with the authors' position that while slums are poor places to live, they do not cause social pathology? Why do you take the position that you do?

2. Can you build a case for the idea that urban renewal is a good thing?

3. What is a slum? This is not as easy as it sounds. Is it just an area of poor housing? A high crime area? A subculture? Where are the boundaries?

4. What do you think of public housing? Should we reconsider the idea?

5. Given the inflation in housing costs, what do you think that the homes of the future will be like? Where will the poor live?

6. Do socialistic societies have housing and neighborhood problems? Do all citizens enjoy comfortable housing at reasonable cost?

7. Is there a practical way to eliminate all federal intervention in the housing market?

SUGGESTED PROJECTS

1. Assume that you want to buy a house for $50,000. Talk to a realtor or a loan officer at a financial institution and find out how much you will actually pay for the house over the period of the loan.

2. Interview a local public official involved in urban renewal. Find out about a local project. How much has it cost in public funds? How long did the project take to be completed? What was done with the property? Where did the residents go?

3. Arrange a visit to a local public housing unit. Visit a vacant unit and compare it to the house in which your parents live.

FOR FURTHER READING

Martin Anderson. *The Federal Bulldozer*. Cambridge, Mass.: The MIT Press, 1964. An important seminal study of urban renewal by one of the first critics of the program.

Claude Brown. *Manchild in the Promised Land*. New York: Macmillan, 1965. A first-hand experience of life in an urban ghetto. Highly controversial when it was published, this book still upsets many people when it shows up on high school reading lists.

Chester W. Hartman. *Housing and Social Policy*. Englewood Cliffs, N.J.: Prentice-Hall, 1975. A useful introduction to the area of housing. Hartman is a longtime critic of national housing policy.

Chester Hartman, ed. *America's Housing Crisis*. Boston: Routledge and Kegan Paul, 1983. A collection of activist writings from a radical anti-Reagan perspective.

Raymond J. Struyk and Marc Bendick, Jr., eds. *Housing Vouchers for the Poor*. Washington, D.C.: The Urban Institute, 1981. A detailed reader covering the findings from EHAP.

Raymond J. Struyk. *A New System for Public Housing*. Washington, D.C.: The Urban Institute, 1980. An argument for the revitalization of public housing.

John Pynoos, Robert Schafer and Chester W. Hartman, eds. *Housing Urban America*, updated second edition. New York: Aldine Publishing Company, 1980. A reader with a wide variety of articles on housing written from different perspectives.

8

Social Welfare Policy and Social Service Delivery

In OUR INTRODUCTION WE MADE THE point that service delivery systems were related to social welfare policy both as outcomes and as sources for policy change. The relationship of service delivery to policy is probably most clearly seen in those agencies that are committed to the delivery of concrete services related to a more or less clearly defined social welfare program, for example, financial aid, employment, or adoption services. These kinds of services are directed toward relatively well-understood ends, and it is easy to see that policy considerations shape the questions of eligibility, the nature of the service and the treatment goal. It may be a little harder to grasp the relationship of service delivery to policy in "pure" counseling services. In this chapter we want to think about social welfare policy as it relates to those aspects of service delivery most relevant to clients or patients—the service act itself. If the aim of social welfare policy is survival through mutual aid, then service delivery should reflect that concern.

Social workers have been helping people for so long that they may not see that the direct treatment of individuals and groups takes the form that it does because of policy choices. Here we are not talking strictly about eligibility determination or the content of the service, although these elements are involved. We are interested in the situation in which service takes place—the interaction between client and social worker in some kind of agency or institution. While this part of the social welfare enterprise is usually seen as strictly a clinical matter, it is possible to discern patterns in the various acts of service delivery that are the result of choices. These choices, whether explicit or implicit, follow guidelines that properly are matters of policy.

A Simple Illustration

In order to make this illustration concrete, let us consider what happens in a visit to a social agency. We will use a family counseling agency for our example, but one might have a similar experience in some other place.

Mr. X thinks that something has gone out of his relationship with Ms. X, to whom he has been married for ten years. He thinks that they are growing apart, and he believes that their communications have become increasingly cold and hostile. Mr. X has talked to the pastor of the church that he attends occasionally. The pastor has suggested that a family social agency might be of help. Accordingly, Mr. X telephones a local United Way family counseling agency and is offered an appointment.

At the time of the appointment, Mr. X appears at the agency office. He is courteously received and after a brief wait, is ushered into an office where a social worker invites him to discuss his difficulty. Mr. X is encouraged to talk about how things look to him, and the social worker helps him to define his problem into manageable form. During this interview, certain things will be tentatively decided. The counselor and Mr. X will try to arrive at some kind of working hypothesis about what to do. The advisability of Ms. X's participation will be discussed. Further appointments, if there are to be any, will be scheduled. After about fifty minutes, the interview will be ended with the social worker's promise that the discussion will be resumed at a later scheduled time.

While we do not argue that the above scenario is either typical or universal, it does happen with consistency. There may be other elements in the process, depending on the nature of the problem or the nature of the agency. That is, if the problem had been financial instead of interpersonal, and if the agency had been a public welfare office, there would have been forms to fill in and a process initiated by the social worker that would result in eligibility determination and some kind of payment if appropriate. If the agency had been a group-serving agency, there would be additional variation because a set of people would be involved as client. In principle, though, the "intake" process would not ordinarily be very different.

What occurred in the encounter between the social worker and Mr. X was influenced by a number of social welfare policy choices. The example is so commonplace that the choices that have been made have become obscure as *policy* choices.

Policy Choices in Service Delivery

Putting to one side our example, let us look at some choices that have to be made within a service delivery system. We will return to the example later in the chapter.

Some years ago, James K. Whittaker identified several "Dilemmas of the Helping Person in an Age of Ecological Crisis."[1] These dilemmas are still very difficult to resolve, and will probably be serious issues far into the future. Society vacillates between the horns of each dilemma, depending on the current values, without reaching any permanent resolution. Here are Whittaker's issues:

> 1. How does one continue to justify any form of treatment or remediation when massive social problems like poverty, inferior education, and urban blight so clearly demand large-scale programs aimed at basic systematic change?[2]

Here, Whittaker has raised the old, but still quite valid, question of whether or not one should take the social engineering or the case-by-case approach to helping people. William Schwartz has addressed the same issue and has suggested that "the practitioner is required neither to 'change the people' nor to 'change the system' but to change the ways in which they deal with each other."[3]

Social workers, like many others in the helping occupations, have never formally resolved this issue. For the most part, social workers have operated on a case-by-case approach although there have been periodic episodes of public social action. Most recently, we saw one of these periods in the 1960s. Although there are a number of activists today who are social workers, the overall direction of the field is toward case-by-case treatment. The United States in general seems disenchanted with the social engineering approach,[4] and Schwartz's "mediator" concept has not been used as a practical basis for social service delivery organization despite its theoretical appeal.

2. At what point, then, should the "rights" of society supersede those of the individual?[5]

Although Whittaker poses this dilemma in the context of the ecology movement's campaign for limiting family size by official policy vs. the notion of individual self determination regarding births, it obviously has larger implications. While this is a general problem for Americans, it is especially poignant for social workers. On the one hand, social work has a long tradition of favoring individual self-determination and individual right, including the right to fail. On the other hand, social work has also supported mandatory governmental programs that require universal participation and provide universal benefit. Few have noticed that there is an inherent contradiction. If a society enforces its "right" and responsibility to protect its members on a universal basis, it must do so in ways that inevitably restrict individual choice.

As an example, consider OASDHI. Members of the work force are required to pay into the system. Defenders of the system argue that if individuals were given a choice, some would prefer to take the money now and would not save for their old age. Opponents argue that if individuals want to spend their money now, then that is their decision. Nearly all social workers support the mandatory participation in social insurance. At the same time, most social workers also argue that the individual must be free to determine his or her own future. This dilemma is not easily resolved at the treatment level, either. Some social workers see themselves as agents of society's concern, while others see themselves as agents of the client, facing society's lack of understanding and unrealistic demands.

3. How does one continue to work within the system (in this instance, the social welfare system) when in many instances the most serious pathology lies not within individual clients, but within the very social service network of which the professional is a part?[6]

Here, Whittaker has captured a nagging dilemma of long standing. During the 1960s, one was acutely faced with this question in dramatic ways. On one campus in the Midwest, students tied colored cloths around their arms during demonstrations; those who were still willing to work "within the system" wore one color and those who were for tearing the system down wore another. Actually, this distinction may be false. In effect, everyone who continues to remain in the United States works within the system unless he or she is an agent of a foreign government or a member of a guerilla movement. This is so because American society has legitimized a certain level of radicalism since the days of Thomas Paine, Samuel Adams and Henry David Thoreau. Civil disobedience is really "within the system," since for this to be an effective technique, the system must recognize one's disobedience and move to censure or imprison the disobedient. Although there are sanctions against extremely violent disobedience when it is perceived as extremely threatening, American norms have allowed people to take more extreme positions than any other country's norms, save perhaps the United Kingdom's. While we cannot offer a solution to this issue either, it is clear that most social workers have opted for "working within the system" and have, in fact, maintained a fairly conservative posture with respect to service delivery systems.

It is difficult to work for change when one is an employee, but some social workers do it. Many simply leave the social welfare field if they find it too uncomfortable and follow some new occupation. Most, fortunately or unfortunately, come to terms with things as they are.

4. But how valid is this concept of target philosophy today? Have not many of the social problems we face been shown to be interrelated?[7]

In this dilemma, Whittaker is raising the question of whether or not it ought to be social work's policy to continue to identify pieces of a problem for interventive purposes or to try to work with the whole problem. Should we continue to offer services to individual poor people, or should we focus globally on the problem of poverty? Whittaker suggests that we may still need to think in terms of target populations, but we may have to carefully redefine what we mean. In the years since Whittaker wrote his book, clinically oriented people have, by and large, quietly committed themselves to working with a traditional target population while more indirectly expressing their concern with overall problems. This shift may seem more apparent when we consider Whittaker's final dilemma.

5. A final dilemma for the helping professional concerns his commitment to social action. Given the maze of problems besetting our social welfare system and the particular dilemmas faced by the practitioner operating within that system, is it any longer possible to separate social concerns from professional life?[8]

It seems to us that this question is increasingly answered "yes" by most social workers.[9] Today, there is only a trickle of students interested in social policy and planning as a career. By far, the larger number of social work students have opted for purely clinical training. We have seen the development of a national Clinical Register to enable the special identification of persons with clinical skills. There is a growing interest in fee-for-service social work practice. The new specialty of industrial social work has developed in which social workers are employed by firms as part of employee benefit services. Interest in social change is increasingly limited to efforts to include groups (e.g., women) into the system, but there is little discussion of radical system change.

In summary, we can say that while these dilemmas remain unresolved in any final sense, there is a discernible swing toward treatment as the primary professional activity with social reform seen as a lesser concern. At some future time, the pendulum can easily swing back toward reform, depending upon the historical situation.

A Sample Analysis

Let us return to Mr. X and his problem in the light of the above discussion. We stated our example in as general a way as possible. Almost any treatment method would fit into the service framework as we have outlined it. This is deliberate, since we want to talk about service policies rather than treatment methods. We will list what we believe to be the policies followed by the hypothetical agency in our example.

1. *Service is to be rendered on a case-by-case basis.*

   The current practice in social work usually involves some initiative on the part of the client in locating the service. Even when a referral is made (as the pastor did in our example), the client must initiate contact. The client comes to the practitioner by appointment, and most interviews take place in an office. This service pattern follows the policy of most professionals and semi-professionals. The customer, client, or patient goes to the practitioner and is served individually on a regular basis. Only in rare cases does any service come to the consumer. Unless one is dealing with an emergency or repair of a large appliance like a furnace, everything comes into the shop. The use of house calls, either by a physician or by the television repair service, is discouraged by staggering charges. In an older day, the physician went to the patient, the "law merchant," as early attorneys were called, was available in the marketplace, and the social worker made home visits.

   While a slight variation might occur in an agency primarily engaged in serving groups, the process would not be radically different. Had Mr. X gone to a group-serving agency, he might well have had an individual interview, then be referred to a group which would meet on some kind of a schedule. In effect, each group would be treated as a case.

2. *A determination shall be made of the appropriateness of the service requested.*

   When a social worker talks to a client, a decision must be made about whether or not the client meets some criterion for eligibility for an agency's service. The agency has some kind of mission: it may be protective services, counseling, or homemaker services. The service delivery world is specialized, and clients must be eligible in some sense in order to receive the service. "Eligibility" can be understood from a number of angles. In one agency, a client is eligible if he or she is poor and falls below a certain income limit. In another agency, eligibility rests on whether or not the client displays certain problems or symptoms. In still another, one would be eligible because he or she had a marital difficulty. In any case, the determination that a need exists is an essential condition of the service. One must be part of a target group.

While those in social work would like to think in terms of prevention, the plain fact is that the service delivery system is attuned to a remedial approach. The same is generally true of other professions and technologies. For instance, while medicine has tried very hard to get people to think of health maintenance, most people do not relate to health professionals when they are well. In another area, only the most sophisticated consult an attorney to avoid legal problems. Prevention may not really be possible in most fields except in a very limited sense.

3. *Evaluation and interventive action (or diagnosis and treatment, if the reader prefers) should be based on an accurate understanding of the client or patient as revealed in the case history.*

As the social worker and the client spend time together, a good deal of material will accumulate about the client's problem. This probably will include how the problem has developed, how it manifests itself, some inferences of the cause of the difficulty, and what the client has done about the problem. This material is intended as the basis for deciding how the case should be handled. In most treatment approaches, some kind of ongoing record of all of this is kept. While there may be great variety in the material (for example, a psychosocially oriented social worker's data may differ from that gathered by a behaviorally oriented worker), it will all find its way into a more or less stylized case record. Entries will also be made, as time progresses, on any changes that take place.

4. *Treatment consists of a series of fifty-minute sessions that will continue at appropriate intervals until client and worker agree that treatment goals have been met.*

Regardless of the treatment orientation of the social worker, a more or less common policy can be discerned. Few social agencies deviate from the standard fifty-minute hour. The weekly appointment has become traditional for clients that are involved in any intensive treatment process. This policy is followed by both publicly supported and privately supported agencies for both individuals and groups (although groups may have longer sessions). Public agencies whose load is too heavy to actually see clients weekly would follow this policy if they could.

It would be possible to extract more policies from the service delivery act, but these will suffice to show the direction of the discussion. It is important to remember that we are not looking at the service delivery process with an intent to judge one treatment method over another. Our interest is limited to the policy issues that guide the provision of any or all treatment approaches. These common patterns constitute social welfare policy even though social workers do not always explicitly acknowledge them as such.

The Office-Practice Model. If we could put a name to the constellation of policies that we have extracted from the service delivery example that we used above, it might be best considered as the "office-practice" approach. The question then becomes, "How good or how desirable a service delivery policy is the office-practice model?" We could proceed to answer this question by applying our policy analysis approach to this model. However, policy analysis and the formulation of alternatives makes the most sense when done on a comparative basis. As an exercise, we will compare the office-practice policy of service delivery with what we will call the "drop-in" counseling model. Bear in mind that we are not espousing any particular style of service delivery, but are trying to show how to do policy analysis.

The Drop-in Model. Suppose that you are on the staff of the agency consulted by Mr. X for his marital difficulty. At a staff meeting, the question is raised about the efficiency of your service policy. Is "office-practice" the most desirable service delivery approach? A small group of the staff offers to look into the problem. They come up with a proposal. Suppose that the agency proceeds on the assumption that the need for counseling service is to be determined by the client and that the agency will attempt to provide service on the schedule most convenient to the client. Instead of a formal appointment schedule, the agency posts the hours that it will be open, and the clients drop in for service when the need arises. Treatment consists of an informal process rather like an ongoing crap game. The clients can come in whenever they like and talk to a social worker. The clients decide when they have had enough and come and go whenever the agency doors are open. They may ask to see a social worker alone if they wish, or they may join in a free floating group session if it meets their needs. If a client requests a specific resource, the social worker will refer the person to that specialized service.

Analysis of the Office-Practice and Drop-in Models

Now that we have identified a "standard" policy and an alternative, we can proceed to analyze the two with a view to making a policy decision. Of course, since this is a hypothetical situation, our analysis is not as precise as it would be if we were actually analyzing a policy decision in a real agency.

1. *Is the policy compatible with contemporary "style"?*

   The office-practice model of service delivery is compatible with contemporary style. In many areas of their lives, Americans receive services based on the office-practice model. Consider the example of the automobile repair service. The customer brings in the vehicle because he or she is dissatisfied with its performance. The service manager listens to the engine, asks some questions about the automobile's performance and writes down the symptoms. He or she then decides if the needed repairs can be made in the shop or if more specialized work needs to be done elsewhere. A record is kept of the work done as "treatment" is undertaken.

Periodic maintenance at regular intervals may be suggested in order to ensure optimum functioning. This example is not intended to compare people with automobiles or service managers with social workers. The point is that people in technological societies are accustomed to obtaining services this way. There is no clash with contemporary style.

On the other hand, the drop-in approach is gaining in popularity. Crisis clinics, drug abuse centers, and some services to the aging are structured to take advantage of our more informal life-style. Note the dramatic change in the retail grocery business that has occurred since World War II. Very few people now shop in a grocery store where one waits to see a clerk who fills individual orders! In a sense, the supermarket concept (which is now extended to hardware, notions, and clothing) is the largest drop-in service in the country.

Even professionals have learned to accommodate to customer demand. There are now places where one can buy various kinds of insurance, stocks, and bonds in shopping malls. There are dental clinics where one can go without appointment and free-standing emergency medical clinics open at convenient times.

Therefore, our agency planning committee could agree that the drop-in approach fits contemporary life-style as well as or better than an office-practice approach.

2. *Is the policy compatible with important and enduring cultural values, particularly equity, fairness, and justice?*

The problem with the traditional office-practice approach, as we see it, is that it is difficult for many potential consumers to get to the service if it is confined to the traditional eight to five schedule. Only those who are unemployed and those who can afford to take time off from work can use the service. Also, personal troubles do not always conform to appointment schedules. For the kinds of problems that social workers handle best, a more flexible approach makes sense. Surely, it would be equitable to provide for services when the clientele could take advantage of it. The traditional system of offering a fifty minute appointment at some time in the future may be outdated and unresponsive to human need. As with a toothache, fifteen minutes now may do a lot more good than an hour two weeks from now. As there have been changes in American style, there have been changes in the way Americans value services. The drop-in approach appeals to the values of efficiency and practicality, material comfort, freedom, and individuality.

3. *Is the policy compatible with social work's professional value and ethical system?*

There is nothing in the National Association of Social Workers' code of ethics that would invalidate either the office-practice or the drop-in approach. However, social workers have a historical tradition of carrying service to people "where they are" geographically and psychologically. If consumers are demanding services at times and in places more convenient to their life-styles, then social work should try to accommodate them.

4. *Is the policy acceptable to those in formal decision-making positions?*

In this case, the formal decision-making body is probably an agency board of directors or a state department. Since we are talking hypothetically, it is impossible to answer this question. In the real world, it would be necessary to propose this change in policy to the decision-making body and make a case for it, at least on a trial basis. There are some logistical problems having to do with the hours the agency was open, availability of clerical staff, and maintenance. If these problems could be solved, we see no obvious objection that could be made.

5. *Does the policy satisfy relevant interest groups?*

When an agency considers a policy change, there are a number of groups other than the staff that must be considered. Would the present clientele of the agency continue to use the agency's services if the delivery system were changed? What would be the concerns of the neighbors of the agency if it were to be open say from eight in the morning until midnight? Would contributors and volunteers react negatively? Would the significant people in the community believe that the appropriate service needs are being met? If satisfactory answers to these questions were obtained, the drop-in approach would be viable. If there were serious objections, it would be an uphill battle.

6. *Is the policy based on knowledge that has been tested?*

Obviously, the office-practice approach has been tested over time and it works. The question is whether or not the drop-in approach would work better. In the applications in which it has been tried, the drop-in approach has proved a useful way of delivering service.

7. *Is the policy workable in the real world?*

Of course, since it has been used in a number of applications as we have mentioned above. There is an obvious problem in using a drop-in approach to counseling. How can continuity be assured? That is, suppose that a couple is actively engaged in a disagreement. They decide to go to a drop-in counseling center, just as they might go to a drop-in medical clinic for medical care. They arrive at the center and are seen by social worker A. Social worker A helps them deal with the immediate problem, but recognizes with the couple that further sessions would be profitable. When are they seen for a further conference and can it be assured that worker A will see them? This would not seem to be an insurmountable problem, but they would have to come back when worker A is on duty or accept that if they came back at some other time, they might have to talk to worker B.

A second practical problem arises. Agencies using the old office-practice approach could schedule clients or patients in such a way that they had virtual anonymity. The junior author of this book recalls once having to juggle appointments for four people so that they would not encounter each other in the waiting room. A drop-in service might make this kind of maneuvering a bit difficult.

Another practical problem relates to the location of some agencies. While many are accessible, we know of a number of offices that are not. Examples that come to mind include a mental health clinic in an older residential neighborhood that is housed in a comfortable 19th century mansion. Parking is very difficult, and clients often must leave their cars several blocks away. In another case, an excellent family counseling agency is in a downtown office building. This agency is reachable by public transportation, but suitable parking is very expensive and inconveniently located for the kind of service delivery system that we are proposing. It is inconvenient enough for the office-practice model. We think that it might be worthwhile for agencies to consider the possibility of locating branch offices in readily accessible places, including shopping malls. Some public agencies have located outreach offices in neighborhoods with a high concentration of clients, but continue to cling to traditional fifty-minute hours by appointment. Not all clients require fifty minutes, and, as we have argued, appointments are not always a functional idea with many clients.

In short, we think that a drop-in social work service is workable if social workers are willing to be flexible. Some agencies have been operating on this basis for years and we think that more ought to try it.

8. *Does the policy create few problems for both the public and the intended beneficiaries?*

We can see no problems in using the drop-in policy other than those that we have already mentioned above under other questions. Certainly there are no obvious hardships to anyone in the client category. The only problems that we can anticipate are essentially mechanical, and they could all be worked out, given a constructive attitude on the part of staff and administration.

9. *Is the policy effective?*

In those applications where drop-in service has been tried, it has enabled the consumer to obtain more convenient service. Remember that in this case, we are not considering whether or not a given *treatment* approach is effective. We are interested in whether or not a given *ser-*

vice delivery approach results in reaching the people for whom it is intended. Obviously, a pilot study is needed.

10. *Will the programs derived from the policy be efficient?*

As in the previous question, it would be necessary to actually try out a drop-in approach and see if it resulted in more service for less cost. Clearly, if it were much more expensive and saw fewer people, it would not have an efficiency advantage over the office-practice approach.

What Policy Decision Should Be Reached?

This hypothetical run-through is of limited value because it is only an example. In the real world there would be some firmer answers. From the sketch that we have provided, it can be seen that the application of our policy analysis scheme has provided a basis for dealing with a policy choice even when some of the inputs are nonrational (for example, questions of style and values). We have, at least, raised some of the right questions that would have to be answered in contemplating a policy change.

While in a number of programmatic areas of social welfare there are many alternatives that have been proposed, there are relatively fewer innovations in service delivery policy. The major arguments center around the effectiveness of clinical methods rather than service delivery modes. We think that clinicians ought to expand their concerns to service delivery. While we would not recommend that every agency immediately initiate a drop-in policy, we do think that it is time to begin to think innovatively about how to provide services in places and at times that are convenient to the client. We also think that agencies should be flexible to client needs, and less formalistic about the practical aspects of getting services to the clientele.

Some Larger Service Delivery Questions

A number of service delivery policy questions can (and should) be submitted to policy analysis. In the absence of adequate attention to policy, it is our impression that most service policies are set by trial and error, tradition, and a certain amount of faddishness. This is unsound. It is every bit as important for service delivery to be based on good policy as it is for it to be based on good clinical method.

Gilbert and Specht, in their book *Dimensions of Social Welfare Policy*, have summarized the policy effects of current social service delivery networks:

> In the heat of controversy, the criticism of service-delivery intensifies. Such criticism tends to focus upon the characteristic failings of local service delivery systems which include *fragmentation, discontinuity, unaccountability, and inaccessibility.*[10]

Given these criticisms, it follows that "the ideal service-delivery system is one in which services are *integrated, continuous, accessible, and account-*

able.[11] The difficulty is that this is not a simple choice. Gilbert and Specht point out that "taken separately each of these ideal elements strains against one or more of the others."[12]

Gilbert and Specht summarize the policy choices as they see them:

1. *Reduce* fragmentation and discontinuity by increasing coordination, opening new channels of communication and referral, and eliminating duplication of services (possibly *increasing* unaccountability and inaccessibility).
2. *Reduce* inaccessibility by creating new means of access to services, and duplicating existing service efforts (possibly *increasing* fragmentation).
3. *Reduce* unaccountability by creating means for clients or consumers to have input into, and increased decision-making authority over, the system (possibly *increasing* fragmentation and discontinuity).[13]

Policy selection based on either the "naive criteria" or the "naive priority" method would miss the complexity that Gilbert and Specht's more sophisticated approach reveals.

Gilbert and Specht have summarized proposals for policy change in the following typology:

A. Strategies to restructure authority for, and control of, policy making
   1. Coordination
   2. Citizen participation
B. Strategies to reorganize the allocation of tasks
   3. Role attachments
   4. Professional disengagement
C. Strategies to alter the composition (i.e., number and types of units of the delivery system)
   5. Specialized access structures
   6. Purposive duplication[14]

In the discussion that follows this typology, Gilbert and Specht engage in an analytical comparison of each alternative within the strategies listed above. We will summarize their main points in the discussion below and intermingle some comments of our own.[15]

Coordination vs. Citizen Participation

There is often very little coordination among social service agencies. It is not unusual to find an individual who is receiving service from several agencies who do not communicate with each other about the case. There is another side to this issue. Agencies may plan new programs that wholly or in part duplicate something already being done. Because there is no coordination in planning, the duplication may waste scarce community resources. There is a corollary in health care when two nearby hospitals both purchase an expensive piece of equipment that is used only half of the working day.

There are two basic ways in which coordination can be brought about. One is through administrative centralization of services, exemplified by the Local

Authority and Social Services Act of 1970 in Britain. This act created Local Authority Social Service Departments which integrated a number of governmental services on the local level. In effect, a number of agencies were combined into one multi-purpose organization under a single administration. While this action will provide better coordinated services, there are two dangers. First, there may be considerable conflict among units, particularly over budgets. Second, the client now has no choice but must use the multi-purpose agency.

A second approach to coordination is the development of neighborhood service centers as has been done in some communities in the United States. This is a federated approach, since each agency retains its own organizational structure while it shares a geographical location in a neighborhood center. Coordination efforts like this are agreements between agencies. They do not necessarily involve any decision by the clientele. The citizen participation movement would involve the inclusion of the clientele in some decision making about service delivery. Some federal programs in the United States have required that citizens be included in the decision-making bodies that operate agencies. In practice, it has been difficult to ensure a broadly based level of citizen participation. Obviously, if citizens actually participate in service delivery planning, then coordination becomes more difficult because there are more interests involved.

Some Comments: First, the above summary does not do justice to Gilbert and Specht's discussion. The reader should consult the original.

We will try to contribute something to the resolution of this dilemma from the viewpoint of our analytical criteria. First of all, it seems to us that citizen participation, despite its failings, is more compatible with contemporary style than an approach wherein all the planning is done by agencies. Consumerism is not a passing fancy, but an idea whose time has clearly come. Americans are weary of solutions "from the top." Consumerism is an important social value and is perceived to be more equitable, fair and just. It is also compatible with the values that social workers espouse in the name of client self-determination. Citizen participation is (theoretically at least) acceptable to those in formal decision-making positions today. We suspect, however, that it is really not as popular as people publicly say that it is. Citizens would no doubt like to have more control over public policy, but entrenched professional groups may really not like the idea any more than physicians or attorneys do. The proliferation of consumer lawsuits suggests that experts and decision makers are likely to be attacked in court when they exceed their authority or fail to fulfill their obligations. Citizen participation may reduce the occasion for lawsuits against service systems. Both approaches have been tried in the real world and both are workable. The major problem with any citizen participation scheme is that decisions are apt to be made very slowly. The relative slowness of decisions is apt to create problems both for the public and the clientele over the short run and efficiency may suffer. Further, it is possible that increased citizen participation in service delivery policy would create some problems, for example, fragmentation and discontinuity. On the other hand, it seems to us that a policy of citizen participation has so much going for it to ensure accessibility of services and accountability that social welfare decision makers at all levels ought to support efforts to improve the quality and quantity of citizen participation rather than to support more efficiency in coordination by professionals.

One can argue that, as a result of citizen participation, more social workers will leave agencies and work on a fee-for-service basis. While middle-class consumers may be the group most likely to use private practitioners, third-party payments may bring the fee-for-service social work within the reach of many. This would enhance the autonomy of the social worker and lead to the decrease of the present semi-professional status of social work. Some kind of voucher payment system could be provided for those unable to pay as is currently done in medicine. Of course, certain public services of a protective nature (child welfare, probation and parole services, and some kinds of mental health services) would have to be continued. This will not threaten professional autonomy any more than the presence of public health services and legal aid threatens medicine and law, provided that the majority of trained social workers are in private practice as other professions are.

Role Attachments vs. Professional Disengagement

Gilbert and Specht here deal with the problem of reallocation of tasks to come to terms with the problem of accessibility. The central idea in the notion of role attachment is that "professionals" have too much social distance between themselves and their clientele. Therefore, the indigenous nonprofessional aide role has been created as a bridge or attachment service for the lower-class client. There are three problems. The poor may end up getting amateurish services. Second, the indigenous aide may not be accepted by the professionals. Third, the indigenous aide will want to become a professional because there is more money and status and will move out of the aide role.

The second policy, professional disengagement, involves simply a turning away by practitioners from traditional agencies to private practice supported by fees from those who can pay and a voucher system for those who cannot. The trouble is, Gilbert and Specht point out, professional disengagement will not turn people who have specialized in some field into generalists. Therefore, accessibility to needed services will not necessarily be enhanced nor will fragmentation be lessened.

Some Comments: Here again, we have oversimplified Gilbert and Specht's careful explication of the issues. It appears that Gilbert and Specht have looked at these two policies from the standpoint of what we have called equity and justice, workability, economic feasibility, and to a lesser extent, efficiency. However, they have been unable to resolve the dilemma.

Of the two policies, a movement toward professional autonomy, subject to consumer control, seems more compatible with contemporary style. With the provision for consumer control, equity, fairness, and justice are better served by the professional who is forced to deal with the public directly. The use of an indigenous professional as a go-between cannot help but emphasize the gulf between client and worker. The autonomous professional idea is compatible with social work's value system, although it is at variance with contemporary practice, since most social workers are employed by governmental and privately sponsored bodies where their autonomy is open to question. The use of indigenous nonprofessionals has always been a source of concern in social work since it tends to be exploitative. The nonprofessional often ends up as little more than a "gopher" (go-for) who occupies a clearly subsidiary position in the operation. Further, the nonprofessionals are usually aware of their "handmaiden" role and frequently come to resent it. The idea of becoming disengaged from agencies is becoming more popular among social workers. There is an increasing number who work in private practice, usually in a private psychiatric clinic, at least on a part time basis. The indigenous nonprofessional cannot really give satisfactory service to the clientele simply because he or she lacks direct access to goods and service. The nonprofessional merely has access to those who have access, and this is not good enough. Clients want to see someone who is in charge. There is little in it for nonprofessionals themselves, as Gilbert and Specht point out, since nonprofessionals usually do not stay in the role. The autonomous professional who must learn to relate to the clientele is probably the better solution.

There is little good research on the comparison between the use of citizen-controlled professionals as opposed to service delivered through nonprofessionals who provide access to professionals. However, the literature seems to indicate that the use of indigenous nonprofessionals has not proven workable on any large scale. As we pointed out above, nonprofessionals become discontented and the service they give is often of uneven quality. Because nonprofessionals have a high turnover rate, their use is not efficient. The autonomous social worker who is forced to come to terms with the clientele in order to earn his or her bread and cheese ought to reduce service problems.

Gilbert and Specht raise two more problems that we have not discussed. They suggest that private social services would not prevent the "private practitioner from imposing his particular brand of service upon the client" and it might tempt the practitioner to continue service in order to collect a fee. Actually, there is nothing to prevent a practitioner from pursuing an unproductive approach under the present system. In a private fee for service system, the practitioner who ignored the needs of clients in favor of an ideological commitment to a particular brand of therapy would be out of business. A narrow focus would not be protected by an agency as is now the case. As for the fee question, only the gullible would continue to pay a fee for a service that was doing no good.

We think that the problem of role allocation would be best served by the organization of service professionals into a fee-for-service group practice, again excepting those professionals employed in protective services. Eligibility determination, for those concrete services where needs must be determined by law, is an administrative function and should be handled by management-oriented people. Human service tasks should be handled by persons trained in human service. Rather than depending on indigenous nonprofessional aides, it is more productive to educate professionals who are able to relate to a wide range of clientele through training and experience. If the members of the service profession were trained in specialties, this would speak to the problem of access and continuity of service. The client would not have to hunt for, say, a skilled family counselor since there would be one or more in the group. The same would be true of other specialties, not unlike a modern medical or dental clinic which houses several subdisciplines. With a well-run group practice, the client would have access to a skilled professional with expertise in the area of the problem and could continue to see that professional over time. If additional expertise were needed, it could be obtained in the same group without any need for the client to find his or her way through a maze of agencies spread out over a large geographical area.

Specialized Access Structure vs. Purposive Duplication

With this issue, Gilbert and Specht deal with the problem of fragmentation, inaccessibility, and discontinuity of service. They see two current ways of handling the problem. One is the information and referral service, which performs a sorting and brokering function. The other approach is what they call purposive duplication, or, more plainly, a duplication of services on purpose. Information and referral services, say Gilbert and Specht, only add to fragmentation of service. An information and referral agency performs little service beyond what the title implies. Thus, it becomes another step that the client must take before finding where to go with the problem for which he or she seeks help. The duplication of services, say Gilbert and Specht, is "enormously expensive."

Some Comments: As one might suspect, we favor purposive duplication. It better fits contemporary style in that most services in other areas of human life in the United States and the Western world are duplicative. One may shop in a number of grocery stores, and in most towns there is more than one garage. Only in very remote areas does anyone have a monopoly on any kind of service, and even in these cases, some options exist. Gilbert and Specht make a distinction between two forms of purposive duplication—competition and separatism. Competitive services increase choice and keep competitors on their toes. Separate services do not seek to enter into competition with existing services, but seek to provide an alternative for disadvantaged groups that cannot or do not care to use existing services. Either format fits contemporary style. It is analogous to, say, the clothing industry. One can purchase off-the-rack or go to specialty shops that have unique (but not always expensive) fashions for particular groups of customers.

Equity, fairness, and justice are more nearly served by purposive duplication if there are genuinely competitive services. Purposive duplication is compatible with social work values as well as those of the larger society. Duplication is politically acceptable to formal decision-making groups. It is flexible enough to satisfy most interest groups. Certainly, purposive duplication has been tested in many areas of modern life. It is clearly workable and would create few problems for either the public or the intended beneficiaries. Genuine competition is cost effective and should motivate social workers to be efficient. Of course, competition may mean that inefficient and ineffective services would go out of business, but we frankly think that this is entirely appropriate. The alternative is to maintain services that are inefficient and ineffective just because they have always been there. This is not defensible. No agency, service, or social work practitioner should have a unilateral right to continue when benefits do not accrue to the consumer. Competing services have a better chance of efficiency than monolithic services that are the only game in town. Access services may only add another screen between the client and service and may make service delivery problems worse. The duplication of services on purpose would put all social workers on the firing line with no artificial screen.

Conclusion

This has turned out to be a rather radical chapter. It will help for us to summarize where we are in order to effect some closure. Obviously, we think that service delivery policy needs a good shaking up. In our opinion, service deliverers have made the most conservative and least risky choices possible. There is some danger, we believe, that service delivery can slip backward thirty years unless some new elements are considered. We think that this consideration can best be helped by raising questions about our present practices through the application of our policy analysis model, however imperfect it may be.

If we take seriously Gilbert and Specht's contention that fragmentation, discontinuity, unaccountability, and inaccessibility are the major problems in service delivery, we think that one is led into consideration of some radical reforms. It is certain that more of the same will only intensify the problems. It appears to us that a different delivery system is worth thinking about. We recognize that the whole delivery system would not change overnight, even if we could prove our case absolutely. We do think that some innovation is in order.

It seems to us that the innovation with the best chance of success is the autonomous group of specialized social workers who earn their living by fees. This kind of service delivery system would maximize citizen participation because the citizen would have direct participation in the system by choosing to whom to pay a fee and from whom to accept service. This approach would result in genuine professionalization of social work, since social workers would finally have control over their own practice and not be responsible to a board of directors who may or may not be empathic toward the social worker's aims. There would still be accountability, but one would have to be accountable to the client who is, after all, the most important person. If competition is good for physicians, grocery stores, and brokerage firms, it is good for social workers.

This innovation is not without its dangers. We think that Gilbert and Specht's recognition of them is pertinent. Clearly, they are factors to be watched. We take the position that these dangers are preferable to the present tendencies in social welfare service delivery. Some change is involved, but there is a considerable drift toward private practice among skilled clinicians now. Certain precautions must be observed. Protective services, as we have noted, will have to be continued. Eligibility for certain benefits will remain, but eligibility determination can be handled by persons trained to do so. Most services of this type are now staffed by persons not specifically educated to provide counseling and treatment services. Unfortunately, they are not always trained in the administration of benefits, either. Specific training for the administration of benefits would certainly result in improved benefit administration. Gradually, we would see persons trained in counseling, therapy, group methods, and even policy and planning services moving to private practice. Fees, vouchers, prepaid services and third-party payments would promote citizen participation and a measure of consumer control over the nature and quality of service. Peer review (instead of administrative supervision) could be built in for additional quality control. All these changes would be more compatible with our criteria than the present system where the consumer has very little to say about services that affect his or her life. Professional disengagement from traditional agencies and governmental services would render social workers truly autonomous and even increase the status of those who remained in protective services. A physician is still respected as a practitioner of an art, even when he or she works for a governmental body. The independence of physicians in general supports this respect. Finally, the existence of more than one firm of social workers would mean competition, but would allow for separation of distinctive and particular services. We would hope that some social workers would be motivated to offer their services on a drop-in basis at the nearest shopping mall, right next to the dental clinic and the discount broker's office!

We realize that what we propose is a dramatic change. We think that it would work to the benefit of clients and their families. We believe that it represents a genuinely professionalized social service delivery system. It is something to think about.

REFERENCES

1. James K. Whittaker, *Social Treatment* (Chicago: Aldine, 1974), Ch. 1.
2. *Ibid.,* p. 7.
3. William Schwartz, "Private Troubles and Public Issues: One Social Work Job or Two?" in Robert W. Klenk and Robert M. Ryan, *The Practice of Social Work,* 2nd ed. (Belmont, Calif.: Wadsworth, 1974), p. 97.
4. Nathan Glazer, "The Social Policy of the Reagan Administration: a Review," *The Public Interest,* 75 (Spring 1984), pp. 76–98.
5. Whittaker, *op. cit.,* p. 11.

6. *Ibid.*, p. 14.
7. *Ibid.*, p. 17.
8. *Ibid.*, p. 19.
9. David C. Phillips, "The Swing Toward Clinical Practice," *Social Work*, Vol. 20, No. 1 (January 1975), pp. 61–63.
10. Neil Gilbert and Harry Specht, *Dimensions of Social Welfare Policy* (Englewood Cliffs, N.J.: Prentice-Hall, 1974), p. 109.
11. *Ibid.*, p. 110.
12. *Ibid.*
13. *Ibid.*, pp. 110–111.
14. *Ibid.*, p. 111.
15. This material is summarized from Gilbert and Specht, pp. 111–123.

QUESTIONS FOR DISCUSSION

1. Is the "drop-in" model adaptable to public welfare practice?

2. Discuss the question of whether or not social workers should concentrate on social reform or individual treatment.

3. Can one change service delivery policy from within an agency? How?

4. Could social welfare agencies be restructured in some way to deal with interrelated social problems?

5. Would the creation of multiservice centers really be a change in service delivery policy? In what way?

6. Should social work practice become more "customer oriented" as the authors advocate?

7. How do you react to the idea of a service delivery system whose main component is fee-for-service group social work practice? Do you consider this "real" social work?

SUGGESTED PROJECTS

1. List several policy issues, other than the ones in the text, that affect the delivery of social work services.

2. Select an alternative to one of the above and analyze its probable success using the policy analysis model outlined in this book.

3. Invite a practicing social worker to class to discuss the relation of social policy to social work practice.

4. Design your own innovative service system. Use the analysis model presented in this book as your guide.

FOR FURTHER READING

Neil Gilbert and Harry Specht. *Dimensions of Social Welfare Policy.* Englewood Cliffs, N.J.: Prentice-Hall, 1974. A scholarly treatment of social policy and the social service delivery system. See especially Chapter 5, "The Structure of the Delivery System."

———. *The Emergence of Social Welfare and Social Work.* Itasca, Ill.: F.E. Peacock, 1976. A book of readings that relates social work and social services to a policy background.

Alfred J. Kahn. *Shaping the New Social Work.* New York: Columbia University Press, 1973. A collection of essays on the impact of social policy on practice concerns. It is now possible to judge the accuracy of some of the gloomy predictions it made over ten years ago.

Arnold M. Levin. "Private Practice is Alive and Well," *Social Work,* Vol. 21, No. 5 (September 1976). Still very ably states the case for the place of private practice in social work.

Social Work, Vol. 26, No. 1 (January 1981). Second special issue on conceptual frameworks. A collection of invited papers on the future of social work. See especially the articles on social work practice.

Robert O. Washington and Beverly Toomey, eds. *Social Work in the 1980's.* Davis, Calif.: International Dialogue Press, 1982. A volume of papers looking to the future of social work during this decade. Some of the articles may be more hopeful than the situation may justify.

Part III

Social Action, Planning, and Administration: Some Bridges from Policy

The first three of the four chapters in this unit introduce the fields of social action, planning, and social administration. These chapters are intended to serve as bridges from social welfare policy analysis and formulation to the implementation of policy. Each chapter is, of course, only a kind of primer, since these are complex subjects. We assume that students in schools of social work will take courses in these subjects after they have completed this course. Readers who are not in formal educational settings will find these chapters a general outline that will suggest further directions for independent study.

We have added a final speculative chapter to this unit in which we try to forecast the trends that we think will be followed in the next few years. The reader is encouraged to write his or her own final chapter, since to be able to do so is the major gain that we hope for from this book.

9

Influencing Decision Making
in Public Policy

THE ANALYSIS AND FORMULATION OF ALTERNATIVE social welfare policies remain academic exercises unless they lead to change in official public policy. This chapter deals, in broad outline, with the connections between policy formulation and the decision-making process.

How Are Policy Decisions Made?

It is oversimple to say that public policy is made by law, although that may be technically correct. We prefer to express it this way: Policy is made through a decision-making process. Enactment of law, the rendering of judicial decisions, and/or the issuance of administrative guidelines are outcomes of the policy process. Here we want to address some concerns about how those decisions are made.

It is only possible in one chapter to sketch the influence process. Our remarks will be general and will constitute a guide or outline, not a comprehensive picture.

The Nature of Power

We have the "gut feeling" that many social workers misunderstand the nature of power and its role in decision making, so we want to begin with our understanding of the concept. Power is the ability to persuade.[1] The aim of using power is to get one decision made over another.

This is not the way that many people think of power. We have all heard people say, "You can make changes. You have the power to do it!" Persons making this statement apparently think that changes can be made if only the right person issues the orders or if the right body makes a decision. The exercise of power is simply not this easy. What actually happens is that people only accept new ideas when it is in their best interests to do so or when they have no other choice. They do not accept new ideas because it is in someone else's best interest and of no benefit to the decision maker. Franklin D. Roosevelt could not have inspired the changes in the United States in the 1930s if the American people had not believed that there was something in it for them and found themselves in fundamental agreement with his policies. What is often regarded as charisma is, in fact, the ability of a leader to ascertain the direction of the general will.

Force is not enough to get people to do something over time. While it may work over the short run, force is resented and tends to breed resistance. Persuasion, on the other hand, is something other than mere force. Richard Neustadt, in his highly regarded study of presidential power, argues that persuasion is contingent upon bargaining and reciprocity.[2] A can persuade B if A controls some important part of B's future. Both have something to trade. In Neustadt's words, "Influence derives from bargaining advantages; power is a give-and-take."[3]

This view of power may take some getting used to. Neustadt quotes President Harry Truman: "I sit here all day trying to persuade people to do the things they ought to have sense enough to do without my persuading them. . . . That's all the powers of the President amount to."[4] Mr. Truman's frustration captures the problem. The exercise of power is not just issuing orders, not just the perquisite of a position, not just a legal responsibility, and not just charisma, although each of these things enters into the picture. Persuasion is also more than just simple arm-twisting. It is a matter of convincing people that what they are asked to do is in their best interest and should be done.

The Decision-Making Process

With the above argument in mind, consider some common models of decision making that have been identified. Lawrence D. Mann has provided a useful summary which we have followed.[5] The reader should study Mann's article in order to get the full discussion.

- ## The "Traditional" Model

    A group of citizens, motivated by public interest, form a planning group. They engage a planner, make decisions by logic and rationality, and submit a benevolent plan that is untainted by politics.

Mann suggests that such plans "gather more dust than sentiment." He argues that this is an incredibly naive view of the decision-making process. In the real world citizens are seldom benevolently disinterested, and plans are not made on the basis of nonpolitical rationality.

- ## The "Power Pyramid" Model

    A few industrialists and businessmen, aided by tame politicians, make all decisions and enforce them on those lower down in the social structure.

This model is easily recognizable as being rooted in the work of Floyd Hunter.[6] Many social workers readily accept this view. Political scientists have been highly critical of the model's simplicity. Mann, following the critique of Herbert Kaufman and Victor Jones, agrees that Hunter assumed that there was a power elite before he looked for it and that the model is "just too pat to have occurred in the real world."

- ## The Yale Polyarchic Power Model

This approach is based on the work of Robert Dahl and his associates at Yale:

> The fundamental idea is that different issues each have a "distinct leadership pattern with very little overlap between issue areas." Or, to put it simply, every issue has a different set of decision makers.

- ## The Qualified "Diffused Influence" Model

This is similar to the "Yale" model described above. The difference is that in this model, influence is even more diffuse. Following the ideas of William L. C. Wheaton, Mann says:

> Influence is spread among a multiplicity of interest groups that change in size and importance over time. Coalitions or constellations of these groups constantly form and reform, depending upon the issue. Since communication is not constant, the effectiveness of the decision-making process is varied.

This model has a great deal of appeal when one looks at reality (which is after all the acid test of an explanatory model). Unless one has become a true believer in an alternative model (and hence a zealot), there is a certain appeal in the notion of a pluralist decision-making process that is open to inputs from various interest groups and coalitions. The model suggests that decisions are not just "locked up" by elites but can be affected by consumers and their advocates.

- ## The "Decision Process" Model

Based upon the work of Roscoe Martin and Frank Munger, Peter Rossi, and others, this model suggests:

> Decision making should not be viewed in structural or pattern terms at all, but as a process. This is a systems approach which sees decision making as a flow in which the final decision is a product of a series of interactions between or among various systems that have an interest in the decision.

Social workers should not have trouble understanding this view of decision making, because it is akin to the notion of visualizing social casework, group work, or community organizations as processes. The client (or group, neighborhood, community) and the social worker start at one point, move through phases of interactional change, and emerge at some future point which is different from the initial one. In other words, decisions are not all of a piece, but are outcomes of prior decisions which are related to still prior decisions.

It is this view that has influenced our approach to social policy analysis and formulation. Obviously, one's view of decision making is crucial to how one operates in the social action arena. If, for example, one believes that decisions are made by a static power elite, then strategy is pretty much limited to either "lick'em or join'em." That is, one either beats the power structure in some kind of contest situation or infiltrates them and takes over the decision-making process. The danger of this view, of course, is that it rests on the deceptive notion that power is a possession and can be used at will—a notion that we have rejected earlier in our argument.

Acting on the notion that decision making is a flow or process, we will discuss some tactical issues and then return to some observations about when these tactics can be used to influence decision making.

The Tactics of Influence

The social worker who is interested in influencing the adoption of one policy over another has a considerable number of approaches from which to choose. We are following Arnold Panitch's lead in this discussion, but have departed from him somewhat.[7] He should not be held accountable for our digressions.

We have arranged these tactics in a rough order of the intensity of involvement and risk. That is, the further down the list one goes, the more time and energy will be expended and the greater the risk to one's safety. This does not mean that any of these tactics is safe, because there is always the possibility that danger can escalate out of proportion to one's activities in any change-oriented process.

The Case Conference. It is possible for policy issues to be addressed as an outgrowth of a single case. An individual (or group or neighborhood association) may not be receiving adequate service. The place to try to get policy change is through a conference that includes the agencies that logically should be offering the service. Even in large federal programs, changes have been made as the result of recognizing that what is dysfunctional for one client may be dysfunctional for many.

Fact-Gathering. Here again, this does not sound like a tactic at first hearing. However, the social worker interested in social policy change should maximize his or her role as a source of information at stages in the decision-making process. Although facts by themselves seldom persuade anybody, they are useful in ordering priorities, supporting points of view, and defending against opposing viewpoints. Very simply, having the right information in a form that can be used properly gives one leverage and influence for change. Knowledge can be persuasive when it is used by the right people at the appropriate time and place.

Position-Taking. When a group wishing to make a change takes a position by issuing a statement or a report, they have gone on public record as a participant (at some level at least) in a change process. Taking a position draws the lines for the contest. It clarifies one's own objectives and provides a point of identification. The influence generated from taking a position depends upon the importance of the one taking the position. While it is sometimes possible to influence change by issuing a position statement, this act is usually not enough by itself. It is, however, an important step in gaining recognition and legitimacy on the issue.

Committee Work. At some point in the policy change process, those committed to an alternative have the opportunity to make inputs to study and planning committees. The knowledgeable social worker probably has, by this stage, some direct experience with the policy problem, has made some kind of study of the problem, and has a position on the alternative that represents a change toward more effective policy. Committees, whether they be local, state, or national in scope, are a step in the decision-making process. We do not think that many important decisions are made in formal committee meetings. However, by providing a forum for the public discussion of ideas, committees of various kinds serve to publicize potential alternatives and get them into the decision-making process. Social workers can serve on such committees or act as consultants to committees on which they are not eligible to serve as regular members.

Petitions. Many organizations committed to social change and/or policy change engage in petitioning. This process serves to proclaim public support (if the petitioners are perceived as important or threatening) for a policy alternative. It informs decision makers that there are people "out there" who have a stake in the decision. Occasionally a petition is effective, but it is usually not enough by itself. Petitioning must be seen as just one step in the influence process.

Media Campaigns. The use of radio, television, and newspapers can be an important part of the policy change process. Again, publicity, stories, and pictures bring issues to public attention. They help create a climate in which change is possible through the mobilization of public opinion. Although "public opinion" is a vague and often elusive concept, it is quite clear that on key issues, public support (or at least public acquiescence) has been of great value. The passage of Medicare legislation in the 1960s certainly owed something to the presidential use of the television medium.

Expert Testimony. When a policy alternative has been around long enough to be "seasoned" (and we cannot give a definite time limit for this seasoning process) and if it is deemed by decision makers to have merit, it will move into a formal consideration process. Legislative bodies (boards, city or community councils, and legislative committees) will conduct hearings. Social workers are often in a position to give expert testimony on the feasibility and desirability of the alternative. While no legislative body would adopt a policy simply because a social worker said it was good, inputs from social workers and their allies may be quite valuable.

Lobbying. More is required than having a good proposal that has received wide public support for policy to be changed. As we have repeatedly said in this context, there are a number of factors that bear upon policy decisions. Assuming that the policy is one that meets the tests that good policy should meet, it still needs to be sold. Here is where the going begins to get a bit rough. A determined group must be prepared to spend a lot of time selling their proposal to a decision-making body. Formally, this involves lobbying— but it may not mean lobbying with official public figures. It may involve direct selling to those to whom the public official will listen. This takes time, money, and work. Social workers may be in a position to do their own lobbying, but they often hire the services of a professional lobbyist.

Part of the lobbying process may involve the building of a coalition. Social workers have found it difficult to enter into cooperative influence efforts. In the past few years there has been a renewed interest in the coalition as a tactical entity.[8] Social workers can gain more leverage if they are able to find other groups with common concerns on an issue. A large enough coalition may be able to swing an election. It is most effective if an interest group can elect their own representative. Teachers' organizations have been especially adept in getting legislators elected from the ranks of teachers themselves. Since social workers are not as large a group as are teachers, it is unlikely that they will be able to elect people to decision-making bodies without a good deal of help. The coalition provides a base for a wider appeal, making possible the election of social workers or those who will support social workers' goals. The coalition has other uses too, particularly in bargaining.

Bargaining. A few years ago, Brager and Jorrin wrote what we believe to be a definitive discussion of bargaining.[9] There are some underlying assumptions to the bargaining process. First, it is assumed that the parties want to reach some accommodation. Both sides may not get exactly what they want, but there is the expectation that a resolution of differences is preferable to continued discomfort. A second assumption is that both sides have something to trade.

Initially, it is clear that those who are maintaining the current state of affairs have the superior bargaining position. They are in office and consequently are better organized and command more resources. However, as Brager and Jorrin point out, there are points of leverage that can be turned to the advantage of a change-oriented group. Most establishments do not want their public images tarnished. They do not want to be involved in lawsuits and "fair hearing" procedures. They do not want to be seen as ogres or to be personally embarrassed. In short, those who support the current policy—whatever it is—are vulnerable, particularly when the policy could be unfair, unfeeling, or embarrassing in its application.

A change-oriented group has something to trade. They can offer peace and quiet along with other social rewards that appeal to the public and private image of those who make decisions. However, the relatively lesser amount of influence possessed by those who want to see changes means that they have to be highly committed and willing to take risks.

The challengers will be in the position of making demands. There are three important points made by Brager and Jorrin about the process:

1. Making extreme demands seems to lessen the disadvantage of the more powerless group in initiating action. The initial demands may be unrealistic so that the real beginning is made by the establishment that replies. In effect, the opponents appear to be the real initiators of change.

2. Making extreme demands allows some testing and some give and take to occur. One can always reduce demands, but can seldom expand them.

3. Demands define the limits of trading. They are maximum positions that cannot be exceeded.

Some community groups (and some national movements) produce a whole "laundry list" of demands. Brager and Jorrin suggest that it might be more effective to keep to one or two basic demands with some embellishments for trading purposes.

Should pressure groups focus on the problem to which policy changes are to be addressed? Or should they present their own proposal? We are assuming that most groups entering into bargaining have a policy alternative. On the other hand, Brager and Jorrin point out that there are strategic advantages in forcing the opponent to make all the moves. We acknowledge this, but would prefer to suggest a firm proposal. Brager and Jorrin suggest that offering a proposal demonstrates commitment and seriousness of purpose.

In any case, the willingness and the ability to negotiate with establishments of various kinds is an important tool of those who would change social policy. Consumers may have more power than they suppose, particularly if they have built an effective coalition.

Demonstrations. The mass demonstration is still a technique to be considered even though it has suffered from overuse in the past ten years. Obviously, there is considerable risk involved in this strategy. There is the danger of violence and of reprisals on the job. However, if the issue is important enough and a change-oriented group believes that the resulting publicity will enhance their ability to influence decision making, they may want to organize a public demonstration. We have some reservations about organizing client groups for mass demonstrations. It seems very important to us that any clients who participate in a public demonstration know that they are taking a risk. It should be obvious that a professional who mounts a campaign of policy change should not use clients to further personal ambition.

Class-Action Suits. Policy changes can be initiated by legal action. In recent years we have seen the desegregation of southern schools and changes in women's rights begun as the result of judicial decisions. The class-action suit, in which a suit may be brought on behalf of a group of people who have similar situations, has recently become a powerful legal weapon. The limitation on pursuing policy change through legal action is that the issue must ultimately rest on a constitutional ground. Suits are expensive and time consuming. Persons entering the legal arena must be prepared for considerable struggle and a certain amount of adversity. Nevertheless, *where grounds exist,* judicial decisions are a fairly certain way of changing inequitable or unjust policy.

Disruptive Tactics. The most dangerous tactic that can be used by a change-oriented group involves disrupting the operation of an organization or political body. By disruptive, we refer to something more active than a demonstration or vigil. Harry Specht, who has written on this topic, includes these milder forms of protest.[10] We are using the term to mean actual disruption: strikes, boycotts, sit-ins, and civil disobedience. The object of these tactics is to shut down the operation so that it can no longer function as it normally would. The danger, as Specht points out, is that disruption may allow one's opponents to change the issue from the policy under consideration to that of the "rabble" in the streets. Obviously, those who are really promoting a policy (rather than taking an "ego trip") should not use this strategy if there is any danger of the issue becoming lost. The strike and the boycott would seem to be the effective choices (where they are applicable) simply because they hit pocketbooks quicker.

We have not included insurrection in our list of tactics. There are two reasons. First, we are talking about change rather than destruction. Second, and we believe Specht would agree with us, insurrection is uncertain and can lead to fascism. We continue to believe in the fundamental health of this society, although we recognize the need for change. We do not think that insurrection is a viable strategy for bringing about the ends that we consider desirable.

Centers of Decision Making

In some countries it appears that policymaking is the responsibility of a very few people. As we have argued above, we think that it is more practical to think of decision making in the United States as a diffuse, multilateral process. In policymaking there are a number of decision makers on a given issue and the nature of the decision-making group changes over time. Business, labor, agriculture, veterans' groups, religious bodies, consumer groups, and others all have their own agendas. Each group tends to equate its own agenda with the public interest.

Broadly speaking, because of the political structure of the United States, there are three arenas in which these groups seek to make their influence felt: legislatures, courts, and administrative structures. Although these centers of decision making exist on several levels, we are going to treat them as if this were not so; that is, for discussion purposes we are going to talk as if one court is very much like any other court and that the city council is comparable to the

Congress. While there are differences, the similarities among these groups are close enough for our purposes.

The Legislative Arena

Legislative decision making tends to be done through consensus and compromise. Both are lengthy processes. The slowness with which decisions are made allows time for influence. Because legislators want to stay in office, they will listen to significant voices. It is important for those who are pursuing policy change to have one of the significant voices. Our legislative system is most responsive when interest groups intervene with timely concerns. The system fails when interest groups miss their opportunities and fail to mobilize themselves. Traditionally, we think of the American Medical Association and the National Association of Manufacturers as the most skilled in influencing legislative decisions. Recently, we have seen women's groups engage in successful policy change.

Of the tactics we have discussed, some are more appropriate for influencing legislative decisions than others. Fact-gathering is important, at least for the purpose of presenting a case for a policy change. Position-taking raises the visibility of the issue. Media campaigns, expert testimony, and the formation of coalitions for lobbying are primary methods in working with legislative bodies.

Judicial Intervention

Most of us were not taught to think of judges as policy decision makers. We were taught that the legislature enacts laws, and the courts enforce them. Courts do, in fact, make policy decisions by the way they interpret laws and apply them. This is most obvious in those instances where there is an absence of clear-cut legislative intent or where legislative or executive policy violates constitutional protections.

Although the interpretation of the law tends to follow precedent, historical events and political pressures do enter in. The judges of today are not the same people who addressed civil rights questions in the 1880s. Clearly, the Supreme Court under Chief Justice Warren Burger is a different court from that of Earl Warren's years.

It would be deceptive to assume that judges have the ability to act arbitrarily. They can only deal with cases brought before the court that fit into their jurisdiction. Their decisions (except for the Supreme Court) are subject to appeal. Judges keep one eye on the appellate courts when they rule, since the prestige and status of a judge is related to the frequency with which his or her decisions are upheld on appeal. But the judge's other eye is on the public. Judges value the respect they believe that the public has for them and they are reluctant to make decisions that will be the subject of public ridicule.

Fact-gathering and expert testimony are two cooperative ways of assisting the judicial decision-making process. The class-action suit obviously is an important means of social change through judicial intervention. To be successful, the suit must be based on a violation of rights. A group wishing to press a class-action suit must find a compatible attorney and work within the constraints of the legal system. If the policy change that is contemplated clearly relates to a violation of due process or of legal rights, there is a good chance that the policy can be changed by legal action.

Administrative Structures

The power of the executive—regardless of the level of government—has fluctuated a good deal in the United States. We have seen variations in the "weak mayor" and "strong mayor" systems in city government. Although the presidency is neither "weak" nor "strong" in the same sense, it is clear that the leadership that can be expected from the president varies with the times and the occupant of the office. Franklin D. Roosevelt probably exerted more influence in the office of president than any other occupant. Of course, the Great Depression and World War II were cataclysmic events. Strong administrative leadership was both required and allowed by American public opinion. Truman continued the tradition of strong leadership. Since Nixon's administration, Americans seem less trusting of administrative leadership and more inclined to seek policy change in the courts or in a legislative body. Nevertheless, administrators at various levels do have discretionary authority in certain aspects of policy; and these administrators are susceptible to influence procedures.

The literature on policy change in large bureaucratic structures clearly suggests certain directions. Awareness and use of the informal channels for communications and decision making are very important. Mobilization of support behind the scenes before formal ratification of a new policy in a staff meeting or by an administrator is often vital. Planting ideas with administrators and seeing to it that they get the credit is an ancient strategy that still works. The use of pressure from outside may be helpful but is extremely dangerous to the career of the initiator.

A wide range of tactics can be used in dealing with administrative structures. The case conference is often effective in securing exceptions to general policies. These exceptions often constitute precedents for future policy change. Petitions may have some effect as part of an overall policy change campaign. Very often, administrative structures use study or advisory committees as sounding boards or screens for ideas. Sometimes social workers can be included on such committees and can make significant contributions to change. If a group attempting to change administrative rules or policies engages in bargaining, the media campaign may help build public support. Lobbying is also an effective tactic, provided it is done in a way that allows the administrative structure to save face. In all-out contests, demonstrations and disruptive tactics probably are more effective in embarrassing administrative structures than they are with legislative bodies or the judiciary.

Every group interested in policy change has to decide on its general strategy. A few years ago most change-oriented groups seemed to leap at the chance to take an adversary position and enter into either contest or conflict with decision-making bodies that they were trying to influence. There are times when contest or conflict gets some mileage. At least, the more dramatic tactics certainly get attention. Care must be taken, however, that dramatic approaches are really thought out. In the 1960s it was clear that some activists were interested in their own agenda: making a name for themselves, meeting members of the other sex, taking an ego trip. It is our opinion that the issues in social welfare policy are so vital that one engaged in policy change ought to look for the satisfaction of personal needs at another time and in another place. Hunger, illness, powerlessness, and discrimination are serious problems, and their control requires more dedication than one who is interested in meeting new people is able to give.

We also want to point that contest and conflict are not the only strategies that are effective. A number of the items that we listed as strategies can be carried out as cooperative enterprises. Perhaps decision makers, like the mule, have to have something dramatic done in order to get their attention. At some point, however, conflict must be resolved and a cooperative basis must be found in order to get on with the job.

Alan Filley, whose field is management, has written of the need to resolve conflicts in order to move organizations along in some consistent direction.[11] It is his belief that decisions are best made through consensus and integrative decision making. Filley trains business managers in an approach to conflict resolution that he has borrowed from transactional analysis. He believes that "win-lose" strategies, in which one party beats the other, are inefficient in the long run. Losers in such contests become resentful and ineffectual. He also believes that "lose-lose" strategies should be avoided. These are strategies that result in both sides losing because they have to give up too much and neither emerges feeling intact. A "win-win" strategy pursues its goals of consensus and integrative decision making by keeping the discussion on the "adult-adult" level.

Although we see the need for contests and understand that conflict can arise over social welfare policy issues, we also recognize that at some point the two sides will have to reach some kind of agreement in order to work out what comes next. "What comes next" is planning for the implementation of policy decisions. A model of the planning process is addressed in the next chapter.

REFERENCES

1. Richard E. Neustadt, *Presidential Power* (New York: Science Editions, John Wiley, 1960), p. 10.
2. *Ibid.*
3. *Ibid.,* p. 39.

4. *Ibid.*, pp. 9–10.

5. Lawrence D. Mann, "Studies in Community Decision Making," *Journal of the American Institute of Planners,* Vol. XXX, No. 1 (February 1964), pp. 58–65. This article has been reprinted in Ralph Kramer and Harry Specht, *Readings in Community Organization Practice,* 2nd ed. (Englewood Cliffs, N.J.: Prentice-Hall, 1975).

6. See Floyd Hunter, *Community Power Structure* (Chapel Hill, N.C.: University of North Carolina Press, 1953).

7. Arnold Panitch, "Advocacy in Practice," *Social Work,* Vol. 19, No. 3 (May 1974), pp. 326–332.

8. Charles S. Prigmore, "Use of the Coalition in Legislative Action," *Social Work,* Vol. 19, No. 1 (January 1974), pp. 96–102.

9. George A. Brager and Valerie Jorrin, "Bargaining: A Method in Community Change," *Social Work,* Vol. 14, No. 4 (October 1969), pp. 73–83.

10. Harry Specht, "Disruptive Tactics," *Social Work,* Vol. 14, No. 2 (April 1969), pp. 5–15.

11. Alan C. Filley, *Interpersonal Conflict Resolution* (Glenview, Ill.: Scott, Foresman, 1975).

QUESTIONS FOR DISCUSSION

1. Criticize the concept of power used in this chapter. Suggest an alternative explanation that has usefulness.

2. Which interest groups do you think will rise to importance in the United States in the next five to ten years? Which will decline?

3. Do you think that it might be possible for social workers to join forces with the National Association of Manufacturers or the Chamber of Commerce in a social policy change effort? Can you think of an issue?

4. Do you think that it would be practical for social workers to be directly involved in protests, boycotts, and other confrontation strategies?

5. Can you think of ways to bring opponents over to your side?

6. Can you think of examples of class-action suits that might be pressed to bring about social welfare policy change?

SUGGESTED PROJECTS

1. Talk with community leaders, editors, or politicians to determine which individuals or groups would be most effective in helping to implement a specific policy change, such as a better way of handling counseling needs.

2. Meet with a state senator or state representative to discuss social policy issues in the state. Ask specifically about mental health, public health, corrections, or Medicaid.

3. Talk with an attorney about the procedures and costs involved in a class-action suit.

4. Talk to a U.S. Senator or representative to get his or her thinking on the

comparative strength of business, labor, agriculture, blacks, women, and other national power groups.

FOR FURTHER READING

Wilbur J. Cohen. "What Every Social Worker Should Know about Political Action," *Social Work,* Vol. 2, No. 3 (July 1966). A brief review of the steps in the legislative process by a former secretary of HEW. Cohen includes a section on administration of programs after a bill is passed. The examples are dated, but the article is still useful on the process.

Maryann Mahaffey. "Lobbying and Social Work," *Social Work,* Vol. 17, No. 1 (January 1972). A valuable review of the problem-solving aspects of the political process. Covers the use of cooperation, allies, and knowledge in lobbying. The major tasks of the lobbyist are discussed, and a model for legislative action is presented.

William T. Murphy, Jr. and Edward Schneier. *Vote Power.* New York: Anchor Books, 1974. A simply written but well-researched discussion of how Congress works and how political campaigns can be developed and carried out. The stress throughout is on getting a candidate elected and is aimed at the average citizen.

Rino J. Patti and Ronald B. Dear. "Legislative Advocacy: One Path to Social Change," *Social Work,* Vol. 20, No. 2 (March 1975). An up-to-date and realistic view of the role of social workers in the development of legislative policy, stressing compromise, the value of providing timely and balanced information to legislators and their staffs, and the sensitive use of tactics.

Charles S. Prigmore. "Use of the Coalition in Legislative Action," *Social Work,* Vol. 19, No. 1 (January 1974). A discussion, with examples, of the use of coalitions in policy implementation. The use of a wide range of organizations is stressed.

Alan D. Wade. "The Social Worker in the Political Process," *The Social Welfare Forum,* 1966. Wade discusses the resistance social workers have had to political action, the relevance of political action to policy implementation, and various roles for social workers. An early article in the movement of social workers into political action, but still valuable and pertinent.

Franklin M. Zweig. "The Social Worker as Legislative Ombudsman," *Social Work,* Vol. 14, No. 1 (January 1969). A practical discussion of the work and experiences of four graduate fieldwork students in the offices of federal and state legislators. The use of a wide range of skills is stressed, including conflict strategies.

10

Connecting Policy to Planning

WHAT IS THE RELATIONSHIP OF SOCIAL welfare policy development to social welfare planning? How do social welfare policies become the basis for social programs and welfare services? The answer to the first question can be understood as one explores a series of stages that include the development of a social policy. Social planning usually follows the development of policy, and is the means through which a policy takes on meaning in the form of organized responses to human problems. The first part of this chapter develops that basic idea in more detail. The second part of the chapter examines the tasks that are performed by social welfare planners as they work to translate social policies into human service programs.

Planning: One of Many Stages in Service Provision

In order to undestand our society's response to social problems, it is necessary to view the context in which these problems develop and are treated. Every problem has a history, and most policies evolve over a long period of time as new approaches are taken. Each new policy, however, must be implemented according to some scheme that can reasonably be expected to produce the intended results. Social welfare planning, then, concerns itself primarily with the means through which social policies are actualized.

Planning, generally, is the process whereby one determines where one is going and how to get there. Planning leads to a selection of goals, a timetable for achieving them, and specification of how the goals will be attained. It is possible to utilize the planning process to develop social policy; most often, however, it is used to determine ways to implement social policy.[1] The process of social development and change is represented schematically in Figure 10.1.

Distinguishing Social Problems

At any one time there are many social conditions in our society, most of which are not necessarily viewed as social problems. Under certain circumstances, however, a social condition that had been viewed neutrally in an earlier time may be recognized as a problem that society feels compelled to address in some way. For an essentially neutral condition to become interpreted as a problem, two factors are usually present. First, the condition must produce acute discomfort for an identifiable group of people. Someone, usually quite a few people, suffers in some way. A second factor often present in a condition's

Figure 10.1 *Social Planning in Context*

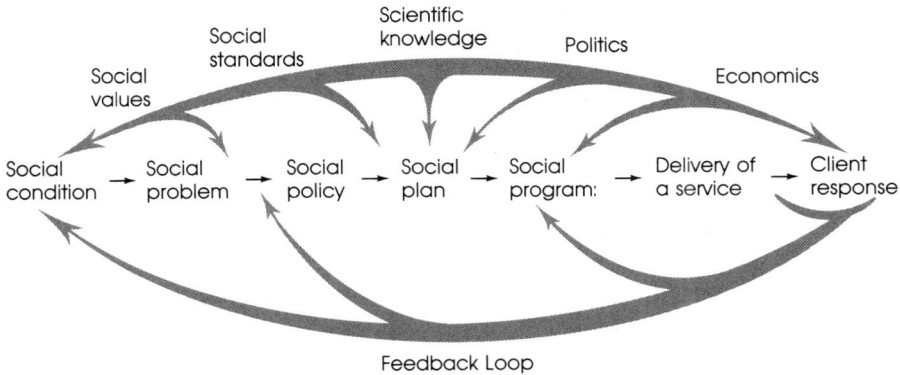

Feedback Loop

Source: Adapted from an unpublished schematic by Raymond Koleski. Indiana University School of Social Work.

transition to a problem status is a belief or conviction that something can be done to alleviate the problem.

Social values and standards provide guidance in distinguishing those situations that are on the way to becoming problems. The existence of outdoor toilets, for example, was not viewed as a problem when our population was widely scattered and when we knew nothing about bacteria. As people crowded their homes closer together, however, it became more difficult to maintain sanitary standards; disease was likely to be associated with too many outdoor toilets, too close together. The social value of maintaining privacy was difficult under such close living conditions. Value was also attached to living near one's work, and as cities developed out of the rural wilderness, it became more valued to live on small land space than to retain some space for one's outhouse. What happened? Eventually, people came to recognize that something that had formerly been seen as a *condition* had shifted to the status of *problem*. The two requirements for this shift had been met. A large number of people were affected, and modern sanitary engineering had made scientific advances that offered a way of dealing with the situation.

A wise local government had to recognize that the problem would only become worse over time. The solution would be a sewer system. First, a timetable would be set for construction in various parts of the city. The policy would have to be refined to take into account sectors outside the city that would be annexed later. As is the case with most social policies, this one had to be concerned with society's responsibility. In this example, a government planned and put into operation a sanitary system.

Merely formulating a new policy did not resolve the problem. Scientific knowledge is particularly influential when a programmatic response to a social problem is being developed. Knowledge of human behavior is especially useful in designing programs to serve people. In this case, it was necessary for the city to compute the cost of installing sewer lines that met desirable criteria. Hills and valleys had to be taken into account; distances had to be measured, and the size and types of pipes needed had to be calculated. An acceptable collection point for the wastes had to be located, and means of disposing of the wastes had to be determined. The city also had to find a way to finance construction. This usually involved extra taxation or special fees. Since the city officials were elected, they were careful to "sell" the tax in such a way as to avoid getting themselves voted out of office at the next election. In sum, a total plan had to be developed, including ways to cope with the politics and the economics of the situation, but using available scientific knowledge.

The expected responses of clients (in this case, residents of the city) were satisfaction with the elimination of offensive odors and reduction in the spread of disease, but annoyance over the cost of connecting to the sewer. Eventually, however, the cost of an indoor bathroom became a moot consideration in the purchase or construction of a home; it was an inevitable part of the home and no longer considered a matter of choice. A new standard was thus set, and a new social value was born. While the rich had indoor toilets and lived inside the city, the poor were likely to live outside the city and continue to use outdoor toilets. Whether one had an indoor toilet became a factor of social status differential in the early development of American cities. The new social condition, as a result of the lengthy process, was one wherein all residents of high-density areas now have indoor toilets.

The example should make obvious the many stages and factors that are necessary in a policy to program to evaluation to reformulation cycle. Planning is one of the very important stages and requires considerable skills. In fact, two basic types of skills are widely recognized as being absolutely necessary for social planners: *analytical* skill, which refers to the intellectual work of the planner, and *interactional* skill, which involves the person-to-person work of getting people organized and working together.[2] Education for social planning roles must include learning opportunities in which students can develop both kinds of skills to a considerable extent.

One of the most appealing aspects of social planning as a career in social work is its complexity. One continually learns about the systems within which social planning is practiced as new factors arise, problems change and social values change. The analytical tasks always present new challenges. Planners learn to think systematically and to take into account all important elements and factors in a given situation. A very special contribution that the social work profession has made to modern concepts of planning is its concern for total communities. The more recent development of systems theory provides a modern rationale for total-community concern, as opposed to small-sector planning.

Social work's values are intricately linked with the highest ideal values of democratic society. It would be considered wrong, for example, to develop services for one group in a community at the undue expense of another. This concern for a total community development perspective is one that guided professional practice long before the general systems theory was popularized and suggested a similar approach. The neckbone is, indeed, connected to the anklebone, and it is up to the astute planner to find the important connections and take them properly into account in any planning venture.

The Use of Planning Theory

Students of social planning have the benefit of perceptions of many planners who have written accounts of their experiences and their research on planning. There are several widely recognized and accepted models of planning process, each produced by a different author or group of authors.[3] No two writers see the planning process exactly alike, although there are many similarities. Some writers are more impressed with the lack of rationality in planning than with its logic. One social planner who had just come through an extensive and intensive experience of helping to implement a new set of social welfare policies at the state level pointed out that, ". . . contrary to rational theories of decision making, one moves from point A to point B very much as if avoiding mine fields rather than following a deliberate course of action."[4] Because of the wide variety of experiences planners have had with their work, it has not been possible to distill them into a neat, simple interpretation of planning. It is, however, possible to interpret planning as a series of practitioner tasks, so long as it is realized that certain steps may be omitted and others retraced until a satisfactory plan has been worked out.

Planning theory typically consists of statements about how planning is or should be done. The statements represent a careful identification of many planning experiences set forth in conceptual terms of what the student of planning should know in order to engage in planning activities. Models of the planning process serve as guides to planners as they decide what must be done at each stage of the process.

Practitioner Tasks

Without stating a comprehensive theory of social planning, it is possible to identify major clusters of tasks that must be performed by the professional planner. The tasks parallel theory, of course, but translate conceptual stages into the specific analytical and interactional tasks that planners must perform. Let us examine these tasks as a way of understanding what the planner actually does. Of course, there will be variations in specific experiences, but the following ten tasks will be fairly typical of many planning experiences.

Identification and Understanding of the Problem

This first task is usually more difficult than it might seem. Planning usually flows from some recognition that a problem exists (see Figure 10.1), but different people will have different views on the problem. The planner must sort them out and determine who suffers and how many people are affected. What are the consequences to persons affected by the problem? What are the consequences to society if nothing is done about it? The planner will also attempt to determine who recognizes that a problem exists and why, and who does not recognize the problem and why they do not.

Problems are usually thought to be rooted either in individual personality, an organization, the social structure, some social institution or a combination of these. The planner seeks the best possible interpretation of how the problem has developed and why it continues to exist. Possible solutions may become apparent as one searches for the antecedents of the problem. It is important to be clear about the possible consequences if no action is taken at all.

Selection of Participants

Most planning ventures involve many persons in addition to the professional planner. Although the planner does not always identify and select all of the important participants in a planning process, there is likely to be some opportunity to influence participant selection. Certain individuals can contribute useful knowledge; others will have influence that will be needed to bring about corrective action. For any given problem it is likely that several persons will have an important stake in seeing it either resolved or left undisturbed. Others will be affected by the manner in which the problem is confronted. The planner can identify persons and groups who have a stake in a particular problem and make an assessment of their potential helpfulness in finding and enacting a solution.

The planner has a major role in actually establishing a planning group to address the problem. In our society it is safe to assume that, with respect to any issue, there are one or more key persons whose influence must be reckoned with if action is to be taken on a particular issue. It is the planner's task to identify the influential people who are important to the particular issue being considered and to help develop ways to deal effectively with them.

Individuals and groups that are powerful are most frequently sought as allies to planning ventures. In some cases, however, a program, service, or change that is known to have powerful opponents may be in the planning stage. In either case, whether the center of power is an ally or an opposition force, the wise planner should have access to the thinking and actions of the power centers in order to keep the planning group working along lines that are likely to be productive. Access to the power centers needs to be established. This is most frequently achieved through persons close to the individuals or groups with power. Such people are often referred to as "gatekeepers." Gatekeepers serve as communication links between influential groups and individuals and a wide array of people.

It is often possible to develop a planning group that is made up of a fairly compatible combination of representatives from all important sectors, including some gatekeepers to appropriate power centers. The group will continue to be assisted by the professional planner, but will take on a character all its own as it proceeds to deal with the planning issues that are involved.

Determination of Goals

What is to be achieved by planning? What are the most desirable outcomes; what outcomes will actually be sought, giving consideration to both obstacles and opportunities? The professional planner has a strong responsibility to learn about and also inform the planning group about programs, services, or organizations in other places that are equivalent to those being planned. The success or failure of others' attempts to deal with a given problem serves to guide local planning. Although it is doubtful that success elsewhere can be imported totally to a local situation, much can be gained from continual adaptation and improvement of good workable examples.

Much like the architect, the planner develops a wide array of working models or program examples through years of study and experience. These then serve as a storehouse of alternative possibilities that can be applied as needed in a local situation. There is ample room for creative development of new approaches to resolving problems, since there are not, as yet, any standard formulas for dealing with most problems. The planner has a professional obligation to continually evaluate the plans that are developed, so that contributions can be made to the literature on workable solutions to the many social welfare problems. One also improves his own effectiveness through continual self evaluation.

The goals that are eventually sought may be considerably modified from the original statement. Most planning ventures, limited by financial and other constraints, rarely achieve what is seen as the ideal. Beginning with an idealized set of goals, however, enables the planner and the supporting group to select those features that are simultaneously most affordable and most workable.

Scientific knowledge for social welfare planning and policy development is rapidly increasing. Large-scale research on the impact of selected policy approaches has the capability of influencing decision makers in their consideration of new and alternative policies. Politicians are elected by majority vote, however, and must consider the wishes of the majority of their constituents who can re-elect them. Perhaps for this reason, elected officials often feel they must be careful not to give too much attention to unpopular social welfare causes. In framing policies and financing social welfare programs, the elected have increasingly attempted to utilize scientific knowledge about the likely benefits of certain policies and programs. When certain bills are being considered by Congress or a state legislature, appropriate committees of those bodies hold hearings on those proposed bills to get the testimony or opinions of interested persons. Increasingly, legislators and congressmen attempt to include the testimony of expert professionals. Often such testimony has genuine impact on the decisions of lawmakers. Ultimately, however, most major decisions of legislative bodies are necessarily framed by a combination of social values and political and economic considerations.

One of the principal reasons frequently cited by professional planners for the lack of scientific certainty about the ways to achieve desirable outcomes is the lack of investment in research. It was pointed out several years ago that "social work functions with the lowest investment in research and development of any major enterprise in the United States—perhaps less than .003 percent of the sums being planned for."[5]

Planners complain that without proper investment in alternative approaches to the solution of social welfare problems, it is impossible to say with certainty which goals and means are most likely to succeed. Each planning effort will, therefore, continue to be handled individually, utilizing existing policies, available resources and the best solutions that can be found which are acceptable to those whose points of view must be taken into consideration.

Determination of Action Needed

Several alternative types of action are possible when considering most social welfare problems, and it is usually important for the planner to be clear about the particular type or combination to be used. The types of action most frequently attempted are *prevention, alleviation, control,* or *correction.*

It would appear desirable to *prevent* problems from ever occurring. Some social welfare problems are thought to have their roots in places that are inaccessible, however, and are not to be tampered with by either policymakers or planners. Good examples of such problems are those that are thought to be rooted in faulty early parent-child relationships. It is possible that a parent may unknowingly contribute to a child's later poor mental health. Although society has established laws concerning both neglect and abuse of children, the laws are not sufficiently developed to detect just which parental behaviors will produce problems for offspring in later life. Early childhood parenting is usually considered to be a domain that official society does not tamper with in any way unless actual legal abuse or neglect is detected. Public social programs that are closest to a child's very early formative years are day care and health clinics, neither of which involve mandatory participation on a wide scale. Prevention of other problems may not be possible because of the lack of scientific knowledge about where to direct preventive efforts and what those efforts should be.

Some problems can be *alleviated,* lessening their impact and severity. Poverty, when defined as the lack of sufficient funds to purchase the necessities of life, can be, and is, alleviated by providing funds for individuals and families. Without supplementary activities and services, however, poverty is neither prevented nor cured by providing money for basic needs. Families can receive public welfare support for years and, unless other special measures are also taken, the families will be just as poor as ever when the financial support is terminated. Alleviation is often the preferred action when other alternatives are either impossible to take or when they are too costly.

Control of certain kinds of problems appears to be the best approach. Health departments utilize a variety of measures to attempt to control to a reasonable level the spread of diseases that cannot be totally prevented.

Some problems can be *corrected* on a person-to-person basis. Poor vision that is caused by certain correctable eye diseases in children has long been a concern of the Lions Clubs of America. Their sight conservation program, providing properly fitted eyeglasses to young children whose parents cannot afford them, can be said to have cured many vision problems. The best examples of corrected problems come from the health field, and include the almost total elimination of smallpox and certain other communicable diseases.

Sometimes whether or not a problem is solved depends upon how it is defined. Public begging or mendicancy, as it was formerly called, has long been considered a nuisance. Public laws were passed in sixteenth-century England to prevent, control, or license begging, yet it persisted until societies found other ways to meet peoples' basic needs. Nevertheless, panhandlers can still be seen in large cities. Few social problems have been totally corrected, although many have been greatly reduced in their severity, through a variety of measures.

Determination of Targets for Intervention

The planner usually thinks simultaneously about desirable types of action and target systems. Target systems are individuals or societal systems upon whom some kind of action is to be taken in order to deal with the problem under consideration. Typical target systems are individuals, families, neighborhoods, subcultures, geographic or functional communities, specific organizations and large institutions. Although some problems may be widespread throughout society, one cannot usually target the entire society to bring about change. In the case of racial discrimination, attempts to correct its ill effects do focus on widespread changes in our social institutions and specific organizations. Individuals and corporate bodies can be and are directed by law to avoid certain practices that are thought to be discriminatory.

In the case of deteriorating housing, the geographic neighborhood is often the target of intervention through slum clearance or rehabilitation. Planners must be careful, however, to be certain that their solutions do not create additional problems that may be worse than the ones being attacked. This is sometimes the case when poor neighborhoods are broken up by new highway construction or renewal projects. Informal networks of mutual assistance and support that sustained residents of a dilapidated neighborhood may be broken up by a forced move to new locations. Multitudes of new social problems have been generated as a result of forced relocation.

Ultimately, all target systems are people systems. It is new behavior that is sought, and the planner must assess whether the necessary resources can be organized and applied to the appropriate target systems to either prevent, alleviate, control or correct the problem under consideration. This particular activity, usually a matter of judgment, is often called "feasibility testing." Goals and plans that are not feasible will need to be revised or adjusted in order to achieve expected feasibility before proceeding.[6]

Evaluation of Available Resources

To take action on many social welfare problems requires a vast outlay of funds. It is not often that planners and planning groups tackle large problems and plan large solutions without assurance of strong and stable financial assistance from a governmental source. Although the planning process may be utilized to develop a recommended policy and budget to deal with a problem, it is most often engaged after basic policies have been determined and budgets fixed, at least for a period of time.

Money is not, by far, the only needed resource in dealing with problems. Although each situation will generate its own list of needed resources, some of those typically in high demand (other than money) are leadership capabilities, professional staff, social climate or willingness to take action, and supportive services and programs that may be needed in providing a continuity of care. Hospital expansions sometimes fail because of an insufficient supply of qualified nurses; entire service programs do not develop within some communities where there is insufficient leadership to bring them into the communities. Whatever the need, all required resources should be identified and plans for their procurement should be made.

The planner is actively involved in all aspects of the developing program. The planner's approach is systematic, requiring consideration of all essential relationships to assure that the planning process will result in effective treatment of the problem. Plans that are simply written notations of a particular individual's ideas about what ought to be done are often doomed to be shelved without even being considered for implementation. The effective planner, however, develops the resources to get the job done along with the intellectual work of planning.

Determination of Strategies

Significant program development through planning usually requires a variety of strategies to bring about the desired changes. Strategies are the short-range actions which, when considered together, move an effort forward toward realization of its larger goals. Examples include news media campaigns, organization of agency coalitions, writing financial proposals, retraining staff through continuing education, and a host of other efforts that contribute toward goal achievement in a larger sense. Each strategic effort is not considered to be an end in itself, but it is contributory toward a more important achievement.

Competent and effective planners rarely proceed very far into a planning venture without developing a general overall map of the entire planning process for the issue at hand. The danger in beginning without thinking far ahead can readily be seen. An analogy can be drawn to an automobile trip that is begun on a particular highway, either because it is beautiful or familiar, without regard to whether it eventually connects with a destination. Some social planners are now utilizing a highly effective approach which involves the use of flow charts, a practice that has been highly developed and is used in manufacturing and in computer technology.

A flow chart in social planning can be used to reflect either simple or very complex involvements of the planning process. It attempts to depict graphically those activities and operations that must be performed within a given span of time. It identifies the individuals and groups that will perform the various operations and the key decisions that must be made in the sequence in which they are most likely to occur. A flow chart of a particular planning process will generally represent the successive stages of a theory of planning that is appropriate to the situation.

Flow charts can be developed to reflect a wide variety of features that the planner finds desirable. It is possible to emphasize the efficient deployment of staff in planning or the intermittent decision role of a board of directors or any combination of those and other dynamics that will occur in the process. Flow charts provide a visual representation of what is to be done, when, and by whom; these can be effectively used in working with planning groups and other decision-making bodies. Through prior agreement on a work plan it is possible to foster and control the timing and substantive input of various interested parties. To provide important persons and groups access to plan development may be crucial; to show them where and when their contributions can be received is to regulate the process efficiently.

Setting of Priorities

Although proper attention to strategies also causes the planner to think about priorities, special attention should be given to this task. There always seems to be fierce competition for scarce resources. As the entire effort is reviewed, those matters that must be given certain attention should be identified and organized into a priority system. New information and increasingly understood external and internal factors may cause priority realignment before final actions. A deliberate pause to reassess readiness to act and to identify key things to be done at this stage is well worth the planner's attention.

Implementation of Solutions

Because action to implement solutions is usually continuous with previous steps, it is not always possible to say just when it begins. Typically, action overlaps with parts of prior stages and becomes continuous with evaluation and replanning. A new set of participants may be brought into the scene as plans are implemented. They are not necessarily planners and people movers; they are more likely to be the service personnel, managers, and others who will establish and maintain that which has been planned. In essence, the implementation stage is the allocation and deployment of resources: money, people, and power.

The professional planner may or may not be intimately involved in implementation of plans that he or she has helped to create. Ideally, the planner should be just like an architect who designs a building and is available to consult with the contractor who is hired to construct it. Last minute changes will be necessary. That which can go wrong, will, and must be reprogrammed at the last minute. Unanticipated resistance will appear in some instances and will need to be handled.

The art and science of program administration comes strongly into play at this point; an entire later chapter will deal with implementation. The close interrelationship of planning and administration can be seen as one traces the path of a social policy's development, the planning that it generates, and the service administration that usually follows. Planning again appears as an essential function of program management, reflecting a continuous cycle of program redevelopment.

Evaluation and Replanning

As indicated earlier, planners need to be involved in evaluating the outcomes of their efforts. Feedback from what we do is one of the most effective instructors. Too often planning and administration become unjoined and a program is later evaluated by persons who had little or nothing to do with its creation. Without involvement in the evaluation process, the planner cannot learn what the mistakes were and how they could be avoided in the future. It may be difficult to determine who was responsible for certain problems; for example, was it faulty planning or faulty administration that resulted in mistakes?

One practice that is not sufficiently utilized in social welfare planning is the development of detailed written specifications for programs that are being developed. The planning team should commit plans to paper in sufficient detail so that it is possible for an administrative team to be clear about what was intended.

Several relatively new approaches in program administration hold promise for assisting with program evaluation, the most notable of which is *management by objectives*. Theoretically, it should be possible to state program objectives clearly and in sufficient detail to control the program they serve. The specific characteristics of the program are therefore designed to achieve the stated objectives. They are periodically evaluated to determine whether that, in fact, is happening. When objectives are not being achieved sufficiently, replanning should produce necessary changes, if all administrative operations are in order. Constant evaluation is essential for the continual improvement of programs and services.

REFERENCES

1. John Friedman, *Retracking America: A Theory of Transactive Planning* (Garden City, N. Y.: Anchor Press/Doubleday, 1973), p. 52.
2. Robert Perlman and Arnold Gurin, *Community Organization and Social Planning* (New York: John Wiley and the Council on Social Work Education, 1972), p. 61.
3. Joan Levin Ecklein and Armand A. Lauffer, *Community Organizers and Social Planners* (New York: John Wiley and Sons and the Council on Social Work Education, 1972), Ch. 8.
4. Aileen F. Hart, "Community Organization, Social Planning and Public Social Service," *Social Development Issues,* Vol. 5, Nos. 2–3 (Summer and Fall 1981), p. 48.
5. Robert Morris, "Social Planning," in Henry S. Maas, ed., *Five Fields of Social Service: Reviews of Research* (New York: National Association of Social Workers, 1966), p. 186.
6. Robert Morris and Robert H. Binstock, *Feasible Planning for Social Change* (New York: Columbia University Press, 1966), p. 80.

QUESTIONS FOR DISCUSSION

1. How can planners anticipate future problems?
2. When does a social condition become a social problem?
3. Can a planner use rationality as the sole basis for planning?
4. Why is it necessary to involve people other than professionals in the planning task?
5. Why do planners not have scientific information available for planning purposes?
6. When does one know whether or not a given plan has succeeded?
7. What kinds of resources are needed in order for planning to be successful?
8. How do flow charts help the planner?
9. What is the role of evaluation in the planning process?

SUGGESTED PROJECTS

1. Contact your local welfare department and request a copy of the Title XX (Social Security Act) plans that have been developed for your area for the current year. Inquire about any forthcoming public hearings on next year's plans that you might attend. Visit their offices and interview one of their planners to develop a written report on how they plan, pursuant to the issuance of Federal policies concerning welfare.
2. Contact the United Way or community council office in your city and make arrangements to attend a meeting of one of their planning task forces. You may be able to review the minutes of previous meetings to get background

material on the matter being planned. Look for information that provides contextual understanding of the planning endeavor. What policy initiated the planning? At what stage of planning is the project? What kinds of help is the professional planner giving the group?

FOR FURTHER READING _____

Edmund M. Burke. *A Participatory Approach to Urban Planning*. New York: Human Sciences Press, 1979. A comprehensive examination and analysis of the rationale and methods for involving citizens in planning that affects them. Burke's extensive experiences as a planner, teacher and White House advisor are richly reflected in the wisdom of this book.

Fred M. Cox *et al.*, eds. *Strategies of Community Organization*, Itasca, Ill.: F. E. Peacock, 1979. A collection of excellent readings that serves as a good textbook on community organization and planning. Although only one chapter focuses exclusively on social planning, the entire book helps to frame the practice of social planning in social work.

Ralph M. Kramer and Harry Specht, eds. *Readings in Community Organization Practice,* 3rd ed. Englewood Cliffs, N.J.: Prentice-Hall, 1983. One section covers various topics related to social planning. The remainder of this book is a collection by many different researchers of outstanding contributions to community organization and social planning theory over the past three decades.

Armand Lauffer. *Social Planning at the Community Level.* (Prentice-Hall Series in Social Work Practice.) Englewood Cliffs, N.J.: Prentice-Hall, 1978. One of the most comprehensive treatments of the theory and practice of social planning.

Robert Perlman and Arnold Gurin. *Community Organization and Social Planning*. New York: John Wiley and the Council on Social Work Education, 1972. A basic textbook that focuses on the relationship of community organization to social planning and policy.

11

Connecting Policy
to Administration

THE OPENING CHAPTERS DISCUSSED THE ROLE of environmental influences on the formulation of social welfare policy. From the criteria for analysis of policy developed in Chapter 3, it is clear that a social welfare policy is to be considered as an input into a system designed to deal with some human condition; that is, a social policy is not an "end" but rather an element of the "means" to the reduction of unemployment or the provision of retirement income. The discussion in this chapter is based on the thesis that administration is the link between the "policy" and the "desired social change." In the absence of effective administration, the intent of the policy will not be realized. Figure 11.1 depicts the relationships that make up the administrative system.

Several elements of this system are critical to the successful fulfillment of any social policy. First, those in the administrative process must recognize the role of social, political, economic, and cultural values. The diagram clearly demonstrates that the values which influence policy formulation also affect the implementation of programs to fulfill the policy. Second, policy creates the need for resource allocation, thus stipulating the primary function of the administration's allocation and coordination of resources. Third, the administrative system is oriented toward a purpose. The purpose receives its direction from, and is organized around, the purpose or mission declared by the policy. Fourth, the administrative system involves the performance of a series of functions (planning, organizing, leading, evaluating) which transform resources into specific services designed to accomplish the mission declared by the policy. Finally, each element of the system is constantly feeding back information and results. For example, feedback about the outcome of service delivery (desired social change) impacts on both the inputs (i.e., values, policy, and resources) and the administrative process (i.e., plans, organization, etc.).

The discussion which follows will clarify and build upon these relationships to increase the reader's understanding of the role of administration. Specifically, the plan for the remainder of the chapter is to sharpen definitions of administration and to look at the functions of an administrator and the activities involved in each of these functions.

What Is Administration?

Definitions of administration or management (for purposes of this chapter these terms are interchangeable) are as numerous as those who write about the subject. Massie, for example, defines management as "the process by which a cooperative group directs actions toward common goals."[1] Peter Drucker

Figure 11.1 *The Administrative System*

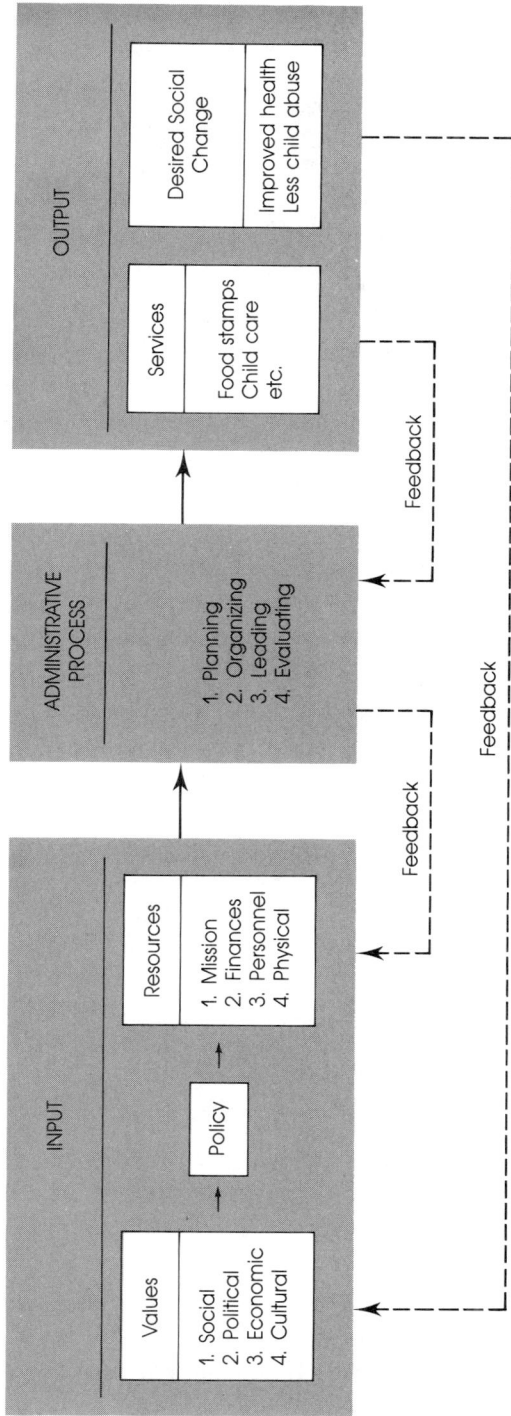

INPUT		ADMINISTRATIVE PROCESS	OUTPUT	

INPUT

Values
1. Social
2. Political
3. Economic
4. Cultural

Policy

Resources
1. Mission
2. Finances
3. Personnel
4. Physical

ADMINISTRATIVE PROCESS

1. Planning
2. Organizing
3. Leading
4. Evaluating

OUTPUT

Services
Food stamps
Child care
etc.

Desired Social Change
Improved health
Less child abuse

Feedback

Feedback

Feedback

defines it as three tasks "equally important but essentially different, which management has to perform to enable the institution in its charge to function and to make its contribution: the specific purpose and mission of the institution, whether business enterprise, hospital, or university; making work productive and the worker achieving; managing social impacts and social responsibilities."[2] Sisk, on the other hand, adopts a more technocratic approach with his definition: "Management is the coordination of all resources through the process of planning, organizing, leading, and controlling in order to attain stated objectives."[3]

These definitions may seem very different, even contradictory. Upon closer examination, however, several common elements appear. First, the stated or implied activity described by each of these definitions is universally applicable. All organizations attempting to achieve a common purpose, whether large or small, require administration. Second, administration is goal oriented. Administration has no life-cycle separate from the goals for which the agency is established. This principle constantly must be kept in mind, since the temptation is ever present to "administer an organization for the sake of administration." When this happens both the organization and its clients or customers are poorly served. The administrative system is a "means" to accomplish the "ends" for which the organization exists—this is its primary and ultimate reason for being.

A third way of looking at administration is that it is a cooperative venture. The organization achieves its goals primarily through the efforts of people. A successful administrative process must cause a convergence of organizational goals and personal goals that will motivate individuals to join in a cooperative partnership. This principle of integration requires "the creation of conditions such that the members of the organization can achieve their own goals *best* by directing their efforts toward the success of the enterprise. . . ."[4] Finally, administration is task directed. The administrator engages in a number of activities related to the establishment of a plan; the development of an organization; providing leadership and direction; and the evaluation and control of performance.

The foregoing discussion has described administration as a cooperative action system. By this we mean that administration includes all activities necessary to transform social policy into the desired social changes. These activities are carried out by administrators, the next topic to be considered.

What Do Administrators Do?

The administrator's primary responsibility is to coordinate the work of others, not to personally perform tasks. On some occasions the administrator will perform tasks, but his or her success does not depend upon knowledge or skills in the field being administered. Rather, the administrator is concerned with the functioning of the organization. The administrator is in a role similar to that of an orchestra conductor. He or she must make sure all of the individuals are going in the same direction so that the performance of each contributes to what is to be accomplished. Adjustments and modifications will be made to achieve the effective functioning of the organization. Therefore, the administrator is responsible for creating an environment that will enable subordinates to achieve agency goals efficiently and in a personally rewarding manner. McGregor has stated "that the limits on human collaboration in the organizational setting are not limits of human nature, but of management's ingenuity in discovering how to realize potential represented by its human resources."[5] How well the environment is designed and maintained will determine the ultimate success or failure of an agency. This environment, at a minimum, must provide each individual within the organization with an understanding of agency objectives and an understanding of how they and their jobs contribute to the accomplishment of these objectives. In addition, the environment must contain a system to motivate individuals to maintain a high level of performance.

The statement of mission or objectives found in public policy pronouncements is customarily a list of broad statements of purpose with which the majority can agree. For example, a public policy may have the purpose of providing superior health care to every citizen. This objective statement, while laudable, is not very operational. With this as your only guidance you could not be expected to move very far toward the accomplishment of the objective. It is up to the administrator to clarify and develop objectives toward which everyone can work. Further, the administrator must ensure that these statements of objectives are clearly understood by all individuals involved in the pursuit of these objectives.

The administrator must ensure that each individual and unit within the agency understands the overall goals and objectives of the organization. Also, they must be made aware of how they as individual units fit into the master scheme. This requires that a set of subgoals be established that, when taken together, will result in the accomplishment of the larger agency mission. Each person in the system should be provided with a set of clear and verifiable goals against which his or her performance will be measured. Similarly, the administrator must ensure that each individual has the necessary information and a scope of authority to perform the tasks assigned. In addition, the administrator has to be aware of the necessary skills required to perform a specific task and be certain that those expected to carry it out possess the skill to do so.

The administrative environment should create a setting in which individuals strive to achieve organizational goals because they have accepted them as their own. In short, the administrator must be a facilitator who can focus an individual's knowledge, skills, talents, and aspirations toward the accomplishment of the organizational mission.

How does the administrator accomplish these goals? To answer this question we will have to look at the roles an administrator fulfills, the activities that occupy the workday, and the administrative functions to be directed.

The administrator-manager is an individual of many identities and is called upon to perform in various administrative roles. Henry Mintzberg has identified ten separate roles that an administrator is likely to be called upon to perform.[6] He has delineated three interpersonal roles, three informational roles, and four decisional roles.

Interpersonal Roles

• The figurehead role

As the head of an organization or organizational unit, an administrator is obliged to perform specific symbolic duties.

> The executive director of the Family Service Association presents certificates of appreciation to foster home parents.

> The commissioner of public welfare receives a call from an angry recipient and he in turn calls the county welfare director of the county involved to advise him of the call.

> The executive director of the United Way presents certificates of recognition to the key people in business who assisted in the annual United Way campaign.

• The leader role

In this role the administrator is responsible for ensuring that the people assigned to the unit perform in a satisfactory manner. As leader, the administrator must motivate and encourage subordinates to achieve organizational goals.

> The director of a community mental health center congratulates the social worker who devised a new and quicker method for summarizing social histories.

> The director of the local community action program encourages the staff to continue with their regular daily responsibilities in spite of adverse public reaction and the threat of financial cutbacks.

> The bureau chief meets with supervisory personnel in an agency and advises them that too much time is being wasted in processing clients' requests for service and that the delay can no longer be tolerated.

• The liaison role

In this role the administrator is concerned with establishing an external information and mutual assistance system.

The superintendent of the boys' training school maintains contact with the local ministerial association and seeks their advice and counsel on programs in the school.

The director of a regional program for retarded citizens contacts the executive secretary of the Chamber of Commerce and advises him that they will soon have graduates from a special training program.

The director of a home for emotionally disturbed children calls the Junior League and seeks their assistance in recruiting volunteers.

Informational Roles

• The monitor role

Here the administrator receives and filters information useful to his or her organization. This information flows both from the formal organizational communication network and the external information system developed in the liaison role.

A memorandum is received from the central office of the mental health department which advises the regional director of changes in the definition of the developmentally disabled.

The director of a private voluntary adoption agency receives a letter from the executive director of the United Fund outlining new guidelines for program budgeting to be required of all funded agencies.

A letter is received by the commissioner of the department of corrections from a private consulting firm seeking permission to interview prisoners.

• The disseminator role

In this role important information that has been gathered is transferred to subordinates who would not otherwise have access to this information.

An announcement of a workshop on transactional analysis is circulated among the professional staff of a mental health center.

A request from the Civitan Club to the superintendent of the state school for the mentally retarded for information on the guidelines for volunteers is forwarded to the supervisor of community services.

A report from a schoolteacher in a residential treatment center is sent to the casework supervisor.

• The spokesperson role

The administrator, in this role, speaks on behalf of the organization to the external environment.

The director of a halfway house for delinquent boys delivers a speech to the League of Women Voters describing the purpose of community-based programs.

The director of a program for unwed mothers is invited to discuss the program on a television talk show.

The executive director of the Children's Aid Society speaks to the board of directors on the developments within the agency during the past quarter.

Decisional Roles

● **The entrepreneur role**

Through decisions to implement new programs or to change existing procedures the administrator acts as an entrepreneur.

The superintendent of the state school for girls lobbies with key legislators to influence their consideration of a bill which would eliminate the commitment of pregnant, delinquent girls to the state school.

The director of a manpower center submits a proposal to the Department of Labor for a federal grant designed to provide training for the hard-core unemployed.

The director of the planning and development commission holds a quarterly "brainstorming" session with the staff for the purpose of coming up with new ideas for dealing with the human service needs in the region.

● **The disturbance handler role**

In any organization some situations have the potential of becoming a crisis. The administrator must respond to such a situation.

The director of social services in a large state mental hospital is confronted with a serious conflict developing between the social workers and the psychiatric residents which must be resolved.

A county welfare director seeks a new approach to handling the conflict between the typists and the professional staff.

The director of a community action program schedules a meeting between local residents and the social work staff to deal with complaints of ineffective service to the community.

● **The resource allocator role**

The administrator must decide within the organization how resources will be allocated among the various unit functions.

The director of a senior citizen center decides to concentrate on the development of new programs and hiring additional professional staff rather than continuing the drive for larger physical facilities.

The administrator of a regional mental health center issues a directive requiring all decisions regarding program development and purchase of equipment to be approved by his office.

The commissioner of the state department of public welfare submits an annual budget request which asks for appropriations to cover an additional one hundred social workers in the child support division of the department and a cutback of fifty social workers in adult services.

• The negotiator role

No organization or organizational unit is self-sustaining or "an island unto itself." Every unit must interface with other parts of the organization as well as with outside forces. The administrator is responsible for the negotiations which maintain the proper environment with those other units.

The chief probation officer of the family court and the regional director of the division of family and childrens' services negotiate which children will be supervised by the court and which will be supervised by the division of family and childrens' services.

The director of a program for inner-city youth confers with the neighborhood school board to negotiate the use of the schools for recreational programs in the evenings and on weekends.

The director of a large multiservice center meets with the union representatives of the Federation of Social Workers to negotiate acceptable standards for the size of caseloads.

It is obvious that, while these ten roles must be performed by any administrator, they cannot be separated and neatly placed in a logbook. The administrator may perform several of these functions simultaneously. For example, when a bureau chief is having lunch with a group of peers, and the topic of next year's budget comes up: Is the bureau chief acting as the liaison, monitor, resource allocator, or negotiator?

It is quite likely that the chief is performing in all of these roles. This suggests yet another approach for understanding the task of administration—to look at the activities engaged in by administrators.

Activities of Administrators

A second avenue leading to an increased understanding of administrators is to view how they spend their time. How a "typical" administrator spends time provides insight into the specific tasks which compose the job of administration. Rino J. Patti has reported on the activities of ninety social welfare managers in the state of Washington.[7] Table 11.1 lists his thirteen functional groupings of administrative activities and the average number of hours spent per week on each activity.

In addition to asking the respondents how they spent their time, Patti asked

Table 11.1 TIME SPENT IN EACH ACTIVITY BY
MANAGERS

Activity	Mean hours
Planning	3.9
Information processing	6.2
Controlling	5.4
Coordinating	3.8
Evaluating	1.5
Negotiating	.7
Representing	1.8
Staffing	.9
Supervising	6.7
Supplying	.3
Extracurricular	1.9
Direct service	4.1
Budgeting	1.0

Source: Rino J. Patti, "Patterns of Management Activity in Social Welfare Agencies," *Administration in Social Work* (Spring 1977), p. 7. Reprinted by permission.

each manager to rank the activities in order of importance to the effective performance of the manager's job. He reported several findings as particularly significant. For example, "Over two-thirds of the managers in this sample judged activities subsumed under controlling, supervising, and planning as the most important ones they had performed during the prior week. Somewhat less than one-half of the respondents ranked coordinating as significant, while one-quarter or less of the managers felt that activities associated with representing, information processing, direct practice, and evaluating were important to effective job performance."[8] It can be seen from Table 11.1 that the three activities ranked most significant, planning, controlling, and supervising, occupied approximately 40 percent of these managers' time each week. This statistic, however, masks the fact that each manager engaged in a wide variety of tasks and activities throughout the survey week. In fact, most studies of this nature, as well as this one, have found a chief characteristic of the job of manager to be rapid change from one task or activity to another.[9] To provide insight into the breadth of activity subsumed under the category headings, Table 11.2 presents a summary of the specific activities engaged in by a typical manager in performance of the major functions.

This and the foregoing section have approached the topic of administration from the perspective of administrator characteristics and activities. The intent was to provide the reader an overview of the nature of the management process itself. Now that you have some understanding of the administrative role it is time to turn our attention to the processes which constitute administration—planning, organizing, leading, and controlling.

Table 11.2 DESCRIPTION OF MANAGEMENT ACTIVITIES

Planning	Determining goals, policies, and courses of action. For example: strategy-setting, staff work-scheduling, grant development.
Information processing	Time spent in communicating information (reading, writing, compiling, telephoning) where the manager or interviewer was unable to specify the specific function these activities filled.
Controlling	Collecting and analyzing information as to how the total operation or major segments of it are going.
Coordinating	Exchanging information with persons within or outside the agency other than subordinates or superiors in order to relate and adjust programs.
Evaluating	The assessment and appraisal of proposals and reported or observed performance.
Negotiating	Conferring, bargaining, or discussing with a view to reaching an agreement with another party.
Representing	Advancing the interests of the agency through contacts with individuals, groups, or constituencies outside the organization.
Staffing	Recruiting, interviewing, hiring, and promoting staff.
Supervising	Leading, directing, training, and reviewing the work of subordinates.
Supplying	Obtaining space, equipment, supplies, and other nonfinancial resources required for the work of the agency.
Extracurricular	Activities done during the work week that would not be part of a job description such as partisan political activity or attending classes.
Direct service	Giving counseling, treatment, or advice directly to a client.
Budgeting	Planning expenditures and allocating resources among items in the budget.

Source: Rino J. Patti *et al.*, *Educating for Management in Social Welfare,* unpublished report, The University of Washington (July 1976), Vol. II, p. 17. Mimeographed. Reprinted by permission.

Administrative Processes

Planning

In a very real sense, planning may be considered the essence of administration. Earlier in this discussion, we described management as the link between social policy and desired social changes. Planning is the backbone of that linkage, in that it is the initial step or function performed by an administrator.

Plans are the means by which administrators extend and put into operation the mission stated in a social welfare policy. This planning function may be separated into the broad categories of strategic and operational planning. Strategic planning is customarily carried out at the highest administrative level within an agency. It begins with the determination of the major objectives of the organization. In this context, an objective is the specific target or need that an agency must achieve in order to continue to exist. Examples of subjects included in strategic plans are matters such as the types of service to be provided, type and number of personnel necessary to perform these services, capital expenditures, and costs associated with each of these activities. Strategic plans tend to be long-range and are mainly concerned with broad statements to provide coordination of the various elements composing the organization. The output of strategic planning efforts is statements of principles which constitute guides for movement toward the accomplishment of agency objectives. We call these statements of principles "policies." Policies act as guideposts for decision making throughout the organization.

Operational planning, on the other hand, involves the translation of objective statements and policy guidelines into action statements. This type of planning has a much shorter time frame than strategic planning, usually one year or less, and is conducted by middle- and lower-level managers. Operational plans are derived from the objectives or strategic plans originating from the upper levels of administration. They are concerned with definite actions which must be taken in order to accomplish the goals established for the unit by the strategic plan.

Operational plans, then, provide the specific program direction necessary to carry out policy statements. Examples of these types of plans are to be found in documents such as procedural manuals, rules, and the unit's budget.

Whether one is attempting to develop an agency-wide strategy or a plan of action for next week, an effective plan specifies the task to be completed (*What?*), the person or persons responsible for completing it (*Who?*), the deadlines for completion (*When?*), and the quantity and quality of performance (*How?*).[10] To accomplish this, the rational planner undertakes five interrelated steps:

1. Identify the problems to be solved and the opportunities to be seized upon.
2. Design alternative solutions or courses of action (i.e., policies, plans, and programs) to solve the problems or seize upon the opportunities and forecast the consequences and effectiveness of each alternative.
3. Compare and evaluate the alternatives with each other and with the forecasted consequences of unplanned development and choose the alternative whose probable consequences would be preferable.
4. Develop a plan of action for implementing the alternative selected, including budgets, project schedules, regulatory measures and the like.
5. Maintain the plan on a current basis through feedback and review of information.[11]

This sequence describes a process not too unlike what you and your family face when attempting to decide upon a vacation trip. Initial consideration must be given to individual family members' preferences—the beach or the mountains. Second, you must choose the goals to be accomplished by the trip—rest and relaxation or sightseeing and activity. Third, basic premises affecting the final decision must be considered—length of vacation possible, money available. Fourth, vacation alternatives that will satisfy the goals set must be identified and compared to determine the best choice—which vacation plan will satisfy the greatest number of family members. After you decide upon the actual trip to be taken, supporting plans must be formulated—development of an itinerary, purchase of needed materials, making reservations. Finally, during and after the vacation, the plan will be evaluated by all members of the family for future vacation planning.

Organizing

The plans discussed in the previous section result in a "road map" leading the agency toward the objectives established by a social welfare policy. If this is the case, then, the organization structure is the vehicle which transports the agency to the objective. The formal organizational structure allocates responsibility, authority, and accountability to individuals within the agency. Through the organization structure each individual is made responsible for a group of tasks which constitutes a job. The structure also extends to each individual the authority to make decisions within the assigned area of responsibility. Finally, the structure makes each individual accountable to a higher authority for the results achieved in the performance of the job.

From this, it may be concluded that the initial task of organizing consists of determining what activities will constitute a basic job. Once again, it should be noted that the activities to be performed must flow from the basic objectives set out for the agency. The collection of activities or tasks that we describe as a job then becomes the foundation for organizing.

Following the grouping of activities or tasks into jobs, a framework must be constructed to specify the relationships between these elements. That is, jobs must be grouped so that the performance of each of the specialized activities fits together in a "chain of command," in which responsibility, authority, and accountability are understood.

Organizationally, the agency will have a wide choice of patterns that will accomplish this goal. For example, a functional pattern may be chosen which logically reflects occupational specialization. Under this pattern all jobs containing like activities are placed in the same department—for example, all fiscal activities. A second structural pattern may group all jobs related to the same service program into the same department. For example, all personnel related to providing day care for children of working mothers may be grouped into one department. Another possibility is to base the pattern of organization on the location of a given set of activities, for example, a county welfare department. Another form of structure might be to organize the agency by client group. All child-care activities, for example, may be placed in a single department.

These structural patterns, while not constituting all the available organizational forms, are representative examples of useful bases for developing effec-

Table 11.3 POTENTIAL RELATIONSHIPS

Number of Subordinates	Number of Relationships
1	1
2	6
3	18
4	44
5	100
6	222
7	490
8	1,080
9	2,376
10	5,210
11	11,374
12	24,708
18	2,359,602

Source: V. A. Graicunas, "Relationships in Organization," *Bulletin of the International Institute* (Geneva: International Labour Office, 1937) in Luther Gulick and Lyndale Urwick (eds.), *Papers on the Science of Administration* (New York: Institute of Public Administration, Columbia University, 1937), pp. 181–187.

tive and efficient work structures. In practice, you are likely to find a mixture of the patterns within any given agency. You may find functional grouping at the statewide level and client grouping at the local level. In short, the form of organizational structure will depend, in the final analysis, on pragmatic considerations.

Whatever the pattern of structure selected, it must clearly establish for each individual within the organization the flow of authority and responsibility, while ensuring accountability of each for his or her performance of organizational tasks. A significant aspect of the interrelationship between authority, responsibility, and accountability is the number of individuals that each manager will effectively be able to oversee. In the development of the organizational structure care must be given to the issue of the span of control which determines the volume of interpersonal activities that a manager is able to handle.[12] As noted in Table 11.3 the number of potential relationships amongst members of a work unit increases geometrically as the number of subordinates increases.

Leading and Directing

The last two sections have shown us that the plan provides the organization with the map of its objectives, and the structure provides the transportation to the objective. In this section, we will see that it is leadership which provides the energy to attain the organization's goals.

The difference between simply "minding the store" and actively striving to

Figure 11.2 *Leadership Style*

(Authoritarian) • (Democratic)

(Task Oriented) • (People Oriented)

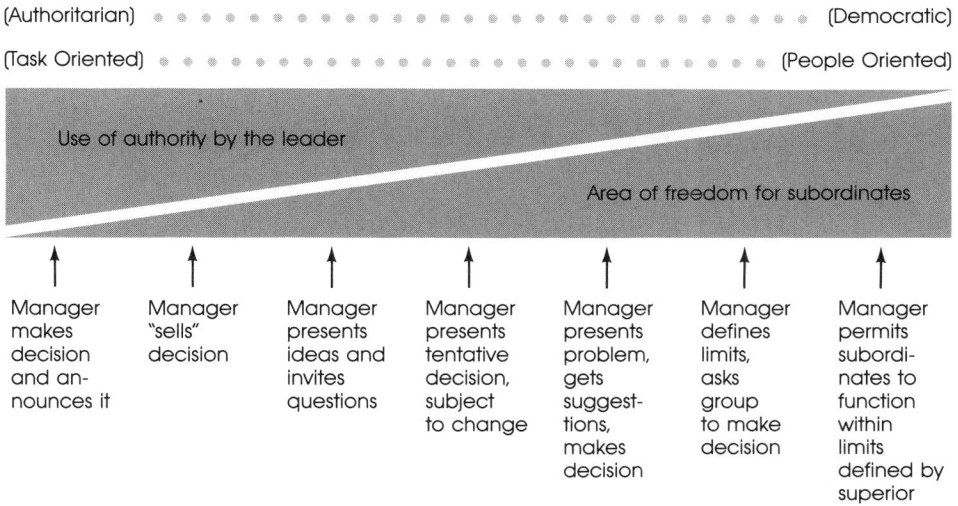

Use of authority by the leader

Area of freedom for subordinates

↑	↑	↑	↑	↑	↑	↑
Manager makes decision and announces it	Manager "sells" decision	Manager presents ideas and invites questions	Manager presents tentative decision, subject to change	Manager presents problem, gets suggestions, makes decision	Manager defines limits, asks group to make decision	Manager permits subordinates to function within limits defined by superior

Source: Robert Tannenbaum *et al., Leadership and Organization: A Behavioral Approach* (New York: McGraw Hill, 1961), p. 69. Reprinted by permission.

achieve goals is the level of motivation found among the personnel in the organization. The administrator, through his or her abilities as a manager-leader, has the responsibility of motivating employees to strive for high performance. Thus, the manager-leader must understand the factors that influence human work behavior.

Managers must think about the people within their organization, yet they must also think of the goals to be attained. Managerial leadership then may be defined "as the process of influencing the activities of a group in efforts towards goal attainment in a given situation. The key elements in this definition are leader, followers, and situation."[13] These three variables interact to affect leader behavior and may result in a variety of styles. Figure 11.2 depicts a leadership style continuum that varies from a task-oriented, highly autocratic style to a people-oriented, highly participative style. The factors of leader, follower, and situation will indicate where on this continuum an individual manager is likely to fall.

The leader's actions at any given time are influenced by his or her own personality and the environment. Since the manager constantly deals with ambiguous situations with a high level of uncertainty, the manager's own feelings of security about his or her position will influence leadership style. The leader's feelings of security, in turn, influence the level of confidence placed in subordinates. Similarly, the leader's own value system and philosophy of leadership will affect the type of leadership. The leader, for example, who believes subordinates to be naturally lazy will likely be much more authoritarian and directive in leadership style than the leader who believes that subordinates have a high degree of commitment and a natural inclination to achieve work goals. This latter manager is more likely to permit subordinates a greater area of freedom and to be more participative in leadership style.

The follower also is influenced by personality and environment. Each of us responds to direction in a different way. Some subordinates have a relatively high need for structure and do not wish to take responsibility for making decisions, but would prefer to remain dependent upon the leader. Others, however, feel a high degree of identification with the organization and feel they possess the ability to deal with most situations. This latter type of subordinate is likely to be very receptive to a democratic leadership style and would reject the highly authoritarian style.

Situational factors are an influential element in leader behavior. The number of individuals involved in a problem requiring action will affect the degree of participation possible. For example, it is unlikely that even the most democratic leader could consult with two hundred field staff about a new program. The pressure of time is also likely to increase the degree of authoritarianism in leadership style. In a crisis situation it is more difficult to involve others. Geographic proximity and the ease with which people can interact also are situational variables that affect the style of leadership. Widely dispersed units or highly mechanized kinds of operations make interaction difficult and thereby reduce the chance for participative decision making.

Earlier in the discussion in this section we mentioned that it is important for the manager-leader to understand and know those who work for him or her. Chris Argyris introduced the concept of maturity in assessing where a follower might be in reference to the work environment.[14] He concluded that as individuals mature they become less dependent on others and should be handled accordingly by the manager. Hersey and Blanchard integrated the concept of maturity into their life cycle theory of leadership and stated that as the level of maturity of the followers increases then the appropriate behavior of the leader should provide less structure (task) and less socioemotional support (relationships).[15] As depicted in Figure 11.3, as the group of followers matures, the leader should adjust his or her style.

Evaluating and Controlling

Throughout discussion of administration we have placed great emphasis upon ensuring that each activity is consistent with the objectives and goals of the agency. How are we to ascertain the extent to which these objectives are being attained? How are we to determine if an alternative program might improve overall service delivery? How are we to provide flexibility in service delivery to meet the changing needs of clients? How are we to respond to the legislative call for accountability? The answer to each of these questions is—through an evaluation and control system.

A primary problem facing all administrators is the determination of the extent to which their unit is accomplishing what it was established to do. A

Figure 11.3 *The Life Cycle Theory*

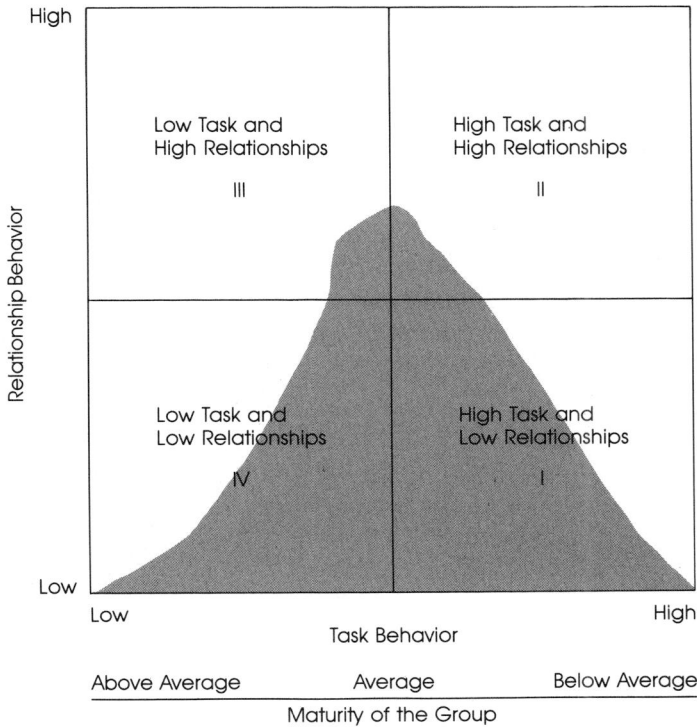

Source: Paul Hersey and Ken Blanchard, *Management of Organizational Behavior: Utilizing Human Resources*, 4th ed. (Englewood Cliffs, N.J.: Prentice-Hall, 1982), p. 152. Adapted by permission of Prentice-Hall, Inc.

good program evaluation system, coupled with adequate managerial control, is an essential element of the administrative system. Such a system contains four critical elements: establishing standards for performance; information-gathering; information analysis; and deviation correction.

Establishing standards for performance involves translating the goal or goals of a program into measurable indicators of success. Care must be exercised to ensure that indicators are developed for all outcomes, both those intended and those not intended. For example, the goal of increasing client purchasing power by 50 percent may have the unintended consequence of increasing price levels, thereby negating the higher income. Unless both of these indicators are considered in evaluating the program, incorrect conclusions will result. A second major factor to be considered is that the goals of many social programs tend to be ambiguous and, therefore, create difficulties in establishing measurable standards. The temptation is great in these cases to substitute hunches and unsupported claims for more objective criteria. This temptation must be resisted if we are to improve the operation of social welfare delivery systems.

The compilation, analysis, and comparison of information necessary for evaluation incorporates most of the commonly used research methods. Information for analysis may be collected from a wide variety of sources, including budgets, published statistics, client records, and interviews. Similarly, there is a wide variety of experimental designs and statistical techniques available for purposes of evaluation. A word of caution is necessary. Many times the evaluator is faced with "information overkill" and must pause to evaluate the contribution of bits of information. For example, a great deal of time and effort can go into the accumulation of very precise financial data related to supplies purchased for a program, only to discover that total funds expended on supplies account for less than 1 percent of total costs. In such a situation, the costs of supplies contribute little to our evaluation of the program. Similarly, the sophistication of the statistical tests performed in evaluation should be comparable to the level of sophistication of the information being measured. Again, much time and expensive effort can be spent in performing intricate and complex statistical comparisons that add little to our basic understanding of the program being evaluated.

The final and perhaps the key element in the evaluation process is that of correction. It must be remembered that evaluation is a tool of management control and, as such, should result in improved program administration. Finding out what is wrong with a unit or program is meaningless unless such knowledge is used to correct the problem and improve the service. It is in this way that evaluation is a means of control. It controls the movement of the organization toward the objective by providing the information to correct the course when there is deviation from the planned progress toward the objective.

Importance of Good Communications

All organizations must ultimately depend upon people to meet their objectives. To perform effectively, these individuals must depend upon the exchange of information and the directions they receive about functions to perform, methods to be used, and progress of the various units within the organization towards goals. In this context the manager is responsible for establishing the type of multidimensional communications network that will ensure unambiguous directions for subordinates as well as maintaining contact with superiors and with other units within the organization. Any communication involves four elements: the person sending the message; the thoughts to be transmitted; the person who is to receive the thoughts; and the feedback system. The communicator must decide who is to receive the message, then must plan carefully what is to be communicated, and how it is to be communicated. The message itself must be free from semantic barriers, such as jargon and technical language, and should be construed with the receiver in mind. The receiver, of course, must be aware of the message, its purpose, and be free of biases that will obstruct reception. Without some form of feedback, it is impossible to determine whether the message has been understood. Some form of feedback should accompany or should be an integral part of any message, since without this feedback we are not certain whether there has been any actual communicating.

There are many barriers to communications, both organizational and human. One need only look at the organizational communications chart of the large organization to see how someone may be omitted from a communications chain and how difficult it would be to develop a truly one-way communication process. Similarly, differences in education, background, and environment of individuals can act to preclude understanding of any communication on personal relationship problems. It is essential for the successful manager to understand the basic principles of communication and to apply these principles in such a way as to stress the removal of these barriers. In short, communication is the glue that keeps the organization together.

Importance of the Administrator

Throughout our discussion of the administrative process we assumed an important element—implementation. A plan must be placed in operation—organization structure requires decision; leadership implies direction; and evaluation must lead to action. Thus, the ability of an administrator-manager to make the correct decision weighs most heavily on the ultimate success of the manager, program, and organization.

Managerial decision making, like any situation requiring problem solving, contains four basic elements. First, the manager must assess the situation and find the element that needs action. This requires an investigation into the causes of unsatisfactory performance to determine what outcome is necessary to a satisfactory solution. Second, the manager must formulate alternative solutions that may yield the desired outcome. The third step in the decision-making process is the analysis of the alternatives. This analysis may range from a simple listing of advantages and disadvantages associated with each alternative to highly sophisticated mathematical formulations. The final critical element in decision making is the choice and implementation of a solution. This involves putting together a definite plan of attack and communicating this decision to all those with a role in the implementation.

In carrying out the responsibilities associated with being a manager the importance of the "people dimension" cannot be minimized. In their study of the most successful corporations in the United States, Peters and Waterman found that the most prevalent theme which characterized these organizations was their "attention to employees."[16] Attention to this theme will enhance the administrative process as it seeks to implement the respective social welfare policy.

REFERENCES

1. Joseph L. Massie, *Essentials of Management* (Englewood Cliffs, N.J.: Prentice-Hall, 1971), p. 4.
2. Peter F. Drucker, *Management: Tasks, Responsibilities, Practices* (New York: Harper & Row, 1974), p. 40.
3. Henry L. Sisk, *Management and Organization,* 3rd ed. (Cincinnati, Ohio: Southwestern, 1977), p. 9.
4. Douglas McGregor, *The Human Side of Enterprise* (New York: McGraw-Hill Book Co., Inc., 1960), p. 49.
5. *Ibid.,* p. 48.
6. Henry Mintzberg, *The Nature of Managerial Work* (New York: Harper & Row, 1973), pp. 92–93.
7. Rino J. Patti, "Patterns of Management Activity in Social Welfare Agencies," *Administration in Social Work* (Spring 1977), pp. 5–17.
8. *Ibid.,* p. 8.
9. For examples of other studies see: Sune Carlson, *Executive Behavior* (Stockholm: Strombergs, 1951); Rosemary Stewart, *Managers and Their Jobs* (London: Macmillan, 1968).
10. Walter P. Christian and Gerald T. Hannah, *Effective Management in Human Services* (Englewood Cliffs, N.J.: Prentice-Hall, 1983), p. 14.
11. Grover Starling, *Managing the Public Sector* (Homewood, Ill.: The Dorsey Press, 1977), p. 128.
12. James L. Gibson, John M. Ivancevich, and James H. Donnelly, Jr., *Organizations: Behavior, Structure, Processes,* 4th ed. (Plano, Texas: Business Publications, 1982), p. 299.
13. Starling, *op. cit.,* p. 346.
14. Chris Argyris, *Integrating the Individual and the Organization* (New York: John Wiley & Sons, Inc., 1964).
15. Paul Hersey and Kenneth H. Blanchard, *Management of Organizational Behavior: Utilizing Human Resources,* 4th ed. (Englewood Cliffs, N.J.: Prentice-Hall, 1982).
16. Thomas J. Peters and Robert H. Waterman, Jr., *In Search of Excellence: Lessons from America's Best-Run Companies* (New York: Harper & Row, 1982).

QUESTIONS FOR DISCUSSION

1. Why should administrators be concerned with social, political, economic, and cultural values? Is it not likely that these things have already received enough attention in the policy formulation and planning process?
2. The authors state that administration is a cooperative venture with staff. In your experience, is this statement a fair description of the true state of affairs?
3. Do you agree that administrators should generally not provide direct services to clients? Would it not make sense for administrators to "get their hands dirty" with some of the work of the agency?
4. Evaluate Mintzberg's ten administrative roles. Can you add to the list?
5. React to Patti's finding that 40 percent of the manager's time is spent in

planning, controlling, and supervising. Does this use of time seem appropriate?

6. Of the styles discussed, what kind of leadership seems most appropriate in social agencies? Why?

7. Discuss the implications of the authors' idea that evaluation is a means of improving program administration. What are the positive aspects of evaluation? In what ways can evaluation be misused?

8. Could health and welfare agencies operate without administrators? What kind of an organizational structure would be possible if there were no administrators or managers?

9. Discuss the implications of the "life cycle theory." Would it be possible to implement the theory in social service organizations? Why?

10. Do you agree with Peters and Waterman that attention should be given to employees? Why is it important for the manager to know his or her people and be concerned about them?

SUGGESTED PROJECTS

1. Visit a social service agency and interview the administrator. Using the Patti model, ask the administrator to rank, in order of priority, the thirteen managerial activities. Discuss each managerial activity with the administrator and then assess the significance of each activity relative to the overall administration of the agency.

2. Using the Mintzberg model of roles, discuss and analyze the managerial functions of a selected administrator in a social service agency.

3. Propose and discuss an administrative system for a county department of public welfare.

FOR FURTHER READING

Michael J. Austin. *Supervisory Management for the Human Services*. Englewood Cliffs, N.J.: Prentice-Hall, 1981. A very useful book. Specifically focuses on the role of the supervisor with emphasis on the management aspects of supervision. A practical approach is taken, thus making the book very beneficial as a guide for effective supervision.

Walter P. Christian and Gerald T. Hannah. *Effective Management in Human Services*. Englewood Cliffs, N.J.: Prentice-Hall, 1983. Both of the authors are practicing managers in human service organizations. They draw from their experience and this is reflected in the pragmatic approach that they take throughout the book. A useful guide for managers and students of management. They include practical appendices for several aspects of the management process.

Walter H. Ehlers *et al. Administration for the Human Services: An Introductory Programmed Text*. New York: Harper & Row, 1976. Extremely useful for students at any level. The book is quite thorough in its treatment of the scope of administration, but requires supplemental support to augment the material. It deals with administration from a traditional perspective and identifies the functions performed by the administrator: planning, organizing, staffing, coordinating, reporting, budgeting, and evaluating.

Rino J. Patti. *Social Welfare Administration: Managing Social Programs in a Developmental Context*. Englewood Cliffs, N.J.: Prentice-Hall, 1983. The author draws upon his years of experience in studying social service organizations and the management of them. The focus of the book is at the level of middle management and addresses the issue of management from a developmental perspective. The author defines and discusses management in three stages: design, implementation, and stabilization. A very helpful and useful book.

Grover Starling. *Managing the Public Sector*. Homewood, Ill.: The Dorsey Press, 1977. Provides a basic understanding of the socio-politico-economic environment of public administration. Introduces the primary management tools in a readable and interesting fashion. The illustrations used throughout the book increase the reader's ability to understand and utilize the basic principles of management in the public sector.

12

Prospects for the Future

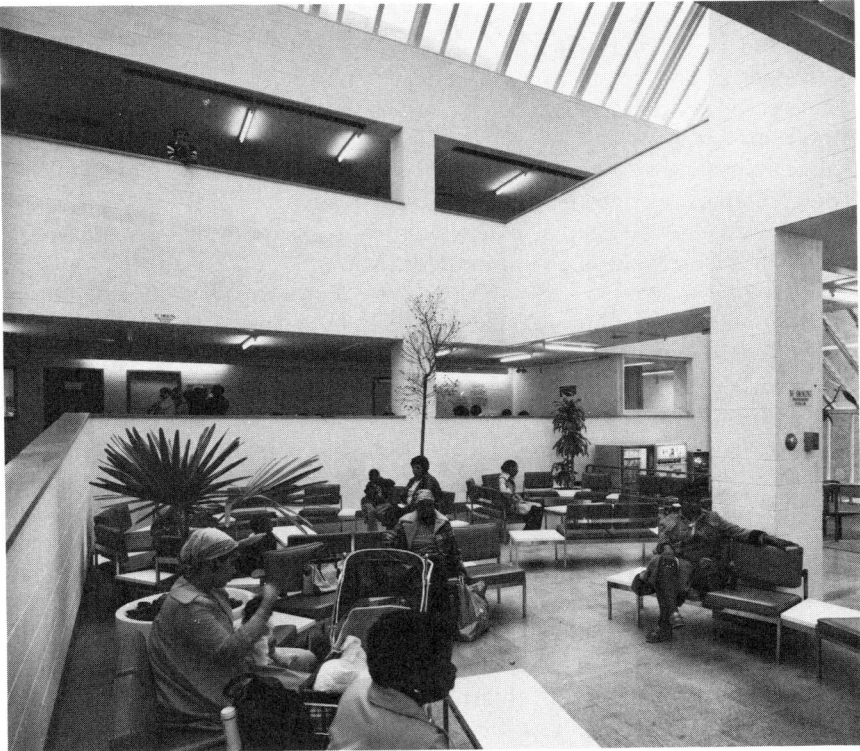

IT IS TIME TO SUM UP where we have been and to look at the future. In this concluding chapter we want to make some comments on the present state of social welfare policy and to speculate on what may be before us. It is, of course, far easier to discuss where we have been than it is to sort out the future. However, we believe that we are obliged to try.

We have made a number of changes from the first edition. These changes involved more than an updating of data. Most of the changes are in response to changes that have occurred in the past several years in the societal conditions in the United States. As we discuss the future, we will review our forecasts in the first edition and try to analyze where we went wrong and where we were closer to reality. We do this, not because we are masochistic, but because a review of this kind is an important part of the policy analysis process. One should not be afraid of looking dispassionately at past errors. There is something to be learned.

In this edition, we tried to select or to devise examples that would be good for learning purposes. As the reader will see, we are not wedded to many of them.

Let us return to our original premise in Chapter 1 and follow it through the succeeding chapters. We began by noting that social services are a given in the modern world. Both conservatives and liberals agree that they are necessary, although not everyone would agree with our belief that they are a natural outgrowth of the need for mutual aid for human survival. Whether one calls it mutual aid, humanism, or a reflection of a specific religion's concern, social welfare is firmly entrenched in modern society.

The key question is not: "Should we have social welfare?" but rather, "What form should it take?" Two other questions are important: "Who should receive the benefits?" and "How should benefits be financed?" In Chapter 2, we argued that these questions were vitally influenced by values. Every society has its own way of defining the nature of its social problems, and each works out solutions (or at least, responses) based on these values. Although societies differ on the nature of social problems, they all institutionalize ways of dealing with them. Sometimes a society's values lead to constructive and successful ways of dealing with problems, and the society and its members survive as a unit and grow as human beings. Sometimes, solutions are punitive and dehumanizing and the society and its members are brutalized. It is our belief that such societies ultimately all fail. They fail because they forget or ignore the legitimate needs of their citizens. It is only when a society's ways work for the benefit of its citizens (as opposed to totalitarian societies which work only for the benefit of their rulers) that both institutions and individuals survive and grow.

Our country has always thought of itself as one of those with the best interests of its citizenry as a paramount concern. Yet, we have a number of conflicting value systems. Therefore, it is not surprising that our social welfare system lurches and stumbles from time to time. We are all mixtures of rugged individualism (even if we do not come from pioneer stock) and selfless concern. At one minute we will complain about welfare cheaters and the next minute we will donate to a fund to send poor children to camp. We oppose governmental intervention in our lives, but we expect the government to "do something" when problems occur. We pay lip service to rationality, but we behave in irrational ways.

In Chapter 3, we presented a model (or pattern) for social welfare policy analysis and formulation that tries to take into account the various factors that bear on social welfare decision making. We think that it is a useful approach to problems, but still far from perfect. With this model, we examined important issues in five areas of social welfare concern. Based upon our discussion of these areas, we offer our analysis of our past forecasting errors and our conjectures about the future.

Major Contemporary Forces Affecting the Future of Social Welfare

First, however, we want to examine some overall forces that are influencing the direction of social welfare policy in the eighties.

1. *The shrinking of federal support.*

    Regardless of which political party controls the Presidency or the Congress, the days of the easy federal dollar are over. There has been a growing disenchantment with federal social welfare activities. We are likely to see more emphasis on private sector initiatives of various kinds.

2. *Changes in demography.*

    Traditionally, social welfare policies in the United States have favored the interests of children and youth. However, in recent years the percentage of elderly in the population has increased dramatically while the relative numbers of children and youth have declined. It is likely that the elderly will get more attention in the future, particularly since they are organized and active in politics.

Income Maintenance

In the first edition, we raised a number of issues. It is worthwhile to review them briefly. We noted that the major income maintenance programs in this country were offered under a mix of auspices. Workers' Compensation is a state program. Unemployment Insurance is a federal/state program and Old

Age, Survivors, Disability, and Health Insurance is a federal program. We recognized that while these programs all were generally aimed at income maintenance, they had different immediate purposes. In all of them, there is a stress on work. One receives benefits because he or she has had regular employment. Further, we said that there was a "preference for minimum benefits."

We then proceeded to forecast an extremely naive outcome. It was our notion that it was likely that these programs would be merged into one federal program financed by taxes on employers and employees, and supplemented by additional funds from the general revenue. We thought that things would move in this direction because we thought we saw signs of some consolidation of government functions in income maintenance.

It is clear to us now that the mix of auspices will continue. Older and more experienced, we see no evidence of any change in the basic pattern of these three programs. Workers' Compensation will continue to be a state program. In this edition, we said that the present system has advantages. It works for most injured workers most of the time. When there are problems, the courts have usually resolved them satisfactorily and the decisions have usually favored the worker. Since coverage is nearly universal, there is general satisfaction with the program. There are problems, of course. Benefits still vary from state to state and they do not replace full earnings loss, nor do they cover the full costs of rehabilitation. While these problems need attention, it is not necessary to change totally the program's general structure in order to deal with them. We noted that there has been some interest in federal standards. However, this proposal appears "dead in the water" at least for now. Even this proposal, which was fairly radical, fell far short of federalization and did not envision merging with the Social Security System. Undoubtedly, the present system will continue because it is acceptable to our present value structure, acceptable to the political and interest groups concerned, economically sound, workable, effective, and reasonably efficient.

The Unemployment Insurance program will likely also be continued largely in its present form. As we have seen in the recent serious recession in the early 1980s, the system can be responsive even in fairly difficult circumstances. While the benefits do not totally replace earnings, they go farther than one might suppose because they are tax-free. If states run out of funds, money can be borrowed from the federal government. In short, this system is compatible with most American values, politically acceptable, workable, effective and reasonably efficient. As we saw in the Alabama example, the system can be responsive to the political process and concerned interest groups can work with it to their mutual benefit. One point may be of interest for the future. Four states (as we mentioned in Chapter 4) now levy some of the UI cost on the worker in the form of a tax on wages and salaries. In Alabama, this tax is scheduled to be phased out. We think that the Alabama legislature may reconsider this phase-out and that other states may favorably consider taxing employees as a means of educating the work force to the cost. As we pointed out, it doesn't matter from an economic point of view, since the worker (and the consumer) pay the cost ultimately anyhow.

The OASDHI program, which has been a benevolent and non-controversial program for most of its existence, has now become extremely controversial. In the first edition, we were extremely critical of the benefit levels. We no longer have this concern. We noted in Chapter 5 that the level of poverty among the aged is now about the same as that of the general population. This progress is attributable in part to the increased benefits received from OASDHI. Given the increased security of private pension plans, the development of Individual Retirement Accounts for everyone, and the increased sophistication of our older citizens, it appears that the bulk of older Americans can now manage to live reasonably well. However, since alternative proposals (including Professor Williams' plan) are not being seriously considered, we think that some reforms of the OASDHI system will still be needed. Furthermore, the problems of the elderly poor remain and additional planning needs to be done on their behalf.

The bi-partisan commission that proposed the reforms of 1983 did some of the things that needed to be done. It was probably sound to add in federal employees and workers in non-profit organizations. It was also necessary to prevent further "opting out" by state and local governmental employees. It also makes sense to increase the amount of wages subject to the tax. This makes the tax less regressive. The regressive nature of the social security tax has been a bone of contention for many years. When the income base was relatively low, a person paying at the current maximum was taxed the same amount as a person making much more. This meant that the tax was a greater burden on the person with the smaller income. Increasing the tax base upward will spread the burden in a way that is a little more fair.

The commission did stop short in one important way. It is clear to everyone that the growth in the rate of increase in benefits will have to be slowed. No one needs to take a cut in present benefits, but they simply cannot grow as fast as they have in the past several years. Before 1972, Congress adjusted the benefit levels annually. In some years, this adjustment was quite generous. In other years, it was less so. When the increases were tied to the Consumer Price Index, part of the idea was to insulate increases from politics. However, as we saw in the early 80s, the increases were still too high, given the amount of money coming in. The current practice of using the average wage increase when the trust fund is low, and the CPI when it is not may still strain the system. Congress will probably have to consider a more effective way of limiting the increases in benefits. Most public and private pension plans have built-in increases that are more modest than the OASDHI increases. Generally, these increases are in the range of 1 and 1/2 to 2 percent annually. Something of this sort may be economically necessary, although it will be difficult to pass limitations of this nature without a lot of struggle and acrimony.

We have been asked by our students if there will be anything when they get old. We are confident that the present system will be fixed or that an alternative will be in place. Our confidence is not so much based on the belief that Congress will act sensibly because it is morally right as it is on the knowledge that older Americans vote. The politicians will fix the system if they want to be re-elected!

So, our forecast in the first edition that WC, UI, and OASDHI would be combined was clearly wrong. How could we have been so far off? We misread the values of the American people. The problems that we saw in the disjointed system simply are not problems to others. The politicians and business people, as well as the rest of the public, are deeply committed to the present admittedly disjointed system. We thought that our proposal was logical and would be more efficient, but we forgot that rationality and efficiency are only two of several criteria. You will have noticed that our forecasts on income maintenance programs are much less adventurous this time. We think that little dramatic change is likely.

Poverty

In the first edition, we argued that the major policy that guided the approach to the treatment of poverty in the United States was either coerced work or stigmatized discomfort. We commented on the moralistic view which interferes with our attempts to deal constructively with the problem. We have seen no reason to change our position. We *have* changed our view that it would be a good idea to shift AFDC recipients to some form of social insurance. In the first edition, we proposed that divorce, desertion, and unmarried parenthood should be seen as risks in the same category as industrial accident, loss of a job, or retirement. Our notion was that these contingencies could be covered using the same money now used for AFDC. In effect, we envisioned the possibility of doing with AFDC what was done when Old Age Assistance, Aid to the Blind, and Aid to the Permanently and Totally Disabled was combined into Supplemental Security Income, but without a needs test. We thought that the idea had the merit of efficiency, since the present system requires extensive investigation. However, it is clear to us that the values of most Americans are contrary to any such change. The idea of any form of minimum income—or anything that looks like it—appears to have reached its zenith with President Nixon's aborted Family Assistance Plan. Such ideas have become extremely unpopular. A number of people have asked us why we didn't discuss the principle of a guaranteed minimum income in the first edition of this book. We omitted it then—and now—because it was never official policy and it is not likely to be so in the foreseeable future. We do not think that either Americans or their representatives will consider any policy for the solution of poverty that eliminates a needs test or work requirements. While there are many social workers who have argued that both are punitive, their argument has never cut much ice with either Congress or the people. Hence we have offered the approach outlined in Chapter 5 that tries to take into account the necessity for a needs test and the value of work, but avoids a punitive approach.

There have been no profound policy changes proposed by the Reagan administration with respect to poverty, other than the "Enterprise Zone" idea. At this point, it appears that Mr. Reagan will continue to count on economic growth to reduce poverty through expanded employment opportunity. Theoretically, if unemployment is reduced, this will leave the available welfare resources to the "truly needy." Mr. Reagan's critics have charged that his economic policies have resulted in more, rather than less, poverty. Given the difficulties in deciding just who is poor, this is an argument that is not likely to be satisfactorily resolved.

Poverty remains an extremely difficult problem to solve. It is too much, perhaps, to hope for the elimination of all poverty. The social mechanisms of all societies seem to create new poor as the old poor move out of poverty. It is important to note that socialist countries, who pride themselves on their provisions for the poor, have not yet solved the problem of poverty.

We think, then, that the present program will continue with very few changes. There may be some tightening up of eligibility requirements and some fresh attempts to provide additional opportunities for work training, but we see nothing very constructive or new in the near future.

Health and Mental Health

As we said in Chapter 6, the health field is probably the most volatile of all those with which social work and social welfare are concerned. While there are some hopeful signs, the problems that we have discussed are still serious. One gets the feeling that the decision makers in health care have desperately tried one thing after another to control prices, but without really thinking through the implications of their policies. No solution has been found to the uneven geographical distribution of health care, and the two-tiered system of health care seems to be increasing the differences between services available to the poor and the non-poor. The policy of deinstitutionalization seems firmly entrenched, despite the way in which it has worked out for some very unfortunate people, and very little has been invested in a remedy.

The rising price of health care and the increasing difficulty of paying for it raise the question of rationing. Will high-quality health care (particularly high-tech procedures including transplants, high-risk nurseries and expensive drug therapies for chronic diseases) become primarily a service for the more affluent parts of our society? Will we increasingly find health care denied because of our inability to pay the inflated costs?

In the first edition, we believed that there was a good chance that the United States would soon adopt some form of national health insurance. We thought that the various proposals that were circulating at that time would "shake out" to a proposal in which persons with an income would pay a premium for health insurance coverage while the government paid the premiums for the unemployed and the poor. We thought that the plan would include a certain deductible amount that the more affluent would have to pay and that there would be a co-payment feature for the balance. In effect, this would have been Medicare extended to everyone, with the federal government paying the bill for the poor. We believed that a plan of this sort would be promoted both to pay the cost of medical care and to reduce the health care gap between the poor and the non-poor. Clearly, we were wrong in our expectations. The push for national health insurance has slowed considerably, partly because of the cost and partly because the country has taken a turn to the political right. It is doubtful if much headway will be made by the champions of national health insurance for some time to come, if ever.

Further, we expected too much of the National Health Planning Act of 1974. The programs provided by that law did not redistribute health services as effectively as we had hoped they would, although there were instances of improved services in some localities. Health services probably did not become more efficient as a direct result of the Act, and prices were not slowed appreciably. We were correct, we think, in recognizing the potential of the Health Maintenance Organization. We still believe this to be a viable approach to the major problems of providing health care.

For the future, we expect a wider acceptance of the HMO concept. The available evidence suggests that the HMO can provide high-quality care while holding down costs. If the federal and state governments will purchase memberships for those who are unable to pay and a way can be found to prevent overloading any one HMO with all the chronically ill persons in the community, then the HMO can provide decent health care for both the poor and the non-poor. Perhaps it will also be possible to use the HMO concept to integrate rural and urban services, but this is a tough problem and it will not lend itself to an easy solution.

We think that the expansion of HMOs and the alternative Preferred Provider Organizations will come about with health plans for employees and individuals through pressure from consumers, companies, and governmental bodies. However, HMOs will remain private businesses. We do not see a future for direct federal financing of HMOs, even for start-up costs. There may be an attempt to use the tax currently supporting Medicare for the purchase of HMO membership for older people. There has been some talk of using Medicaid funds to do the same for the poor. We think that these ideas will become more attractive during the next few years as a means of reducing the costs of health care.

We do not look for dramatic changes in mental health care in the near future. The great breakthroughs have been made and further reductions in mental disorder will be less dramatic. The focus will be on medical rather than psychological treatments. While there may be some further integration of mental health care with general health care, we suspect it will be slow. We think that deinstitutionalization will continue as an overall policy and that we will not see the reemergence of the large mental hospitals as we knew them thirty years ago. Some people, unfortunately, will continue to be lost in the system, and we are not hopeful that any really sizeable attempt will be made to rescue them. Perhaps social workers can have a crucial role in bringing these people's problems to a more satisfying conclusion.

In summary, we can forecast that medical prices will stabilize and might even decline in the aggregate, relative to other prices, and that there may be some adjustment in the maldistribution of health services between rich and poor. Problems will remain in the geographical maldistribution of services and in the mental health care of those lacking community and family support.

Housing and Living Space

The federal government and the housing and financial industries will continue their present relationships and most Americans will continue to benefit from it. The major problems will continue for the poor. We suspect that there still will be difficulty in providing safe, clean housing for those who cannot afford to buy it on the private market.

Public housing will not be a resource for the bulk of the poor in the United States. While existing units will be used as long as they are habitable, new construction will probably be limited to facilities for special groups—the elderly and the handicapped.

The general belief that public housing concentrates the poor and intensifies their problems will remain persuasive among legislators. Further, the cost of new construction on a mass basis will be seen as prohibitive.

In the first edition, we opted for a policy of subsidizing the consumer, following the lead of Arthur P. Solomon. You will recall that the idea was to provide direct housing grants to the poor and then to let them shop for housing in the market. The present policy, as we outlined in Chapter 7, differs in that the current practice is to pay the subsidy to the landlord. We still think that subsidy of the consumer is the best policy and we will be interested to see if it surfaces as a live proposal in the next few years.

Service Delivery

In the first edition, we envisioned that private practice would be the growth area in service delivery and that agency-based practice would tend over time to be limited to protective services, corrections, and some mental health applications. We still think that this is an accurate forecast of the future direction of service delivery. In Chapter 8, we mentioned the new field of practice in industry. This setting is close to private practice. Further, most of the clinical social workers that we know engage in some private practice. We have seen a number of our colleagues move into full-time jobs outside the traditional tax-supported or contribution-supported agency system. We recognize that there are many social workers who do not support this change. The fear is that if social workers become concentrated in private practice, the poor and other relatively less powerful groups will be denied both direct therapeutic services and social advocacy. This will not necessarily happen. In Chapter 8, we recognized that provisions need to be made for the poor, but we repeat our contention that this can be done through a voucher system similar to what we recommended for housing. It is our observation that the poor utilize a service better when they select it and have some consumer leverage. In this the poor are very like the non-poor. The junior author had some years of experience in privately supported family counseling agencies that charged fees. The fees were on a sliding scale ranging from $.50 an hour to $25. These agencies charged everyone some fee, including AFDC recipients (who were charged the minimum, of course). The clients universally used the time better than those in agencies that were more "charitable." Free services tend to be poor services unless they clearly serve a social purpose, as in the case of protective services and others that have a clear societal mandate.

We still think that service delivery needs a good shaking up. Even medicine, which has been an extremely conservative field, has felt new winds blowing in terms of service delivery. No longer does medicine project the image of the old country doctor carrying his largely ineffectual nostrums from house to house in his little black bag. The new free-standing emergency clinics that offer to see a patient within twenty minutes at a lesser fee than he or she would pay in an emergency room suggest that medicine has become more flexible. Can we not think as creatively?

We can be proud of the multipurpose crisis center and the increased flexibility of business hours that some agencies have instituted. We hope that the waiting list, the fifty-minute hour for everybody for every purpose, and the interminable course of weekly interviews will eventually pass. Surely, some clients need only fifteen minutes once in a while, while others may need two hours on a frequent basis. Some clients' problems can be handled on a group basis and we should enlarge our use of groups far beyond what we have done. Surely, we are capable of more flexibility.

Certainly the increase in private practice in social work can be a good thing, unless practitioners get greedy. The opportunity is there for the kind of group practice that is more in keeping with the modern era. One can dream of a facility to which one would turn for help, staffed with specialists in specific problem areas who offer services on individual, group, and community levels. This is not as wild as it may sound. There are organizations in existence now that approach this pattern. Surely more social workers will be encouraged to try it in the future.

Conclusion

We affirm the position that we took in the first edition. If there is a key to the future, it is best expressed in the value of self-determination. Probably the most critical thing that one can say of social welfare policy in the United States is that the ghost of a more paternalistic era still lingers over it. Social workers will be under increasing pressure to demonstrate what they can do. We can no longer plan *for* peoples' needs. We must plan *with* them and treat them in the same way that a good business treats its valued customers. One does not demean or paternalize a valued customer, but treats him or her with respect as a person one is glad to serve. This is not a bad model to follow.

Fortunately, consumers are not as voiceless as they once were. Blacks, women, the old, the handicapped, and others will no longer settle for indifference in either programs or services. As new policies are needed, social workers and other personnel in the social welfare enterprise must be ready with useful ways to analyze and formulate them so that the human services are genuinely helpful to those who use them.

QUESTIONS FOR DISCUSSION

1. What do you think that OASDHI will look like by the year 2000? Will the system survive?
2. Are the authors too pessimistic in their forecasts for programs dealing with poverty? Why or why not?
3. What is your opinion of the future of national health insurance?
4. Given the rising prices of land and relatively high interest costs, what would you forecast that the federal government will do about housing in the future? Do you think that the present policies will continue or do you see changes?
5. What do you see as the future of social work as a profession?

SUGGESTED PROJECTS

1. Invite some individuals to class who are involved with each of the five policy areas discussed in this book. Ask each to discuss his or her ideas about the future in his or her area of expertise.
2. Do your own forecasting. Organize a panel discussion using students who are prepared to discuss the future of selected areas in social welfare.

FOR FURTHER READING

Daniel Bell. *The Coming of Post-Industrial Society*. New York: Basic Books, 1973. A look at the year 2000 by one of the country's most respected thinkers. Now that this book has been around for a while, it is instructive to see if Bell has been successful in identifying any currently observable trends.

Harleigh Trecker, ed. *Goals for Social Welfare 1973–1993*. New York: Association Press, 1973. A look at the future from 1973 by a number of prestigious social work educators. Are these forecasts "on track"?

Index

1 2 3 4 5 6 7 8 9 0

DATE DUE